UNGRADING

TEACHING AND LEARNING IN HIGHER EDUCATION
James M. Lang, Series Editor

Other titles in the series:

Radical Hope: A Teaching Manifesto
Kevin M. Gannon

Teaching about Race and Racism in the College Classroom:
Notes from a White Professor
Cyndi Kernahan

Intentional Tech: Principles to Guide the Use of Educational
Technology in College Teaching
Derek Bruff

Geeky Pedagogy: A Guide for Intellectuals, Introverts, and Nerds Who
Want to Be Effective Teachers
Jessamyn Neuhaus

How Humans Learn: The Science and Stories
behind Effective College Teaching
Joshua R. Eyler

Reach Everyone, Teach Everyone: Universal Design
for Learning in Higher Education
Thomas J. Tobin and Kirsten T. Behling

Teaching the Literature Survey Course:
New Strategies for College Faculty
Gwynn Dujardin, James M. Lang, and John A. Staunton

The Spark of Learning:
Energizing the College Classroom with the Science of Emotion
Sarah Rose Cavanagh

UNgrading

Why Rating Students Undermines Learning (and What to Do Instead)

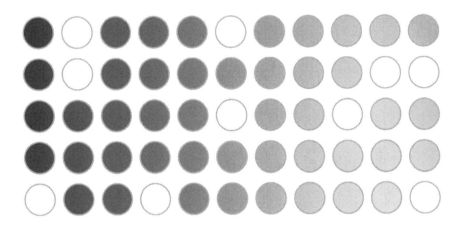

EDITED BY

Susan D. Blum

With a foreword by Alfie Kohn

West Virginia University Press · Morgantown

Copyright © 2020 by West Virginia University Press
Foreword copyright © 2020 by Alfie Kohn
All rights reserved
First edition published 2020 by West Virginia University Press
Printed in the United States of America

ISBN
Cloth 978-1-949199-81-9
Paper 978-1-949199-82-6
Ebook 978-1-949199-83-3

Library of Congress Cataloging-in-Publication Data

Names: Blum, Susan Debra, editor. | Kohn, Alfie, writer of foreword.
Title: Ungrading : why rating students undermines learning (and what to do
    instead) / edited by Susan D. Blum ; with a foreword by Alfie Kohn.
Description: First edition. | Morgantown : West Virginia University Press, 2020. |
    Series: Teaching and learning in higher education | Includes bibli-
    ographical references and index.
Identifiers: LCCN 2020022379 | ISBN 9781949199819 (cloth) | ISBN
    9781949199826 (paperback) | ISBN 9781949199833 (ebook)
Subjects: LCSH: Grading and marking (Students)—United States. | Students—
    Rating of—United States.
Classification: LCC LB3060.37 .U55 2020 | DDC 371.27/20973—dc23
LC record available at https://lccn.loc.gov/2020022379

Book and cover design by Than Saffel / WVU Press

To our students—
may you be rewarded by deep,
meaningful, and joyful learning

You do what you can within the confines of the current structure, trying to minimize its harm. You also work with others to try to change that structure, conscious that nothing dramatic may happen for a very long time.

—Alfie Kohn, *Punished by Rewards: The Trouble with Gold Stars, Incentive Plans, A's, Praise, and Other Bribes*

CONTENTS

Foreword xiii
Alfie Kohn

Preface xxi

Introduction: Why Ungrade? Why Grade? 1
Susan D. Blum

PART I
Foundations and Models

1   How to Ungrade 25
    Jesse Stommel

2   What Going Gradeless Taught Me about
    Doing the "Actual Work" 42
    Aaron Blackwelder

3   Just One Change (Just Kidding): 53
    Ungrading and Its Necessary Accompaniments
    Susan D. Blum

4   Shifting the Grading Mindset 74
    Starr Sackstein

5   Grades Stifle Student Learning. Can We Learn to
    Teach without Grades? 82
    Arthur Chiaravalli

PART II
Practices

6   Let's Talk about Grading 91
    Laura Gibbs

7   Contract Grading and Peer Review 105
    Christina Katopodis and Cathy N. Davidson

8   Critique-Driven Learning and Assessment 123
    Christopher Riesbeck

9   A STEM Ungrading Case Study: 140
    A Reflection on First-Time Implementation
      in Organic Chemistry II
    Clarissa Sorensen-Unruh

10   The Point-less Classroom: 161
    A Math Teacher's Ironic Choice in Not
      Calculating Grades
    Gary Chu

PART III
Reflections

11   Grade Anarchy in the Philosophy Classroom 173
    Marcus Schultz-Bergin

12   Conference Musings and the G-Word 188
    Joy Kirr

13   Wile E. Coyote, the Hero of Ungrading 204
    John Warner

Conclusion: Not Simple but Essential 219
Susan D. Blum

Acknowledgments 229
Contributors 233
Index 237

FOREWORD

———

Three concepts emerged independently in different fields: quantum leaps (in particle physics), punctuated equilibrium (in evolutionary biology), and paradigm shifts (in the history of science). All converge on the revelation that change doesn't always take place incrementally. Sometimes things stay pretty much the same for a long time, and then suddenly— ka-pow!—rapid transformation seems to come out of nowhere.

This notion is intriguing precisely because it's so counterintuitive. And it's counterintuitive because evolution is a lot more common than revolution in everyday human affairs. Most people, including teachers, don't wake up one morning prepared to adopt radically different practices. And gradual change is fine—as long as we don't underdo it. In other words the first tentative step we take shouldn't be the extent of our journey.

I'd like to describe nine specific ways this principle might play out where grading is concerned. In each case I've taken the liberty of describing a two-step process to call attention to the insufficiency of the first step.

(1) We start by worrying about grade inflation before gradually coming to realize the real problem is grades themselves. The trouble isn't that too many students are getting As but that too many students have been led to believe the primary purpose of schooling is to get As. Making it more difficult to receive a high grade (in the name of academic rigor or high standards) doesn't solve the underlying problem and also makes things worse by ensuring grades will be even more salient to students.

(2) We acknowledge that ranking students or grading them on a curve—in both cases setting them against one another for artificially

scarce distinctions, thus rigging the game so that not everyone can succeed—is not only counterproductive for learning but also, frankly, immoral. So we make sure everyone can, in theory, get an A. Only then do we realize that rating, too, is a problem, even if a less egregious one than ranking. We've eliminated the strychnine of competition, but there is more to be done if we're still dispensing the arsenic of extrinsic motivation. Judging students on a relative basis (so that each comes to be viewed as an obstacle to the others' success) compounds the damage done by grades, but it doesn't exhaust the damage done by grades.

(3) Step one: after reading the research showing that grading has three predictable effects—less interest in learning, a preference for easier tasks, and shallower thinking—we stop using letters and numbers to rate what students have done and instead use descriptive labels such as "needs improvement," "developing," "meeting/exceeding expectations," "proficient," and "mastery." Step two: we realize these labels are just grades (on a four- or five-point scale) by a different name and that we need to get rid of them too.

(4) First we dispense with ratings in favor of narrative reports. But then we realize narratives are still monologues. If we prefer dialogue, we have to do more asking than telling. That means engaging in conversations (conferences) with students rather than firing off comments for them to ponder.

(5) Another variation of the preceding progression: if the first step is to move from grades to (qualitative) feedback, the second is to ask whether what we're *calling* feedback—a term that, strictly speaking, refers to information—is really just a judgment. We may decide it's impossible or undesirable to completely avoid evaluation in our comments to students, but that's a decision that needs to be defended. We should stop calling it feedback if it's not purely descriptive. And we may want to adjust the ratio of genuine feedback ("Here's what I've noticed . . .") to judgment ("Here's what I like and dislike about what you've done . . .") that we're offering.

(6) Old-school grading strikes us as creaky and unfair, so we shift to some version of what is called "standards-based" grading—a reasonable first step. But eventually it occurs to us that this solves none of the most serious harms caused by grading. Those harms weren't due to a lack of

precision; in fact, more precision in the form of quantified ratings can actually exacerbate the negative effect grades have on students' intrinsic motivation and depth of understanding. Similarly there are only limited benefits to assorted other minor changes: true, it's hard to defend giving students zeros (which can sink their grade point averages irrecoverably), merely averaging the marks on multiple assignments to yield a final grade (which ignores improvement), factoring things like attendance or behavior into grades, or denying students the chance to rewrite a paper or otherwise bring up a grade (which implies we're more interested in playing "Gotcha!" than in assessing their best effort). But ultimately these are all peripheral issues. Eventually, perhaps reluctantly, we see the need to move on to step two—eliminating any sort of grading—if we're truly committed to creating a focus on learning.

(7) We begin by accepting the idea that a "growth mindset" is desirable, and we set about helping students to see the role of effort in determining success. The next step, though, is to realize this whole framework has the effect of blaming individuals for lacking the correct attitude or orientation—and, consequently, of shifting our focus away from systemic barriers. An emphasis on defective mindsets (or a tendency to accuse students of being insufficiently motivated) conveniently lets us off the hook. It is popular for the same reason we may be tempted to believe that the problem is grade-grubbing students rather than grade-giving instructors and institutions.

(8) It occurs (or is suggested) to us that even though we're required to turn in a final grade for students, we're not required to decide unilaterally what that grade will be. So we stop using grades as bribes or threats. We meet with students individually and ask them to propose course grades for themselves, while reserving the right to decide whether to accept their suggestions. This is an excellent first step—on the path to relinquishing veto power. Ultimately ungrading—eliminating the control-based function of grades, with all its attendant harms—means that, as long as the noxious institutional requirement to submit a final grade remains in place, whatever grade each student decides on is the grade we turn in, period.

(9) Clarity begins at home, as the old saying almost has it. We start by understanding what is going on in our own classroom and act

accordingly; that's logical because it is where we enjoy at least a measure of autonomy. We eliminate grades on individual assignments, do what we can so the prospect of final grades remains as invisible as possible for as long as possible, and allow students to choose those final grades. But the second step—which is in fact a long, hard, uphill climb, and is no less urgent for its difficulty—is to look *beyond* our own classrooms, to stop seeing that noxious institutional requirement as a fact of life like the weather and start seeing it as a policy that can be questioned and ultimately reversed. So we press administrators for the right to offer our courses only on a pass-fail basis. (It's remarkable how many educators who understand the destructive effects of grades have never attempted this.) Simultaneously we organize and mobilize our colleagues to work for the abolition of letter and number grades altogether. That may mean setting up a faculty-student committee to investigate how other schools have gone grade-free and to explore better ways to report information about students' progress. Classroom ungrading is, let's remember, just a stopgap measure, an attempt to minimize the damaging effects of the final grade. And individual courses taken pass-fail may seem less consequential than graded courses to students who have been socialized to think grades matter more than learning. Our classrooms are the low-hanging fruit, but that fruit isn't enough for a full meal. By all means, pick it—and then go get some ladders.

The various two-step advances I have described are meant to get us closer to wiping out grades once and for all. But to read the chapters of this remarkably useful and heartening collection is to be reminded that this daunting goal is itself part of an even more ambitious journey. Because much has been written elsewhere about these topics—and because this is, after all, only a foreword, not a book in itself—I will briefly describe only two dimensions of that journey.

First, an impressive collection of scholarship in educational psychology has distinguished practices that encourage students to focus on their academic performance from practices that encourage them to focus on the learning itself. *The more their attention is directed to how well they're doing, the less engaged they tend to be with what they're doing.* In fact, getting students to keep taking their temperature, so to speak, has a range of disconcerting effects—on intellectual development, curiosity, risk-taking, psychological health, and relationships with fellow learners.[1]

This body of research is either unknown to, or overlooked by, even some critics of grades, who embrace alternative evaluation strategies that do nothing to ameliorate—and may even exacerbate—a preoccupation with performance at the expense of learning. Rubrics are a case in point: they just offer a wider variety of (standardized) criteria for judging students. Even if we have the good sense to strip them of numerical ratings, a critical first step to detoxifying them, rubrics are all about evaluation. They offer umpteen different axes along which to make students think about their performance—often at the cost of becoming less immersed in what they're doing.

The same is true of any system that assigns points to students for completing various tasks to the instructor's satisfaction—an extrinsic inducement (a doggie biscuit, so to speak) if ever there was one. And it is also true of replacements for traditional grading such as peer evaluation and self-evaluation: these are, again, important first steps to the extent that they shift the power dynamic in the classroom. But ideally we want to be careful not to overdo *any* evaluation lest students become too focused on whether they're measuring up and thus are less *caught* up in intellectual discovery. (Again, empirical research attests to the fact that these two things tend to pull in opposite directions, even if we'd like to believe otherwise.)

The first challenge, then, is that getting rid of grades is not enough if our classrooms are still more about performance than learning. The second challenge is this: while it isn't easy to figure out how to assess learning in a constructive (or, at least, not destructive) way, it is even more challenging to create a curriculum that's worth learning. As one contributor to this volume (Aaron Blackwelder) remarks, "Assigning grades was the easy way out of doing the actual work of teaching. . . . When I eliminated grades, it tested my creativity and patience. I was forced to rethink what went on in my class." And that, presumably, is when the real work began.

To create a culture of vibrant intellectual discovery, getting rid of grades is necessary but far from sufficient.

- **We need to grapple with curriculum (what we're teaching).** If a disproportionate amount of time is devoted to memorizing facts, we can get only so far by abolishing grades.

- **We need to grapple with pedagogy (how we're teaching).** Are we still lecturing—which, as the writer George Leonard observed, is the "best way to get information from teacher's notebook to student's notebook without touching the student's mind"?[2]

- **We need to grapple with assessment.** Tests are a deeply flawed way of evaluating students and have been abandoned by many thoughtful educators in favor of more authentic and informative types of assessment. That raises the question, Why bother to get rid of a defective method of reporting achievement (like grades) if we're still using a defective method of assessing achievement (like tests)?

- **We need to grapple with issues of control**—whether decisions about these and other issues are made *for* students or *with* them. (Consider that many instructors still prepare a detailed syllabus: a week-by-week summary, along with a list of rules and threats, whose tone often resembles "something that might be handed to a prisoner on the first day of incarceration" and whose very specificity signals that we don't care who these particular students are—what they know, what they need, what interests them—because the course has already been prepared.)[3]

When high school or university teachers protest that it is unrealistic to get rid of grades because students wouldn't do the reading or even show up without them, these teachers are, on one level, offering evidence about the harm grades have already done to these kids. (Why in the world would we then compound the damage by continuing to employ what we know crushes intrinsic motivation?) On another level, though, they may be unwittingly raising questions about their own teaching. If my curriculum and pedagogy aren't sufficiently engaging, is that an argument to rely on grades to coerce students into doing what I want? Or should I gulp and ask some serious questions about the quality of my curriculum and pedagogy? Moreover, as another contributor to this volume (Marcus Schultz-Bergin) points out, even if it is true that grades might induce some students to do more "work," that doesn't mean they will have learned more.

The first few times I was invited to speak to college faculties about grades and other issues, I dived into the arguments and research I had already used when writing to K–12 educators in order to see what was relevant. The answer, I quickly concluded: just about everything. That's true partly because much of the research (notably on the effects of grading) has been conducted on college students as well as younger children—with essentially the same results. Indeed, some research has focused specifically on older students and demonstrated a strong inverse relationship between a learning orientation and a grade orientation. Other studies, meanwhile, show that undergraduate and graduate grade point averages are lousy predictors of just about any postgraduate outcomes—further reason to eliminate final course grades as an institutional feature.[4]

Many of the chapters in this book offer even more compelling evidence that the case against grades applies across ages (equally relevant to those teaching in high schools and universities) and across disciplines (quite a number of which are represented here, in the humanities, social sciences, and natural sciences). The writers you are about to meet draw on research, common sense, examples set by other educators, and their own experimentation to point the way to moving away from grades. They have sometimes engaged in tough introspection about what they've been doing for years, and you may well resonate with their doubts, their hesitations, their epiphanies. Many have come to realize that (a) grades have been driving much of what happens in their classrooms, (b) this is a serious problem, and (c) it doesn't have to be that way. Each contributor describes a somewhat different journey; at least one of them may offer a model you decide to follow—one step at a time.

Alfie Kohn

NOTES

1. I review some of this research in my book *The Schools Our Children Deserve*, chapter 2.

2. Leonard 1968.
3. The quotation is from "Death to the Syllabus!" by Mano Singham (2007). Of course an enormous amount has been written about pedagogy, curriculum, assessment, and decision-making issues in higher education, and the importance of challenging traditional assumptions and practices in each of these areas. I'll mention only two sources here: Finkel 2000 and Meyers 1986. I reviewed the case against lecturing, and described projects to create alternatives, in my 2017 essay "Don't Lecture Me!"
4. For example, see Milton, Pollio, and Eison 1986. Meanwhile a review of thirty-five studies revealed that academic indicators (grades and tests) from college accounted for less than 3 percent of the variance in eventual occupational performance as judged by income, job effectiveness ratings, and job satisfaction. Moreover, these indicators had no predictive power whatsoever for MDs and PhDs. (See Samson et al. 1984.) Other studies have found similar null effects in the careers of lawyers and doctors.

SOURCES

Finkel, Donald. 2000. *Teaching with Your Mouth Shut*. Portsmouth, NH: Heinemann.

Kohn, Alfie. 1999. *The Schools Our Children Deserve*. Boston: Houghton Mifflin.

Kohn, Alfie. 2017. "Don't Lecture Me!" https://www.alfiekohn.org/blogs/lectures/.

Leonard, George. 1968. *Education and Ecstasy*. New York: Delta.

Meyers, Chet. 1986. *Teaching Students to Think Critically*. San Francisco: Jossey-Bass.

Milton, Ohmer, Howard R. Pollio, and James A. Eison. 1986. *Making Sense of College Grades*. San Francisco: Jossey-Bass.

Samson, Gordon E., et al. 1984. "Academic and Occupational Performance: A Quantitative Synthesis." *American Educational Research Journal* 21(2): 311–21.

Singham, Mano. 2007. "Death to the Syllabus!" *Liberal Education* 93(4). https://is.gd/cKmEOs.

PREFACE

As this book goes to press, we are in the midst of the Covid-19 pandemic. This has affected higher education more than anything since, well, we aren't sure. Possibly the Black Death, or the world wars. As schools everywhere move entirely online, one topic has been prominent in the considerations about how to proceed: what should we do about grades?

Individual faculty are struggling to reassess their own class policies, and institutions have also been anguished as they consider whether courses should be pass-fail (or no credit), and if so, whether this should be optional or mandatory.[1] Students calculate the consequences of opting for Pass rather than a letter grade. The deeper question, sometimes raised and often skirted, is of what grades mean at all.[2]

Postgraduate educational institutions such as medical schools, which rely on baccalaureate institutions to sort students for them, are taking varying stances on what to do with the grades from the spring 2020 semester. Some have announced that they will accept pass-fail grades even for the prerequisite courses usually accepted only if they have traditional grades (though notably Harvard Medical School announced this only after initially saying that such grades would be accepted only if the pass-fail was mandatory).[3] The University of Michigan Medical School announced that they would accept courses with pass-fail grading, whether they were mandatory or optional.[4] Grades affect athletic eligibility, visas for international students, internships, jobs, financial aid, transfer to four-year colleges, and more.

Discussions about the meaning and necessity of grades have many dimensions: Is it equitable to grade when students' conditions are so various? What, exactly, are we assessing? If students fail to appear in synchronous meetings, should they be penalized? What about uneven access to digital materials? Many enduring levels of inequity are becoming apparent in this particular moment. But should we, assuming an end to the lockdown, just go back to business as usual? What if the usual is problematic?[5]

Those of us involved in ungrading are able to weather this disruption much better than those wedded to conventional precision grading. But we hope that the conversations remain focused on the deeper question of what the nature of the enterprise is, as a whole, and of how varying assessment and feedback methods contribute to the real learning of real individual learners, rather than imposing an arbitrary method of sorting. As Jen Newton wrote on Twitter, "Grades are made up. That's it, that's the tweet."[6]

Even in this unfinished, unchosen experimental moment, which will endure we know not how long, we hope our contribution to this conversation can help clarify some of the issues, reveal underlying assumptions, and lead to a true change in how educational institutions, educators, and students can work together for healthy learning.

Susan D. Blum
May 4, 2020
South Bend, Indiana

NOTES

1. Laura Gibbs, one of the contributors to this volume, collected the policies of hundreds of institutions for several weeks at https://www.diigo.com/user /lauragibbs?query=%23PNP.
2. On potential consequences, see Lilah Burke, "The Asterisk Semester," *Inside Higher Ed*, April 13, 2020, https://www.insidehighered.com/news/2020/04 /13/how-will-passfail-affect-students-future.
3. On medical schools in general, see Burke, "The Asterisk Semester." On accepting pass-fail, see Harvard Medical School, "Prerequisite Courses," https:// meded.hms.harvard.edu/admissions-prerequisite-courses, current as of April 28, 2020. A month earlier, they had limited which courses they would accept. See Matt Reed, "Harvard Gonna Harvard," *Inside Higher Ed*, March 31, 2020, https://www.insidehighered.com/blogs/confessions-community-college-dean /harvard-gonna-harvard.

4. University of Michigan Medical School, "Requirements," https://medicine.umich.edu/medschool/education/md-program/md-admissions/requirements, current as of May 4, 2020.
5. Cathy N. Davidson and Christina Katopodis, "In a Pandemic, Everyone Gets an Asterisk," *Inside Higher Ed*, March 23, 2020, https://www.insidehighered.com/views/2020/03/23/during-covid-19-crisis-higher-ed-should-rethink-how-assess-test-and-grade-students.
6. Jen Newton (@jenrnewton), April 27, 2020, 1:10 p.m., https://twitter.com/jenrnewton/status/1254820335536439296.

———

WHY UNGRADE? WHY GRADE?

Susan D. Blum

———

From birth onward, humans, in their healthiest states, are active, inquisitive, curious, and playful creatures, displaying a ubiquitous readiness to learn and explore, and they do not require extraneous incentives to do so. This natural motivational tendency is a critical element in cognitive, social, and physical development because it is through acting on one's inherent interests that one grows in knowledge and skills.

—Richard M. Ryan and Edward L. Deci, "Intrinsic and Extrinsic Motivations: Classic Definitions and New Directions"

———

Instead of focusing on getting a good grade, I focused on actually learning the material. I was less stressed out, and more interested in the actual class content.

—Undergraduate in my grade-free (until the end) class, Fall 2018

———

Humans, in recent memory, invented a way of looking at students' learning. We in the United States call it *grading*; in Canada, the United Kingdom, and elsewhere, they distinguish between *marking* on particular

I

assignments and final _grading_. Though grading seems natural, inevitable, a part of the very fabric of school, it isn't. It was created at a certain moment, for certain reasons not entirely well thought out, and then became embedded in the structures of schools for most students.

But because we invented it, we can uninvent it. We can remove it. And many of us believe we should.

There's a growing movement at this end of the second decade of the twenty-first century. I call it _ungrading_. Others call it _de-grading_ or _going gradeless_. Though the destination tends to be generally the same, there is variation in the routes, the reasons, the contexts, and the specific ways various individuals at different levels of education enact our changes. This book is an effort to assemble some of the practices faculty have devised to question the apparent centrality of grades as an unchanging, unyielding fact of schooling (according to both teachers and students).

After I published a short article online in 2017 called "Ungrading: The Significant Learning Benefits of Getting Rid of Grades," I was invited to a secret Facebook group called Teachers Going Gradeless, TG2.[1] There was already a group that Starr Sackstein had been part of called Teachers Throwing Out Grades. Since then I've discovered more and more evidence of faculty going gradeless—most at the secondary (middle and high school) level, but increasingly in higher education. Much of the material in this book is available as blog posts, podcasts, Twitter threads, and interviews. Little has been published in print or peer-reviewed formats. We've retained some of the flavor of those posts, to keep the sense of energy and conversation of each author.

Almost everyone I approached was delighted to contribute to this book (those who declined had other commitments) and excited to push the conversation into a broader public realm. We believe that putting these pieces together produces a picture of what is possible—a picture greater than any individual alone can produce.

All the authors included in this book are troubled by some of the consequences of and reasons for grades. It could be because grading dehumanizes and flattens nuances in students' practices and understanding. It could be the mechanistic approach, derived from the factory model of education, that we wish to challenge. It could be that we are concerned about the fixation on grades, which leads to cheating, corner cutting, gaming the system, and a misplaced focus on accumulating points rather than on learning. It could be that people wish to be more responsive to individuals in the classroom, to be more informative about feedback, to join students in a collective effort that isn't primarily focused on assessment, evaluation, sorting, ranking. It could be that people are rebelling against audit culture, or what Jerry Z. Muller in his book *The Tyranny of Metrics* calls "metric fixation."[2]

It could be that people are propelled by insights—robust insights—from the last fifty years of educational psychology, findings on motivation research that show a loss of intrinsic motivation when extrinsic motivations are dominant. It could be that they are influenced by progressive educators such as Alfie Kohn. It could be that they are concerned about how, when comments on papers are accompanied by grades, students disregard our comments—often not even reading them and certainly not using them to improve or learn more deeply. This finding has been shown over and over again beginning with researchers such as Ruth Butler.[3] Those who focus on increasing students' intrinsic motivation often tap into students' curiosity (which exists as a motive not only in humans and other primates but in all mammals and even birds).[4] They attend to social and emotional rewards of learning and also to authentic application.[5]

Obviously the effort to make education more genuine, authentic, effective, engaging, and meaningful is scarcely new. Numerous educational challenges have existed since conventional education as we know it has become more ubiquitous. Under the labels of *progressive, democratic, humane, Deweyian, utopian, experimental, open, experiential, feminist,* or *anarchist* education, all kinds of other frameworks have existed. Entire schools have been constructed without grades—Montessori, Reggio Emilia, Waldorf, Summerhill, Sudbury Valley, Big Picture Learning— and all of these schools have wonderful things to offer. They add up to something important and revelatory. But they are far from the majority, and they tend to be smaller than average, somewhat out of reach of the bulk of students, and sometimes expensive, even with financial aid and even though many were initially started expressly to serve children from low-income families.[6] Still, there are whole classrooms and programs, some public, trying to create student- and learning-centered grade-free educational settings, emphasizing mastery rather than arbitrary deadlines and measures, learning rather than compliance.[7]

At the level of higher education, too, some institutions are either entirely or optionally grade-free, emphasizing narrative evaluations. Grade-free institutions include Hampshire College, Evergreen State College, Deep Spring College, New College of Florida, Alverno College, Fairhaven College of Interdisciplinary Studies at Western Washington University, Prescott College, Antioch University, and Goddard College. Others, such as Sarah Lawrence College and Reed College, record grades but don't automatically report them to students. Brown University gives students the option to take most courses for satisfactory–no credit. For a time the University of California, Santa Cruz, was grade-free but changed its policy.[8] Entire organizations of college teachers have questioned the need for grades.[9]

Most elite medical schools (eighteen of the top twenty medical schools) use only pass-fail grades for preclinical courses.[10] In 2017 as many as ninety-six medical schools used simple pass-fail systems; twenty-six used honors, pass, fail; and thirteen used honors, high pass, pass, fail. Only twenty-eight used numerical or letter-grade systems.[11] The argument is that students' grades in basic science courses show no meaningful correlation with their later quality as practicing physicians. Medical schools have also largely eliminated a focus on grades because they have been plagued by high rates of suicide; these reforms aim in part to ameliorate some pressures by creating more cooperative communities—something that surely is relevant for institutions serving undergraduates, said to have "epidemic" levels of anxiety.[12]

Aiming to reduce the focus on grades and internal competition, some elite law schools—Harvard, Yale, Stanford—have likewise modified their grading systems, though they have basically replaced a letter-grade or numerical system with another system with verbal labels. Harvard moved to honors, pass, low pass, and fail; they have no curve and no class rankings, but students still get GPAs, and the words are converted to 4 (honors), 3 (pass), 2 (low pass), and 0 (fail). Yale has only pass and fail for first-semester students; thereafter the evaluations are pass, low pass, and honors. Stanford has honors, pass, restricted credit, and no credit. These systems are both evidence of discomfort with grades and retention of the essential process of sorting.[13]

Grades are attacked for a variety of reasons, sometimes while faith is retained in their usefulness and necessity. Sometimes it is because there is no consensus on what grades are in the first place. Attempts at consistency and uniformity have tended to fail, or at least falter, leading to lack of clarity about their meaning (and student lore about which faculty are easy graders). Complaints about grade inflation circulate in society and administrations (though grade inflation is really grade compression, as a smaller range of grades is actually employed for most students).[14] Grade compression is a complaint especially at elite schools.[15] The problem with grade compression, critics argue, is that students are harder to distinguish. In going gradeless, most of the authors of this book act on the conviction that our principal task is educating all students, not ranking them.

Some colleges have systemic regulations aiming to combat grade inflation, sometimes by restricting high-level (i.e., A) grades and sometimes by requiring a fixed distribution (30 percent A, 30 percent B, etc.) or a preestablished median. However, not all colleges do this, and communication of the meaning of grades may be challenging. Perceiving that outsiders may regard their grades as lower than those at other universities, Dartmouth (and also Cornell in the past) includes information on students' transcripts not only about students' own grades but also about the median, for the professor or the college, to contextualize the stricter system. The University of California, Berkeley, has been mandating a lower set of grades to fight grade inflation; some students avoid Berkeley entirely to avoid getting "deflated" grades.[16] Princeton in 2004 implemented a cap on A-range grades, mandating that only 35 percent could be at that level; it is considering rescinding the policy.[17]

All this is to show the long-standing discomfort with grades as they are and the manifold attempts to improve, or save, them, as those aiming to combat grade inflation are really committed to doing.

WHERE DID GRADES COME FROM IN THE FIRST PLACE?

It is helpful to know a little about the origin of grades, seemingly lost somewhere in the mist of time, so natural have they come to seem.[18] It appears that grades began as a way of simply conferring exceptional recognition on some individuals who stood out in examinations. But under the model of other industrial systems, grading took hold of most levels of education by the early twentieth century. There had been a few precursors in formal educational systems, but largely this was a novel approach, not undertaken with any sort of plan. Previously there had been one truly rank-conscious educational system, in imperial China. In higher education, China had administered examinations (Civil Service Examination, *keju*) for over thirteen hundred years, with various rankings that determined bureaucratic and professional placement.[19] The current incarnation, the *gaokao*, is the subject of much critique but also defense for its relative fairness.[20]

In the European context, medieval and early modern universities had public oral examinations—"marked" at Cambridge with letters and pluses and minuses. These examinations were really more like debates than like our familiar examinations. There may have been some written examinations, especially in mathematics, as early as the sixteenth century, with some kind of ranking of students at Cambridge, but it is only in the eighteenth and nineteenth centuries that written examinations became dominant at institutions such as Oxford and Cambridge, likely because of the increased numbers of examinees, where the scale made oral examinations impractical. (Some minor vestige of oral examinations, especially for higher levels such as the dissertation, remain.)

Though there is little concrete evidence for it, some attribute the practice of grades to the chair of mechanical engineering at Cambridge, William Farish, who is reputed to have used marks for individual examination questions beginning in 1792. In contrast, Oxford downplayed ranking. Ranks using Greek alpha, beta, and gamma existed, but all students could be ranked alpha. In many European universities, especially in Germany, examinations were often simply pass or fail; students were permitted to retake their examinations until they received a satisfactory result. But things were different in the United States.

Yale began to differentiate students into four classes in the late eighteenth century. Harvard began in 1830 to use a twenty-point scale for rhetoric examinations. The fluctuation between numbers and letters has been ongoing. The University of Michigan used a numerical system, then in 1851 switched to a pass–no-pass system, and in 1860 returned to a numerical scale of 100.

Our familiar letter-grade system started in 1897 at Mount Holyoke College and has spread to most schools. This style of evaluation has been tinkered with, but along with tinkering has come much serious questioning of both the method and purpose of grading.

THE ENDURING TENSION BETWEEN PROGRESSIVE AND SCIENTIFIC APPROACHES

There have been, for a hundred years, those who believe human learning and schooling can be broken down into little bits and assessed, just like other types of production, using principles of *scientific management*, or the Taylorian method of breaking factory production and other tasks into smaller ones and maximizing efficiency, normed outcomes, curves, and the like.[21] One of the names associated with this is Edward Lee Thorndike, from whom we have inherited our standardized and normed tests.[22]

Intelligence tests, originally designed to sort out people with the capacity to overcome their impoverished backgrounds, measured an individual's score on a test against a "normal" person of that age, resulting in a quotient, hence the *intelligence quotient*. IQ and even the notion of *general intelligence*, or *g*, have been criticized as being racist, classist, sexist, ableist, and more.[23] They derive from the notion that there is a single, fixed amount of intelligence—fixed mindset—and that every individual can be arrayed against all others in an objective distribution.

Because some human traits, such as height, may be distributed along a bell-shaped curve, and because normed tests (such as IQ tests) have been made to conform to such distributions as well, some believe human "aptitude" falls into a bell curve (normal distribution curve or Gaussian curve). But the belief that this applies to human learning is a claim and an assertion, not a finding.[24] The twentieth-century rise of a focus on assessment stems in large part from the scientific management views of schooling as consisting of a limited number of identical, measurable tasks, along with the notion that scarcity and competition are the essence of schooling. And a twenty-first-century push for assessment (of entire systems) is largely seen as having failed.[25]

Contrasting with scientific management approaches to education have been contrary strands from the beginnings of what has come to be called *progressive education*, exemplified in the work of John Dewey who questioned many dimensions of our formal schooling, including the idea that schools should be separated from the world and that the focus should be on abstract, "academic" learning. Instead, Dewey favored integrating learning with life and embracing practical learning. He experimented with this in the University of Chicago Laboratory Schools, which he founded in 1896.

Enduring tension between the ideas that all students can learn equally well—the more democratic assumption—and that schools should be in the business of sorting has given us arguments about cooperation and competition, abundance and scarcity, citizenship and credentialism, democracy and meritocracy. It is here that we see questions about vocational versus academic preparation, about education preparing for work or further school or for citizenship and fulfillment, about ability grouping or equity. (These assumptions vary globally.)

A relatively recently established but very exciting field that contributes to this work in higher education is the scholarship of teaching and learning (SoTL). Scholars such as Sarah Rose Cavanagh, Joshua Eyler, Oscar Fernandez, Kevin Gannon, Kelly A. Hogan, Mays Imad, James Lang, Saundra McGuire, Jessamyn Neuhaus, Rebecca Pope-Ruark, Viji Sathy, Thomas Tobin, Daniel Willingham, and many others have written about and given faculty development workshops on "how humans learn," based on rigorous work in cognitive science, neuroscience, and the "learning sciences," plus a deep commitment to inclusion and equity.[26] Much of this work focuses on innovative pedagogy, including flipped classrooms, active learning, peer education—all the new, sometimes-disparaged buzzwords a new generation of young faculty is taking up in earnest. Overall the research on teaching and learning challenges the effectiveness of old teaching methods from the days of medieval lecturing. Books in this series, Teaching and Learning in Higher Education, tend to build on these studies. Sometimes based on experiments and laboratory research, they discuss motivation, social and emotional learning, and more. This body of research overall does not support the old early twentieth-century views of sorting students along bell curves, of threatening and using behaviorist techniques, or of disregarding the social and emotional elements of learning.[27]

Appreciative but slightly critical of such cognitivist approaches, however, are some feminist and critical views of learning. Focused on care, or on the nonpredictability of learning as is evident in, say, composition studies, they challenge the cognitivist approaches that tend to emphasize the individual as the unit of analysis and to rely on experiments conducted in North American college populations (WEIRD—Western, educated, industrial, rich, democratic).[28] SoTL tends to assume the endurance of bounded classrooms and degree-granting institutions—which are, obviously, not required for deep and lasting learning. And studies of learning, they may charge, tend to focus on learning as *information* which may then be assessed through simple testing or limited observations. As John Clifford, a writing teacher, put it,

> Protocols [lab experiments] certainly tell us something, but their web has not been precise enough to catch the important ingredients that go into cognition, memory, perception and attention, to say nothing of intention, desire, self-esteem and all the other variables of the rhetorical situation. . . . The use of protocols is indeed problematic. If writers are forced to order their responses so systematically, isn't their composing behavior significantly changed? Is the context of these experiments relevant to the psychological and social morass of the classroom? The "context-stripping" that their empirical scrutinizing demands casts serious doubts on how closely protocols mirror real classrooms with all their peer pressures, grades, authority figures and motivational nuances, plus the stylistic and rhetorical idiosyncrasies of individual instructors.[29]

It is certainly very difficult to measure the affective and social gains that accompany a rich semester of immersive learning, in contrast to a single laboratory variable-controlled experiment, but that is what some views would require.

Even in terms of cognitive gains in critical thinking, studies have been very difficult to conduct. One of the most famous, that of Arum and Roksa in the much-cited *Academically Adrift*, relied on computer-graded assessments (reliability correlated with human scorers),[30] but this methodology has been deeply criticized in terms of its statistical basis, the use of computer-assisted scoring, and the actual researchers' logic.[31] I dwell on this only to remind you that it is extremely difficult to assess learning, and that methods matter.

Enduring tensions regarding the nature of schools and indeed of the person and society are evident in some of the different models in this book. But despite some disagreements, all the contributors converge in our rejection of conventional grading practices.

CHALLENGES TO CONVENTIONAL GRADING SYSTEMS: FOUNDATIONS

Faculty object to conventional grading systems on a number of grounds, supported by research and scholarship of many sorts. Many of the contributors in this book refer to the topics of motivation (citing Edward Deci, Richard Ryan, Alfie Kohn, and Daniel Pink) and the contrast between *intrinsic* and *extrinsic* motivation. Whether arguing for Kohn's three ideal characteristics of classrooms (collaboration, content, choice) or Pink's three concepts of autonomy, mastery, and purpose, the authors aim to create positive atmospheres devoid of fear and threat and focused on learning.

Inconsistent Meanings of Grades

Incommensurability of grades is another long-standing problem. One professor may include homework in the calculation, either simply points for completion or actual evaluation of accomplishment. One may include all tests while another may drop the lowest score. One may ignore attendance; one may offer extra credit for things like watching a movie or attending a lecture.[32] Many include participation—up to half the points in seminars—which may or may not include attendance; others disregard it. (This may reward students who are extroverts, as well as those who are fortunate enough to avoid serious illnesses, financial challenges, and family responsibilities.) Though some faculty recognize other ways to acknowledge participation and involvement in courses, as a way of acknowledging more differences, abilities, and so on, most commonly *participation* means speaking in class. Attendance is legendarily low in some courses where it doesn't count; when it does count, students may sign one another in for the attendance points. One professor may weight more heavily assignments later in the semester. Some may curve the grades, attaining a predetermined distribution. Some may assess simply for final mastery, while others include intermediate efforts.

Grades, despite their apparent solidity, have been inconsistent from the start. Research from 1912 and 1913—early in grades' ubiquity—jolted the profession. Two researchers attempted to test how much consistency (*reliability*) they would find among faculty evaluating the same papers. They found little agreement in English and history—there was a range of 39 percent—but perhaps, the researchers thought, this resulted from the inherently less clear-cut nature of the subjects. Assuming judgments of math work would be more uniform, they sent out a geometry paper, where they found even *less* agreement: some faculty gave scores of 38 to 42, and others of 83 to 87. Some incorporated neatness or organization, though others did not.[33] Lest you think this would have been improved in the intervening century, Dean Stevenson reported on a September 2019 investigation in which he asked for volunteers to assess student assignments; more than fifty teachers volunteered to participate. The grades they assigned ranged from 1 to 6 points.[34] This shows that it is common for grades to be inconsistent, subjective, random, arbitrary.

Yes, judges can become consistent—but only with a great deal of training, as in the strange task of creating inter-reviewer consistency for SAT scorers, and then evaluating a restricted dimension of the work. Peter Elbow, renowned educator in composition studies, is not impressed: "The reliability in holistic scoring is not a measure of how texts are valued by real readers in natural settings"—where, for example, in "real life" some people may adore and others despise particular movies, music, books—"but only of how they are valued in artificial settings with imposed agreements."[35]

Beyond inter-rater consistency on the same assignment or test, there are many other forms of inconsistency. One example, with huge implications for equity, has to do with well-resourced secondary schools awarding higher-than-perfect ("weighted") grades for honors and advanced placement courses, so a student graduating from such a school may have a GPA above 4.0. Yet a student whose school does not offer many of such courses may, "just by going to the wrong school," have a lower GPA to offer in the college application process.[36]

So what do grades mean? What are they for? And can we accomplish our aims with different methods?

Desire for Substantive Communication

If grades in part are designed to communicate feedback, to say for example, "This is pretty good because you've done this well, and it would be stronger if you did . . . ," then it has been shown for a long time that grades *fail* at this task. Narrative evaluations do, along with conferences and more.

Another problem with grades is the serious question of how to understand the grades of learners with different beginning baselines: if someone begins with a good bit of knowledge and doesn't put in effort, but ends "higher" than someone who started with no knowledge, worked very hard, and made great strides, how should this be evaluated? One way, of course, is to say just that: "You worked very hard and made great strides, and you still have more to learn about X, but I can tell you care about the topic" or "You began as a very accomplished student but didn't put a lot of effort into the class. You may want to assess your interest in the topic, or your time management, or your goals."

The point is, when we grade, we really convey very little information about what is being assessed. But we can convey it in other, fuller ways.

Side Effects, Unintended Consequences, Perverse Incentives

The critique of grades focuses, often, on their failure to produce the desired outcomes—learning—and on their potential negative outcomes. Yong Zhao has suggested that we take seriously the negative "side effects" of educational structures, just as we do with medicine.[37] If cheating is a frequent side effect of a bottom-line mentality, where the goal is the grade, rather than learning, perhaps improvement might be possible if institutions and courses could explicitly focus on learning and either downplay or eliminate a fixation on grades.[38]

We can disagree about whether grades should be what educators distinguish as *formative* (allowing some learning still to occur using the information here) or *summative* (a final pronouncement about what has been done).[39] Writing, composition, and rhetoric teachers usually regard their feedback as encouraging revision, and only the final product gets a grade; the intermediate steps often get a grade simply for completion (contract grading). Narrative evaluations, as long as teachers have the time and freedom to engage substantively in them, accomplish this. But despite the time harried faculty put into writing comments, the sad and enduring fact has been that students rarely read them, as Ruth Butler demonstrated in the 1980s. Comments alone, however, especially when they are used for subsequent tasks—in other words as "formative assessment"—may have some efficacy.[40]

Further evidence about the effects of grades is that grades discourage risk-taking and encourage replication of safe tactics. In studies of divergent-thinking tasks of students in fifth and sixth grades, the more rewards they received, the less creative the process they employed. One explanation is that focus on grades emphasizes teachers' control, and thus produces extrinsic orientation. Praise without feedback is not productive: "Praise did not yield higher subsequent intrinsic motivation than grades and did not even maintain initial interest at its baseline level."[41] Kvale argues that assessments in higher education have focused on control, discipline, and selection, which contradict goals of learning.[42]

There is even a connection between student evaluations of teaching and the deplored grade inflation: if faculty, whose careers depend on students' perceptions, desire to be regarded favorably by their students, there is no better way to do that than to give uniformly high grades. This certainly incentivizes mutual rewarding of high numbers.[43]

Fixation on grades and GPA leads students to seek easy classes. My own students report a frenzy of inquiries during the class registration period, when students ask one another for information about easy classes, the desirable ones that yield high grades with little work. A Reddit thread I observed asked for "Easy Online GPA Booster" courses that offer an A+ and are preferably upper division. Further desirable characteristics are that they have no schedule so they can be completed immediately, that answers are online (Course Hero, Chegg), and that they do not require much writing.[44]

Furthermore, the use of "learning outcomes" and "assessment" for accreditation agencies appears fair, accountable. But it's often merely an appearance of fairness. If someone comes in, say, to a language class as a heritage speaker of a language—a popular tactic for boosting a GPA—then doing well on tests may reveal the initial condition of mastery and little growth. Grading promotes a deleterious focus on an appearance of objectivity (with its use of numbers) and an appearance of accuracy (with its fine distinctions), and contributes to a misplaced sense of concreteness.

Surely no educator worth her salt would consider these to be desirable characteristics of a meaningful learning experience. The authors of this book largely regard many of these negative outcomes as stemming directly from, as ineluctable consequences of, the system of grading.

SOLUTIONS IN THE PLURAL

For all these and other reasons, many are questioning the utility, morality, and negative effects of grades. The individuals contributing to this volume are noteworthy not only because as individuals we are committed to focusing on our students' learning but also because we operate within structures that are conventional. It's one thing to have students who reject the conventional model and select a school that is entirely gradeless. It's another thing to have students, in a conventional system, show up in one person's class and find out that, wow, this professor or teacher is different from the others and ask, How do I navigate this class? For me personally, this is a (sometimes daunting) challenge every semester, when I get a new batch of students who have perhaps never before questioned the conventional structures. We believe it is helpful, for teachers and professors who want to implement a different system, for us to spell out some of the challenges we face, and to provide some of our own solutions, as well as some of the failures, in order to be realistic and give some ideas about approaches to try. Though this is not precisely a how-to book (we don't say, "Do these five things"), we hope readers will appreciate the many practical suggestions in each chapter. The authors of this book's chapters are not uniform in our approaches. We offer honest, earnest accounts of our own trials at creating more effective communication with our students in order to create more learning-focused conditions. In many ways this nondogmatic, problem-based (design-thinking?) approach to learning how to teach in new ways is a model for how our students might learn anything as well: we've recognized a problem, learned about previous research, prototyped solutions, iteratively improved them, shared our experiences, failed a little, risked a lot, succeeded a little more.

Our solutions are not in lockstep: some have prespecified outcomes while others craft them in dialogue with students; some have more fluid notions of what is supposed to be accomplished. Alternatives to conventional grading incorporate a variety of techniques. Some use rubrics while others have rejected this approach. Some employ contract grading; some grade for completion, effort, quality, or quantity. Some administer conventional tests; some measure learning against uniform predetermined learning outcomes and others differentiate goals, using variants of Universal Design for Learning (UDL).[45] Some regard the syllabus as a contract; others see it as a promise. (I frame it as an invitation.) Practitioners vary along a continuum of radicalness, from co-constructing the syllabus (chapter 7, Katopodis and Davidson) to tweaking the existing frameworks. Most emphasize that they trust students.

Each of the authors elaborates on her or his own approach. It is often a personal and sometimes emotional journey, but it is not as lonely as each one of us may have initially thought. There is no uniformity among these approaches—appropriate but worth examining in the future.

A BAKER'S DOZEN APPROACHES

Here we have a baker's dozen faculty reporting on what they have done, in a variety of settings, using a variety of approaches, and reflecting on how it has worked.

Some are old hands, engaging in ungrading for as long as two decades (Blackwelder, Davidson, Gibbs, Riesbeck, Sackstein, Stommel), and some are quite new to the practice (Schultz-Bergin, Sorensen-Unruh). Some teach writing (Blackwelder, Chiaravalli, Sackstein, Warner) and several teach STEM subjects (Chu, Riesbeck, Sorensen-Unruh). Some are at relatively elite institutions (Blum, Riesbeck) and others at relatively democratic/less advantaged ones (Katopodis and Davidson, Sorensen-Unruh). Some use contract grading (Gibbs, Katopodis and Davidson); many use portfolios. One teaches entirely online (Gibbs). Several have developed shorthands for explaining their practices ("all-feedback-no-grades" [Gibbs], "do-review-redo" [Riesbeck]). Some have found nothing but acceptance and appreciation, while others have encountered resistance.

This book includes five chapters from secondary school teachers (Blackwelder, Chiaravalli, Chu, Kirr, Sackstein) who teach writing, social studies, and math. They report on their own practices, and Kirr offers student responses to it. Eight chapters are from faculty in higher education (Blum, Gibbs, Katopodis and Davidson, Riesbeck, Schultz-Bergin, Sorensen-Unruh, Stommel, Warner).

We hope that this set of foundational pieces, presenting a variety of models, along with assorted practices and reflections on this experience, will at least cause you to think, possibly to experiment, and to have conversations about what is at the heart of learning and teaching, and the role of grading or ungrading in this multidimensional, human set of interactions.

If there's something happening here, perhaps you should know about it.

NOTES

1. Blum 2017. See also chapter 3, Blum.
2. Muller 2018. Many critics of conventional schooling draw on the notion of neoliberalism—the creep of economic thinking into realms of human experience that may not be intrinsically economic. Whenever people mention sorting, ranking, competition, branding, and the like, they are inspired by notions of neoliberal thinking, whether or not they acknowledge or know it. See Gershon 2017; Harris 2018; Harvey 2005.
3. Butler 1987; Butler 1988.
4. Eyler 2018; Livio 2017; Panksepp and Biven 2012.
5. For social and emotional rewards, see Cavanagh 2016; for authentic application, see Beckerman, Burbules, and Silberman-Keller 2007.

6. It's not just money that prevents low-income students from attending higher-ranked institutions. See Jack 2019; McMillan Cottom 2019.
7. Spencer 2017.
8. Cappel 1999; College XPress 2018; Rogoff 2001.
9. Jaschik 2009.
10. This is according to Deng and Wesevich 2016.
11. AAMC 2018.
12. For suicide rates and prevention among medical students, see American Foundation for Suicide Prevention 2018; Grossman 2016. For levels of anxiety at undergraduate institutions, see Cavanagh 2019; Kane 2019.
13. Jones 2014.
14. Rojstaczer 2016.
15. Clarida and Fandos 2017.
16. Bullitt 2018; Koti 2015.
17. Kaminer 2014.
18. Much of this summary comes from Blum 2016: 132–34, which draws heavily on Davidson 2011; Durm 1993; Gould [1981] 1996; Lemann 1999; Smallwood 1935; Stray 2001.
19. Elman 2000; Miyazaki [1963] 1981.
20. Heinz 2018; Howlett 2017; Howlett forthcoming.
21. Ireh 2016.
22. Lemann 1999, Levin 1991.
23. Gardner [1983] 2011.
24. Schinske and Tanner 2014.
25. Lederman 2019.
26. Cavanagh 2016; Eyler 2018; Willingham 2009; and many more.
27. Cavanagh 2016.
28. Henrich, Heine, and Norenzayan 2010.
29. Clifford 1984: 17.
30. Arum and Roksa 2011.
31. Astin 2011; Ennis 2012; Possin 2013.
32. Dunn and Halonen 2019.
33. Starch and Elliott 1912; Starch and Elliott 1913a; Starch and Elliott 1913b. This study is frequently invoked. See, for example, Elbow 1994; Kirschenbaum, Simon, and Napier 1971: 258–59.
34. Stevenson 2019. I am grateful to Andrew Burnett for posting about this on Twitter (September 28, 2019), and responding to my request for further information.
35. Elbow1994: 2.
36. Personal communication, Connor Methvin, October 7, 2019.
37. Zhao 2018.
38. Blum 2009.
39. See Black and Wiliam 2009; Taras 2005.
40. Butler 1988.
41. Butler 1987: 481.

42. Kvale 2007.
43. Bunge 2018; Tobin 2017.
44. Gobsmackedplayboy, "Easy Online GPA Booster," Reddit, April 26, 2017, https://www.reddit.com/r/ASU/comments/67s3jq/easy_online _gpa_booster/.
45. Tobin and Behling 2018.

CITED SOURCES AND FURTHER READING

AAMC (Association of American Medical Colleges). 2018. "Number of Medical Schools Using Selected Grading Systems in Pre-Clerkship Courses." https://www.aamc.org/initiatives/cir/406418/11.html.

American Foundation for Suicide Prevention. 2018. "Healthcare Professional Burnout, Depression and Suicide Prevention." https://afsp.org/our-work /education/healthcare-professional-burnout-depression-suicide-prevention/.

Arum, Richard, and Josipa Roksa. 2011. *Academically Adrift: Limited Learning on College Campuses*. Chicago: University of Chicago Press.

Astin, Alexander W. 2011. "In 'Academically Adrift,' Data Don't Back Up Sweeping Claim." *The Chronicle of Higher Education*. February 14. https://www.chronicle.com/article/Academically-Adrift-a/126371.

Bekerman, Zvi, Nicholas C. Burbules, and Diana Silberman-Keller, eds. 2007. *Learning in Places: The Informal Education Reader*. New York: Peter Lang.

Black, Paul J., and Dylan Wiliam. 2009. "Developing the Theory of Formative Assessment." *Educational Assessment Evaluation and Accountability* 21(1): 5–31.

Blum, Susan D. 2009. *My Word! Plagiarism and College Culture*. Ithaca, NY: Cornell University Press.

Blum, Susan D. 2016. *"I Love Learning; I Hate School": An Anthropology of College*. Ithaca, NY: Cornell University Press.

Blum, Susan D. 2017. "Ungrading: The Significant Learning Benefits of Getting Rid of Grades." *Inside Higher Ed*. November 14. https://www.insidehighered .com/advice/2017/11/14/significant-learning-benefits-getting-rid-grades -essay.

Blum, Susan D. 2019. "Why Don't Anthropologists Care about Learning (or Education or School)? An Immodest Proposal for an Integrative Anthropology of Learning Whose Time Has Finally Come." *American Anthropologist* 121(3): 641–54.

Bullitt, Andrew-Iyan. 2018. "Everything a UC Berkeley Student Should Know about Grade Suppression." *The Daily Californian*. April 27. http://www .dailycal.org/2018/04/26/everything-uc-berkeley-student-know-grade suppression/.

Bunge, Nancy. 2018. "Students Evaluating Teachers Doesn't Just Hurt Teachers. It Hurts Students." *The Chronicle of Higher Education*. November 27. https://www.chronicle.com/article/Students-Evaluating-Teachers/245169.

Butler, Ruth. 1987. "Task-Involving and Ego-Involving Properties of Evaluation: Effects of Different Feedback Conditions on Motivational Perceptions, Interest, and Performance." *Journal of Educational Psychology* 79(4): 474–82.

Butler, Ruth. 1988. "Enhancing and Undermining Intrinsic Motivation: The Effects of Task-Involving and Ego-Involving Evaluation on Interest and Performance." *British Journal of Educational Psychology* 58(1): 1–14. https:// doi.org/10.1111/j.2044-8279.1988.tb00874.x.

Cappel, Constance. 1999. *Utopian Colleges*. New York: Peter Lang.

Cavanagh, Sarah Rose. 2016. *The Spark of Learning: Energizing the College Classroom with the Science of Emotion*. Morgantown: West Virginia University Press.

Cavanagh, Sarah Rose. 2019. "The Best (and Worst) Ways to Respond to Student Anxiety." *The Chronicle of Higher Education*. May 5. https://www.chronicle .com/article/The-Best-and-Worst-Ways-to/246226?cid=wcontentgrid_hp_9.

Clarida, Matthew Q., and Nicholas P. Fandos. 2017. "Substantiating Fears of Grade Inflation, Dean Says Median Grade at Harvard College is A–, Most Common Grade Is A." *The Harvard Crimson*. May 26. https://www.thecrimson .com/article/2013/12/3/grade-inflation-mode-a/.

Clifford, John. 1984. "Cognitive Psychology and Writing: A Critique." *Freshman English News* 13(1): 16–18.

College XPress. 2018. "Colleges with Innovative Academic Programs. Carnegie Dartlet." https://www.collegexpress.com/lists/list/colleges-with-innovative -academic-programs/238/.

Davidson, Cathy. 2011. *Now You See It: How the Brain Science of Attention Will Transform the Way We Live, Work, and Learn*. New York: Viking.

Deng, Francis, and Austin Wesevich. 2016. "Pass-Fail Is Here to Stay in Medical Schools. And That's a Good Thing." *KevinMD.com*. August 3. https://www .kevinmd.com/blog/2016/08/pass-fail-stay-medical-schools-thats-good-thing .html.

Dunn, Dana S., and Jane S. Halonen. 2019. "The Extra-Credit Question: Should You Offer It or Resist?" *The Chronicle of Higher Education*. April 3. https:// www.chronicle.com/article/The-Extra-Credit-Question-/246015.

Durm, Mark W. 1993. "An A Is Not an A Is Not an A: A History of Grading." *The Educational Forum* 57 (Spring). http://www.indiana.edu/~educy520/sec6342 /week_07/durm93.pdf.

Elbow, Peter. 1994. "Ranking, Evaluating, Liking: Sorting Out Three Forms of Judgment." *College English* 12. https://scholarworks.umass.edu/cgi /viewcontent.cgi?referer=&httpsredir=1&article=1011&context=eng_faculty _pubs.

Elman, Benjamin A. 2000. *A Cultural History of Civil Examinations in Late Imperial China*. Berkeley: University of California Press.

Ennis, R. 2012. "Grading the Critical Thinking Aspects of the CLA Test." Central Division Meeting of the Association for Informal Logic and Critical Thinking.

Eyler, Joshua R. 2018. *How Humans Learn: The Science and Stories behind Effective College Teaching*. Morgantown: West Virginia University Press.

Gardner, Howard. [1983] 2011. *Frames of Mind: The Theory of Multiple Intelligences*. Reprint, New York: Basic Books.

Gershon, Ilana. 2017. *Down and Out in the New Economy: How People Find (Or Don't Find) Work Today*. Chicago: University of Chicago Press.

Gould, Stephen Jay. [1981] 1996. *The Mismeasure of Man*. Rev. ed. New York: Norton.

Grossman, Dana Cook. 2016. "Reducing the Stigma: Faculty Speak Out about Suicide Rates among Medical Students, Physicians." *AAMC News*. September 27. https://news.aamc.org/medical-education/article/reducing-stigma-suicide-rates/.

Harris, Malcolm. 2018. *Kids These Days: The Making of Millennials*. New York: Hachette.

Harvey, David. 2005. *A Brief History of Neoliberalism*. Oxford: Oxford University Press.

Heinz, Nicholas. 2018. "Failing Grade: How China's All-Important Exam Is Stunting National Growth." *Berkeley Political Review*. December 7. https://bpr.berkeley.edu/2018/12/07/failing-grade-how-chinas-all-important-exam-is-stunting-national-growth/.

Henrich, Joseph, Steven J. Heine, and Ara Norenzayan. 2010. "The Weirdest People in the World?" *Behavioral and Brain Science* 33(2–3): 61–83.

Howlett, Zachary. 2017. "China's Examination Fever and the Fabrication of Fairness: 'My Generation Was Raised on Poison Milk.' " In *Emptiness and Fullness: Ethnographies of Lack and Desire in Contemporary China*, edited by Susanne Bregnbæk and Mikkel Bunkenborg, pp. 15–35. New York: Berghahn Books.

Howlett, Zachary. Forthcoming. *Fateful Rite of Passage: The National College Entrance Examination and the Myth of Meritocracy in Post-Mao China*. N.P.

Ireh, Maduakolum. 2016. *Scientific Management Still Endures in Education*. Department of Education, Winston Salem State University.

Jack, Anthony Abraham. 2019. *The Privileged Poor: How Elite Colleges Are Failing Disadvantaged Students*. Cambridge, MA: Harvard University Press.

Jaschik, Scott. 2009. "Imagining College without Grades." *Inside Higher Ed*. January 22. https://www.insidehighered.com/news/2009/01/22/imagining-college-without-grades.

Jones, Evan. 2014. Which Law Schools Are Pass/Fail? *LawSchooli.com*. March 18. https://lawschooli.com/law-schools-passfail/.

Kaminer, Ariel. 2014. "Princeton Is Proposing to End Limit on Giving A's." *The New York Times*. August 7. https://www.nytimes.com/2014/08/08/nyregion/princeton-considers-end-to-limit-on-number-of-as.html.

Kane, Will. 2019. "Anxiety 'Epidemic' Brewing on College Campuses, Researchers Find." *UC Berkeley News*. April 18. https://news.berkeley.edu/2019/04/18/anxiety-epidemic-brewing-on-college-campuses-researchers-find/.

Kirschenbaum, Howard, Sidney B. Simon, and Rodney W. Napier. 1971. *Wad-ja-get? The Grading Game in American Education*. New York: Hart Publishing.

Koti, Shruti. 2015. "The Truth about UC Berkeley's 'Grade Deflation.' " *The Daily Californian*. May 16. http://www.dailycal.org/2015/05/15/grade-deflation/.

Kvale, Steinar. 2007. "Contradictions of Assessment for Learning in Institutions of Higher Learning." In *Rethinking Assessment in Higher Education: Learning for the Longer Term*, edited by David Boud and Nancy Falchikov, pp. 57–62. London: Routledge.

Lang, James M. 2016. *Small Teaching: Everyday Lessons from the Science of Learning*. San Francisco: Jossey-Bass.

Lederman, Doug. 2019. "Harsh Take on Assessment . . . from Assessment Pros." *Inside Higher Ed*. April 17. https://www.insidehighered.com/news/2019/04/17/advocates-student-learning-assessment-say-its-time-different-approach.

Lemann, Nicholas. 1999. *The Big Test: The Secret History of the American Meritocracy.* New York: Farrar, Straus and Giroux.

Levin, Robert A. 1991. "The Debate over Schooling: Influences of Dewey and Thorndike." *Childhood Education* 68(2): 71–75.

Livio, Mario. 2017. *Why? What Makes Us Curious.* New York: Simon & Schuster.

McMillan Cottom, Tressie. 2019. *Thick: And Other Essays.* New York: New Press.

Miyazaki, I. [1963] 1981. *China's Examination Hell: The Civil Service Examinations of Imperial China.* Translated by C. Schirokauer. Reprint, New Haven, CT: Yale University Press.

Muller, Jerry Z. 2018. *The Tyranny of Metrics.* Princeton, NJ: Princeton University Press.

Panksepp, Jaak, and Lucy Biven. 2012. *The Archaeology of Mind: Neuroevolutionary Origins of Human Emotions.* New York: Norton.

Possin, Kevin. 2013. "A Serious Flaw in the Collegiate Learning Assessment [CLA] Test." *Informal Logic* 33: 390–405.

Rogoff, Barbara. 2001. "Why a Nonconventional College Decided to Add Grades." *The Chronicle of Higher Education.* September 14, p. B17.

Rojstaczer, Stuart. 2016. "Grade Inflation at American Colleges and Universities." GradeInflation.com. http://www.gradeinflation.com/.

Ryan, Richard M., and Edward L. Deci. 2000. "Intrinsic and Extrinsic Motivations: Classic Definitions and New Directions." *Contemporary Educational Psychology* 25: 54–67.

Schinske, Jeffrey, and Kimberly Tanner. 2014. "Teaching More by Grading Less (or Differently)." *CBE—Life Sciences Education* 13(2): 159–66. https://doi.org /10.1187/cbe.CBE-14-03-0054.

Smallwood, M. L. 1935. *Examinations and Grading Systems in Early American Universities.* Cambridge, MA: Harvard University Press.

Spencer, Kyle. 2017. "A New Kind of Classroom: No Grades, No Failing, No Hurry." *The New York Times.* August 11. https://www.nytimes.com/2017/08/11 /nyregion/mastery-based-learning-no-grades.html.

Starch, Daniel, and Edward C. Elliott. 1912. "Reliability of the Grading of High School Work in English." *School Review* 20: 442–57.

Starch, Daniel, and Edward C. Elliott. 1913a. "Reliability of Grading Work in History." *School Review* 21: 676–81.

Starch, Daniel, and Edward C. Elliott. 1913b. "Reliability of Grading Work in Mathematics." *School Review* 21: 254–95.

Stevenson, Dean. 2019. "A, B, C, D, and F: Meaningful Grades or Random Letters?" Paper presented at the National Council of Teachers of Mathematics conference, September 25–27, Boston, MA. https://www.youtube.com/watch?v=UFR93oiw FEk#action=share.

Stray, Christopher. 2001. "The Shift from Oral to Written Examinations: Cambridge and Oxford 1700–1900." *Assessment in Education: Principles, Policy & Practice* 8(1): 33–50.

Taras, Maddalena. 2005. "Assessment—Summative and Formative—Some Theoretical Reflections." *British Journal of Educational Studies* 53(4): 466–78.

Tobin, Michael. 2017. "UO Study Finds Correlation between Grade Inflation and Student Course Evaluations." *Daily Emerald.* July 17. https://www.dailyemerald .com/news/uo-study-finds-correlation-between-grade-inflation-student

-course-evaluations/article_2ec7ac20-f6b1-5e21-bb82-346c859e
9eb5.html.

Tobin, Thomas J., and Kirsten T. Behling. 2018. *Reach Everyone, Teach Everyone:
Universal Design for Learning in Higher Education*. Morgantown: West Virginia
University Press.

Willingham, Daniel T. 2009. *Why Don't Students Like School? A Cognitive Scientist
Answers Questions about How the Mind Works and What It Means for the
Classroom*. San Francisco: Jossey-Bass.

Zhao, Yong. 2018. *What Works May Hurt: Side Effects in Education*. New York:
Teachers College Press.

Part I

FOUNDATIONS AND MODELS

Chapter 1

———

HOW TO UNGRADE

Jesse Stommel

———

Grading has become the elephant in almost every room where discussions of education are underway. As Peter Elbow writes, "Grading tends to undermine the climate for teaching and learning. Once we start grading their work, students are tempted to study or work for the grade rather than for learning."[1] Grading is something we never should have allowed to be naturalized.

Prior to the late 1700s, performance and feedback systems in US education were idiosyncratic. The one-room schoolhouse called for an incredibly subjective, peer-driven, nontransactional approach to assessment. Throughout the nineteenth century, feedback systems became increasingly comparative, numerical, and standardized. Letter grades are a relatively recent phenomenon. They weren't widely used until the 1940s. In "Teaching More by Grading Less," Jeffrey Schinske and Kimberly Tanner cite the first "official record" of a grading system from Yale in 1785.[2] The A–F system appears to have emerged in 1898 (with the E not disappearing until the 1930s), and the 100-point or percentage scale became common in the early 1900s. According to Schinske and Tanner, even by 1971 only 67 percent of primary and secondary schools in the United States were using letter grades. The desire for uniformity across institutions was the primary motivator for the spread of these systems.

An "objective" approach to grading was created so systematized schooling could scale—so students could be neatly ranked and sorted into classrooms with desks in rows in increasingly large warehouse-like buildings. And we've designed technological tools in the twentieth and twenty-first centuries, like massive open online courses and machine grading, that have allowed us to scale even further, away from human relationships and care. In fact, the grade has been hard-coded into all our institutional and technological systems, an impenetrable phalanx of clarity, certainty, and defensibility.

When I first taught fully online, I encountered the horror that is the gradebook inside most learning management systems (LMSs), which reduces students (often color coding them) into mere rows in a spreadsheet. I've watched this tool proliferate into all the institutions where I've worked. Even teachers who don't use the LMS for its decidedly more pleasurable uses have made its gradebook more and more central to the learning experience. To the point that, when I've chosen not to use the institutionally adopted LMS, students sometimes ask after the LMS in its absence. Not because the LMS has any particularly useful magic, but because we've come to expect it—to be comforted by the inevitability of its use. When a grade appears there, we feel a sense of completion, acknowledgment. A reassurance of our place in the education hierarchy, whether teacher or student. In *Now You See It*, Cathy Davidson calls the gradebook a "prop," the "symbol of pedagogical power."[3]

On its surface, the LMS gradebook does not seem all that functionally different from an analog gradebook, which also reduces students to mere rows in a spreadsheet. But most learning management systems now offer (or threaten) to automate a process that is, in fact, deeply personal. The LMS gradebook does make grading more efficient, as though efficiency is something we ought to celebrate in teaching and learning. Assessment is reduced to a mark, and the complexity of human interaction within a learning environment is made machine readable.

According to marketing statements on their public websites, Angel's "automated agents save time," Blackboard facilitates teacher-student "interaction" by "calculating grades," and Canvas calls its tool "speed grader." The problem is not just the fact of grades but the fetishization of them.

Ranking. Norming. Objectivity. Uniformity. Standardization. Measurement. Outcomes. Quality. Data. Performance. Metrics. Scores. Excellence. Mastery. Rigor.

There is no room for student agency to breathe in a system of incessant grading, ranking, and scoring.

WHY I DON'T GRADE

I've forgone grades on individual assignments for over eighteen years, relying on qualitative feedback, peer review, and self-assessment. My goal in eschewing grades has been to more honestly engage student work rather than simply evaluate it. Over many years, this has meant carefully navigating, and even breaking, the sometimes absurd rules of a half-dozen institutions. In "Civil Disobedience," Henry David Thoreau writes, "If it is of such a nature that it requires you to be the agent of injustice to another, then, I say, break the law. Let your life be a counter friction to stop the machine."[4]

When I first taught as instructor of record in spring 2001, I did not give grades. I was inspired by a mentor, Martin Bickman, the only college professor who had not given me grades. Over the years I've taught over one hundred sections of courses at six institutions in various disciplines. I've taught traditional students, nontraditional students, for credit, not for credit, online, in classrooms, as a tenure-track professor, as an adjunct, at small liberal arts colleges (SLACs), at a community college, and at research universities (R1s). I have not always felt I could be publicly open about my approach to grading at the institutions where I've worked.

My ideas about grades and assessment have evolved over the years, as I've become a more confident teacher. But I am even more certain of what I instinctively knew when I taught that first class in 2001: grades are the biggest and most insidious obstacle to education. And they are a thorn in the side of critical pedagogy. John Holt writes in *Instead of Education* that competitive schooling, grades, and credentials "seem to me the most authoritarian and dangerous of all the social inventions."[5] Agency, dialogue, self-actualization, and social justice are not possible (or, at least, unlikely) in a hierarchical system that pits teachers against students and encourages competition by ranking students against one another. Grades are currency for a capitalist system that reduces teaching and learning to a mere transaction. They are an institutional instrument of compliance that works exactly because they have been so effectively naturalized. Grading is a massive coordinated effort to take humans out of the educational process.

Grades are not good incentive. They incentivize the wrong stuff: the product over the process, what the teacher thinks over what the student thinks, etc.

Grades are not good feedback. They are both too simplistic, making something complex into something numerical (8/10, 85%), and too complicated, offering so many gradations as to be inscrutable (A, A–, A/A–, 85.4%, 8.5/10).

Grades are not good markers of learning. They too often communicate only a student's ability to follow instructions, not how much she has learned. A 4.0 or higher GPA might indicate excellence, but it might also indicate a student having to compromise their integrity for the sake of a grade.

Grades encourage competitiveness over collaboration. And supposed *kindnesses*, like grading on a curve or norming, actually increase competitiveness by pitting students (and sometimes teachers) against one another.

Grades don't reflect the idiosyncratic, subjective, often emotional character of learning.

Finally, grades aren't fair. They will never be fair.

All of this demands exactly two pedagogical approaches:

1. Start by trusting students.
2. Realize "fairness" is not a good excuse for a lack of compassion.

My approach to assessment arises from these two principles. While I've experimented with many alternatives to traditional assessment, I have primarily relied on self-assessment, asking students to do the work of reflecting critically on their own learning.

Amy Fast writes on Twitter, "the saddest and most ironic practice in schools is how hard we try to measure how students are doing and how rarely we ever ask them."[6] We have created increasingly elaborate assessment mechanisms, all while failing to recognize that students themselves are the best experts in their own learning. Certainly metacognition, and the ability to self-assess, must be developed, but I see it as one of the most important skills we can teach in any educational environment.

I include the following statement about assessment in my syllabi:

> This course will focus on qualitative not quantitative assessment, something we'll discuss during the class, both with reference to your own work and the works we're studying. While you will get a final grade at the end of the term, I will not be grading individual assignments, but rather asking questions and making comments that engage your work rather than simply evaluate it. You will also be reflecting carefully on your own work and the work of your peers. The intention here is to help you focus on working in a more organic way, as opposed to working as you think you're expected to. If this process causes more anxiety than it alleviates, see me at any point to confer about your progress in the course to date. If you are worried about your grade, your best strategy should be to join the discussions, do the reading, and complete the assignments. *You should consider this course a "busywork-free zone." If an assignment does not feel productive, we can find ways to modify, remix, or repurpose the instructions.*[7]

It's important to note that an ungraded class does not mean grades don't influence the work that happens there. Grades are ubiquitous in our educational system to the point that new teachers don't feel they can safely explore alternative approaches to assessment. In my experience, new teachers are rarely told they have to grade, but grading is internalized as an imperative nonetheless. And student expectations and anxiety can still swirl around them even when they're taken mostly off the table.

Google Trends shows increased search volume around the term *grades* over the sixteen years from 2004 to 2019. It also shows an increasingly furious pattern of search behavior centered each year on the months of May and December, like a heartbeat beginning to race. And this has been

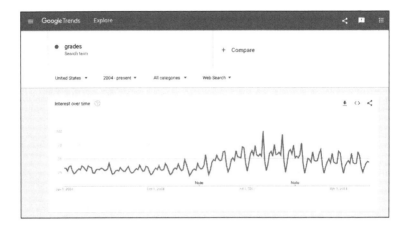

Figure 1.1. Google Trends search for "grades," 2004 to 2019.

my personal experience as well, as I've watched the increasing anxiety around grades become more and more palpable.

I am also finding myself drowning in buzzwords.

Learning Outcomes: More and more, we are required to map our assignments, assessments, and curricula to learning outcomes. But I find it strange that teachers and institutions would predetermine outcomes before students even arrive on the scene. I argue, instead, for *emergent outcomes*, ones that are cocreated by teachers and students and revised on the fly. Setting trajectories rather than mapping in advance the possible shapes for learning.

Grade Inflation: The problem, I'd say, is grades not inflation. And when institutions try to control grade inflation, the results are disturbing, and perhaps also unsurprising.[8] Require teachers to give more B and C grades and they give more B and C grades disproportionately to Black students. We should be *creating opportunities*, not *limiting possibilities* for success. The best feedback I've ever gotten from a student, and something I've since tried to reflect more explicitly in my pedagogy, was: "Jesse's class was one of the hardest I've taken in my life; it was an easy 'A'." Having high expectations and giving mostly good grades are not incompatible.

Grade Grubbing: If this phrase is still in your vocabulary, do a quick internet search for the words *grub* and *grubber*, and I suspect you'll stop attributing these words to students. As educators we have helped build (or are complicit in) a system that creates a great deal of pressure around grades. We shouldn't blame (or worse, belittle) students for the failures of that system.

Objectivity: In brief I do not think objectivity is a virtue if dialogue is what we're after in education. Human interaction is incredibly complex. Authentic feedback (and evaluation) means honoring subjectivity and requires that we show up as our full selves, both teachers and learners, to the work of education. Grades can't be normed if we recognize the complexity of learners and learning contexts. Bias can't be accounted for unless we acknowledge it.

Rubrics: Most rubrics I've seen are overly mechanistic and attempt to create objectivity and efficiency in evaluation by crashing on the rocks of bureaucracy. Learning and human interaction are sufficiently high resolution that a 3×3 grid, or a 5×5 grid, usually fails to capture the complexity of learning or student work. And when rubrics are given in advance to students, they are likely to close down possibility by encouraging students to work toward a prescribed notion of excellence.

Participation Grades: Too many of our conventional practices work to reduce the complexity of learning to its detriment. Grading participation, for example, is an exercise in futility. Different humans engage in different ways at different times, and much of that engagement is effectively invisible to crude quantitative mechanisms. Most grading scales offer way too many demarcations to communicate clearly and way too few demarcations to reflect reality. They frustrate organic participation by foregrounding control. Laura Gibbs writes in "(Un)Grading: It Can Be Done in College," "Because I put myself outside of the grading loop, I can focus all my efforts on feedback and encouragement—on teaching, not grading." [9] We can't participate authentically, can't engage in real dialogue, without first disrupting the power dynamics of grading.

Grades as Motivators: Alfie Kohn writes in "The Trouble with Rubrics," "Research shows three reliable effects when students are graded: They tend to think less deeply, avoid taking risks, and lose interest in the learning itself." [10] Grades do motivate, but they don't usually motivate the kinds of peak experiences that can happen in a learning environment. Something like "have an epiphany, communicate an original thought, sit uncomfortably with your not knowing, or build something that's never been built before" can't be motivated by a grade.

Grading on a Curve: In brief grading on a curve pits students against each other, discourages collaboration, and privileges the students who our educational system has already privileged. Cathy N. Davidson writes, "There is an extreme mismatch between what we value and how we count."[11]

Mastery: I've long argued education should be about encouraging and rewarding *not knowing* more than *knowing*. When I give presentations on grading and assessment, I often get some variation of the question, How would you want your doctor to have been graded? My cheeky first answer is that I am most concerned with whether my doctor has read all the books of Virginia Woolf, because critical thinking is what will help them save my life when they encounter a situation they've never encountered before. I go on to say I would want a mixture of things assessed and a mixture of kinds of assessment, because the work of being a doctor (or engineer, sociologist, teacher, etc.) is sufficiently complex that any one system of measurement or indicator of supposed mastery will necessarily fail.

HOW I DON'T GRADE

As I was preparing to write this piece, I looked through web pages offering advice on grading at a dozen higher education institutions (most from teaching and learning centers). What I noticed is how so much of the language around grading emphasizes efficiency over the needs of individual learners. Nods to fairness are too often made for the sake of defensibility rather than equity. One site, for example, encourages "discussing grades with students" as a way toward making those grades "less likely to be contested." The work of grading is too often framed less in terms of encouraging learning and more as a way of ranking students against one another. Another site argues that "grades should be monotonic: within any pair of students, the student with better performance should not be given a lower grade." Others have headings like "grading as a fair teaching tool," "limit grading time," "responding to grade challenges," "maintaining your sanity," "easing the pain," and "making grading more efficient." What disturbs me is how effortlessly and casually this language rolls off Education's collective tongue. And I'm even more disturbed by how many otherwise productive pedagogical conversations get sidetracked by the bureaucratic dimensions of grades.

The page from the Berkeley Graduate Division offering "Tips on Grading Efficiently," for example, is pretty standard fare.[12] The very first bit of advice on grading for new graduate student instructors raises more anxiety around grades than it alleviates. And at the same time, as is all too common, grading is something new teachers are encouraged to spend as little time on as possible: "Too often, time spent grading takes away from time spent doing your own coursework or research."

Without much critical examination, teachers accept that they have to grade, students accept that they have to be graded, students are made to feel like they should care a great deal about grades, and teachers are told they shouldn't spend much time thinking about the why, when, and whether of grades. Obedience to a system of crude ranking is made to feel altruistic, because it is supposedly fair, saves time, and helps prepare students for the horrors of the "real world." Conscientious objection seems increasingly impossible.

When I talk about why I don't grade, I often hear some version of "but I have to grade" because I'm an adjunct, because my institution requires it, because grading is necessary in my discipline, because wouldn't you want your heart surgeon to have been graded? The need to navigate institutional (and disciplinary) pressures is real, but I would argue teachers grade in many more situations than grading is useful or is required by institutions. When I was a "road warrior adjunct," teaching up to nine courses at four institutions, how I taught and how I talked about my pedagogy were different from one institution to the next. I had to balance my own approach with the specific requirements at each institution. But I can also say that none of the institutions where I've worked has dictated how I had to approach assessment—at every single one there was sufficient wiggle room for experimentation.

Peter Elbow writes in "Ranking, Evaluating, Liking: Sorting Out Three Forms of Judgment," "Let's do as little ranking and grading as we can. They are never fair and they undermine learning and teaching."[13] I believe pedagogy is personal and idiosyncratic. My approach won't necessarily work in each classroom, at every institution, for all teachers, with every group of students. My hope here is to challenge stock assumptions, describe what has worked for me, and explore alternatives that might work for others.

I am often asked if (and how) I deal with student anxiety in an ungraded class. Of course, being asked to do this work is a challenge. For as much anxiety as grades can create, being graded is something most of us find comfortable. Students are increasingly conditioned to work within a system that emphasizes objective measures of performance and quantitative assessment. It's important to acknowledge that these systems have been (in some cases intentionally) crafted to privilege certain kinds of students. It's also important to acknowledge that, in lieu of these systems, there are tacit expectations that still favor already privileged students. Students who are female, Black, Brown, Indigenous, disabled, neurodivergent, queer, etc. face overt and systemic oppression whether expectations are explicit or implicit. Soraya Chemaly writes in "All Teachers Should Be Trained to Overcome Their Hidden Biases," "Training teachers to understand bias will not eliminate it, but it could create an institutional environment in which it is clear that understanding bias and its effects is critically important."[14]

It's also important that teachers (and institutions) open these pedagogical conversations to students. And that whether we're grading or not, we think critically (and talk openly with students) about our approaches, assumptions, tacit expectations, and actual expectations. We don't prepare students for a world of potential oppression by oppressing them.

Over many years I've found that not grading begins a set of necessary conversations among my colleagues, between me and students, and among students in my classes. Currently I have students write self-evaluations two to three times throughout the term. The first of these is usually more directed (with specific questions) than the last (which opens into something more like an essay).

What students write to me in these self-evaluations is profoundly different from the kinds of interactions we would have in a purely transactional system. Their self-evaluations (which I sometimes call "process letters"), and my responses to them, become a space of dialogue, not just about the course, but about their learning and about how learning happens. Not every interaction rises to that level, but many do. With almost every single student, any assumption I might make about them is squashed by what they write about themselves and their work. My view of students as complex and deeply committed to their education is fueled by the thousands of self-reflection letters I've read throughout my career.

At the end of the term, every institution where I've worked has required me to issue a final grade for students. So I ask the students to grade themselves. I wish I didn't have to do this. I wish the conversation I had with students could focus purely on authentic assessment, process, and formative feedback. But I have found that asking students to give themselves a grade also makes the why and how of grades a valuable subject of the conversations we have—valuable because they will go on to be graded in other courses, and thinking critically about how and why grading happens helps that become more productive for them.

I am frequently asked what I do when I disagree with the grade a student gives themselves. What I say is that if I am going to give the responsibility of grading over to students, I have to let go of my attachment to the accuracy of that process. Instead I give feedback, and the need for objectivity or accuracy gives way to a dialogue—one that is necessarily emergent and subjective. I do make clear on the syllabus (and in class) that "I reserve the right to change grades as appropriate." But I do this only very rarely, and I usually have to raise grades (because students are often their own harshest critics). The most common change I make is from an A– to an A for students who offer no good reason other than modesty for giving themselves the A–. (I have observed a distinct gender imbalance in this, with women students much more likely to give themselves an A–.) Ultimately, students get the full range of grades in my classes.

ALTERNATE APPROACHES TO ASSESSMENT

Grading and assessment are two distinct things, and spending less time on grading does not mean spending less time on assessment. Assessment is inevitable. Ungrading asks us to question our assumptions about what assessment looks like, how we do it, and who it is for. There is no single approach to ungrading that will work universally. And ungrading works best when teachers feel they can fully own their pedagogical approaches (which requires administrators and institutions to defend the academic freedom of teachers, especially adjuncts). I encourage teachers not to get too caught up in the mechanics of ungrading, because I agree with Alfie Kohn who writes, "When the how's of assessment preoccupy us, they tend to chase the why's back into the shadows." [15] There are lots of possible paths toward ungrading, and smaller experiments can be just as fruitful as larger ones.

Grade-Free Zones

Sometimes it's hard to imagine diving right into the deep end of ungrading, so try having the first third of the term be ungraded, a sandbox for students to experiment inside before moving on to the more formal activities of a course. Or decide to grade only a few major assignments.

Self-Assessment

I've already talked at length about how I use self-assessment. What I'll add is that this work is both part of my approach to the problem of grades and also an end in and of itself. Ann Berthoff writes in "Dialectical Notebooks and the Audit of Meaning," "Learning to look carefully, to see what you're looking at, is perennially acclaimed as the essential skill for both artist and scientist." [16] Metacognition is a practical skill that cuts across disciplines. bell hooks advocates for "continual self-evaluation" both of a student by the student and of a teacher by the teacher.[17] I would add that we—teachers and students in dialogue—should evaluate our collective work together, the class itself.

Process Letters

If you're only grading a few assignments, you may not feel like you have enough information to determine a final grade at the end of a course. I have students write process letters, describing their learning and how their work evolves over the term. These work particularly well for creative and digital work that might otherwise seem inscrutable within traditional grading and feedback systems. A process letter can be text, including (or pointing to) representative examples of work students don't otherwise turn in. You might also ask students to take pictures of their work as it evolves, add voice-over to a screencast, or document their learning via film (a sort of behind-the-scenes reel for the class).

Minimal Grading

In "Grading Student Writing: Making It Simpler, Fairer, Clearer," Peter Elbow describes what he calls "minimal grading," using a simple grading scale instead of giving students bizarre grades like 97%, 18/20, or A-/B+.[18] Scales with too many gradations make it difficult for teachers to determine grades and even more difficult for students to interpret them. Elbow recommends scales with fewer gradations: turned in (one gradation), pass/fail (two gradations), strong/satisfactory/weak (three gradations). He also describes a "zero scale," in which some work is assigned but not collected at all. This frees teachers from feeling they have to respond to, evaluate, or even read every bit of work students do. And this last, moving away from student work as a thing to be collected, might prove best at creating intrinsic motivation to do the work of a course.

Authentic Assessment

In my film courses, I often ask students to organize a film festival or premiere to share their work for the class. These usually include talk-backs with the audience. Increasingly I don't ask students to turn assignments in to me (aside from their self-reflections). The community of the class becomes their audience. I allow myself space to be one member of that community, a genuine reader of student work. In a service learning course, this community expands beyond the boundaries of the class. In short, how can we create reasons more meaningful than points for students to do the work of a course?

Contract Grading

Grading contracts convey expectations about what is required for each potential grade (see also chapter 7, Katopodis and Davidson). In "A Grade-Less Writing Course That Focuses on Labor and Assessing," Asao B. Inoue argues for "calculating course grades by labor completed and [dispensing] almost completely with judgments of quality."[19] Students work toward the grade they want to achieve, and goalposts don't unexpectedly shift. These contracts can also be negotiated with the class. Either way, contract grading pushes against the relegating of people into categories ("A student," "B student") by keeping the focus on the work rather than the student. Contract grading can be humane in a way that standardized teacher-centered rubrics usually are not. Contracts do run the risk of centering grades even more than traditional grading, but at their best, the negotiating around the contract becomes a way for students to collectively worry the edges of grading as a system.

Portfolios

Increasingly, many corporate e-portfolio platforms are walled gardens, giving students a regimented way of gathering together their work for the purposes of assessment. I prefer more authentic portfolios that have use value beyond the needs of individual, course, programmatic, or institutional assessment. Having students build personal or professional sites on the web, for example, can help them craft a digital identity that exists outside (but also in conversation with) their coursework. The key is to use a portfolio not as a mere receptacle for assignments but as a metacognitive space, one with immediate practical value (as a way for students to share their work with potential collaborators, employers, graduate schools, etc.).

Peer-Assessment

Peer-assessment can be formal (having students evaluate each other's work) or informal (just having students actively engage with one another's work). It can be particularly useful when students work in large groups. I frequently ask students to work on projects that have an entire class (of twenty-five or more) collaborating. When I do this, I ask every student to write a process letter that addresses their own contributions as well as the functionality and dynamic of the team they're working with. With large-group projects, it is hard for me to see what and how each student contributes, but peer-assessment helps me get a view into a process I might not otherwise be able to see. If it is a project students work on across the entire term, asking students to complete process letters multiple times also allows me to get the information I need to step in and help when and where I'm needed.

Student-Made Rubrics

I'll be entirely honest. I'm not a fan of rubrics. Alfie Kohn, in "The Trouble with Rubrics," describes them as an "attempt to deny the subjectivity of human judgment."[20] Rubrics are often recommended as a way to make standards for evaluation transparent, but rubrics have never helped me make sense of grading or being graded. For me learning is just too complex to fit into neat and tidy little boxes. Peter Elbow encourages making rubrics plainer and more direct, a 3 × 3 or smaller grid. The rubrics I find most exciting are ones crafted by students—so that the making of the rubric becomes an act of learning itself rather than a device (or set of assumptions) created entirely in advance of students arriving to a course.

These alternative approaches can work on their own or in combination. With classes of twenty-five or three hundred. (You aren't going to write an individual letter responding to every student self-evaluation in a class of three hundred, but you can write a letter to the whole class, talking about the trends you notice and suggestions for moving forward.) Ultimately any assessment strategy demands us to adapt, in the moment, as we encounter each new group of students. This attention to context, our own and our students', is what critical pedagogy calls for.

The work of ungrading begins with us each asking hard questions about the what, why, and how of grading. Specifically:

- Why do we grade? How does it feel to be graded? What do we want grading to do (or not do) in our classes (for students or teachers)?
- What do letter grades mean? Do they have intrinsic meaning, or is their value purely extrinsic? Does assessment mean something different when it is formative rather than summative?
- How does feedback function in relation to grades? Does grading create a power structure that frustrates authentic dialogue? To what extent should teachers be readers of student work (as opposed to evaluators)?
- What would happen if we didn't grade? How would institutions be forced to rethink their hierarchies and systems for evaluation?
- If grades are going to remain ubiquitous in education, can we be more creative in how we approach them?

At the very least, our talk of grading shouldn't be reduced to our complaining about its continuing necessity.

NOTES

1. Elbow 1997: 127.
2. Schinske and Tanner 2014.
3. Davidson 2011: 107.
4. Thoreau [1857] 2004: 370.
5. Holt [1976] 2004: 4.
6. Amy Fast (@fastcrayon), March 28, 2016, 8:05 p.m., https://twitter.com /fastcrayon/status/714604325146902528.
7. Jesse Stommel, "Intro. to Cinema Studies Syllabus," January 12, 2017, https://medium.com/cinema-studies/introduction-to-cinema-studies -syllabus-22db40cd7172.
8. Nelson 2015.
9. Gibbs 2016. See also chapter 6, Gibbs.
10. Kohn 2006.
11. Davidson 2012.
12. Berkeley Graduate Division, "Tips on Grading Efficiently," https://gsi .berkeley.edu/gsi-guide-contents/grading-intro/grading-efficiently/.
13. Elbow 1994.

14. Chemaly 2015.
15. Kohn 2006.
16. Berthoff 1987: 13.
17. hooks 1994: 17.
18. Elbow 1994.
19. Inoue 2014: 71.
20. Kohn 2006.

SOURCES

Berthoff, Ann E. 1987. "Dialectical Notebooks and the Audit of Meaning." In *The Journal Book*, edited by Toby Fulwiler, pp. 11–18. Portsmouth, NH: Boynton/Cook.

Chemaly, Soraya. 2015. "All Teachers Should Be Trained to Overcome Their Hidden Biases." *Time*. February 12. http://time.com/3705454/teachers-biases-girls-education/.

Davidson, Cathy N. 2011. *Now You See It: How Technology and Brain Science Will Transform Schools and Business for the 21st Century*. New York: Penguin.

Davidson, Cathy. 2012. "How Do We Measure What Really Counts in the Classroom?" *Fast Company*. September 20. https://www.fastcompany.com/1680584/how-do-we-measure-what-really-counts-in-the-classroom.

Elbow, Peter. 1994. "Ranking, Evaluating, Liking: Sorting Out Three Forms of Judgment." *College English* 12. https://scholarworks.umass.edu/cgi/viewcontent.cgi?referer=&httpsredir=1&article=1011&context=eng_faculty_pubs.

Elbow, Peter. 1997. "Grading Student Writing: Making It Simpler, Fairer, Clearer." *New Directions for Teaching and Learning* 69 (Spring): 127–40.

Gibbs, Laura. 2016. "Un(Grading): It Can Be Done in College." *Education Week Teacher*. March 31. http://blogs.edweek.org/teachers/work_in_progress/2016/03/ungrading_it_can_be_done_in_co.html.

Holt, John. [1976] 2004. *Instead of Education: Ways to Help People Do Things Better*. Reprint, Boulder, CO: Sentient.

hooks, bell. 1994. *Teaching to Transgress: Education as the Practice of Freedom*. New York: Routledge.

Inoue, Asao B. 2014. "A Grade-Less Writing Course That Focuses on Labor and Assessing." In *First-Year Composition: From Theory to Practice*, edited by D. Teague and R. Lunsford, pp. 71–110. West Lafayette: Parlor Press.

Kohn, Alfie. 2006. "The Trouble with Rubrics." *English Journal* 95(4). https://www.alfiekohn.org/article/trouble-rubrics/.

Nelson, Libby. 2015. "Black Students Were Hurt Most When Wellesley Tried to Control Grade Inflation." *Vox*. March 13. https://www.vox.com/2014/8/26/6067175/grade-inflation-college-wellesley.

Schinske, Jeffrey, and Kimberly Tanner. 2014. "Teaching More by Grading Less (or Differently)." *CBE—Life Sciences Education* 13(2): 159–66. https://doi.org/10.1187/cbe.CBE-14-03-0054.

Thoreau, Henry David. [1857] 2004. *Walden and Civil Disobedience*. Reprint, New York: Simon & Schuster.

Chapter 2

———

WHAT GOING GRADELESS TAUGHT ME ABOUT DOING THE "ACTUAL WORK"

Aaron Blackwelder

———

THE REVELATION

When I entered the teaching profession in 1998, I envisioned building relationships with students, discussing the intricacies of stories, and inspiring students to explore literature. I imagined my students developing into expressive writers who articulated their deepest thoughts with eloquence. In short, they would become lifelong readers and writers.

My first year in the classroom felt like this. I got to know every student. They showed an interest in books. And though their writing needed some structural and mechanical improvement, they were writing. I didn't know how to use a gradebook, so my focus was on learning, and my passion for reading and writing was evident to my first class. I knew every student's name. I knew their strengths and weaknesses. I knew their hopes and aspirations. It was a lot of work, but it was an amazing year.

However, as years passed, I noticed my students were losing interest in reading. The discussions began to lack depth; the writing became more mechanical. It seemed as though I had to threaten students with consequences, such as detentions, phone calls home, and poor grades, to motivate them. I continued to find easier ways to get students to understand reading and organize their writing. Year after year I found new formulas and tools to help my students, but it was clear the joy of learning had faded from my classroom and my room was more of an assembly line than a flourishing garden.

I began to wonder what was going on. What happened to that joy? Where was all the wonder? Were the kids changing or was it me?

I am a product of the eighties, a Gen Xer to the core. I grew up on John Hughes films. They spoke to the core of who I was and what I wanted to become. Hughes was a prophet to my generation. He embraced my teen angst and challenged me to question the status quo.

One of my favorite Hughes films is *The Breakfast Club.* In the movie the antagonist Richard Vernon, the teacher in charge of detention, complains to Carl, the janitor, about the kids. Vernon sees them as irreverent, lacking respect, and just plain apathetic. Carl reveals something that, though missed by Vernon, was quite profound:

> VERNON: Carl, don't be a goof! I'm trying to make a serious point here . . . I've been teaching, for twenty-two years, and each year . . . these kids get more and more arrogant.
>
> CARL: Aw bullshit, man. Come on Vern, the kids haven't changed, you have! You took a teaching position, 'cause you thought it'd be fun, right? Thought you could have summer vacations off . . . and then you found out it was actually work . . . and that really bummed you out.
>
> VERNON: These kids turned on me . . . They think I'm a big fuckin' joke . . .
>
> CARL: Come on . . . listen, Vern, if you were sixteen, what would you think of you, huh?
>
> VERNON: Hey . . . Carl, you think I give one rat's ass what these kids think of me?
>
> CARL: Yes, I do . . . [1]

These lines resonated with me. They shook me up. Rewatching this scene as an adult, I felt almost as though Carl was talking directly to

Figure 2.1. Mr. Vernon and Carl from *The Breakfast Club*.

me. The kids did not change. I changed. I lost touch. I wasn't someone students wanted to listen to. However, though both Vernon and I care about what our students thought about us, I acknowledge it and reflect upon it to build my practice.

I had lost my focus. I was more interested in keeping a class period busy, justifying the point value of each assignment, how these points would add up to ensure grades were earned. I was more concerned about how my colleagues and administration saw me than my learners. And in order to make my class more rigorous, I scoured student work to find ways to ensure no student earned 100 percent. I was no longer a teacher. I was a gatekeeper.[2] It was apparent to me because the profession was not as invigorating. I felt detached from my students, and school became a power struggle rather than a learning environment.

Most of my conversations with students were about grades. I was hounded with questions like "What can I do to change my grade from an A– to an A?" or "What will my grade be if I choose not to do this assignment?" When I would pass a student failing my class walking down the hall, there was always a mutual understanding that if we did not acknowledge each other we would not have to acknowledge the failing grade. My relationships with students were dependent on the accumulation of points in my gradebook. I felt like a cruel god who was keeping records of my students' sins to ultimately pass eternal judgment on them on the day of reckoning.

Besides this, I noticed that students had turned on each other. I wanted to inspire students to debate ideas around literature, philosophy, and social justice, but instead I heard students discuss who had the highest percentage in the class or who got the top score on last week's test while those with the lowest grades remained silent. Instead of more collaboration, students were in competition with one another. Instead of students being willing to learn from each other, they saw diversity as a threat to their status. This was not what I thought I'd become when I signed my first teaching contract in 1999.

When I realized this, I decided I needed either to leave the teaching profession or to make some major changes. I shared my concerns with my department, and they helped me explore options that would reignite me and transform my classroom.

As a department we began to deconstruct teaching and learning. We read the work of Alfie Kohn, Maja Wilson, Rick Wormeli, and others who wanted to liberate the classroom from a system focused on conformity. We asked the question, What is essential for students to learn? The answer led us to the discovery that learning can be fun.

THE PROBLEM

I came to the conclusion that it was my grading practice driving a wedge between the teacher I was and the teacher I wanted to be. I had turned on the kids. The kids didn't turn on me.

Grades are not an effective tool to communicate learning. Let's say a student gets an 85 percent (B) on an essay. What does the grade suggest? Did the student stop writing and turn in a perfectly written essay when he was 85 percent into it? Did the student fail to capitalize proper nouns and leave out citations? Was the essay late three days and I deducted 5 percent for each day it was late? Was it because I was tired of grading essays and simply threw the same score I put on that student's previous essay? It can be any or all of these. The problem is this grade does not tell the student what was done well and what she could do to improve.

Grades not only fail to communicate learning. They are also a carrot and stick that neither motivate nor promote learning. They diminish it.

I discovered Alfie Kohn's "From Degrading to De-grading." In it he argues the negative effects of grades:

1. Grades tend to reduce students' interest in the learning itself.
2. Grades tend to reduce students' preference for challenging tasks.
3. Grades tend to reduce the quality of students' thinking.
4. Grades aren't valid, reliable, or objective.
5. Grades distort the curriculum.
6. Grades waste a lot of time that could be spent on learning.
7. Grades encourage cheating.
8. Grades spoil teachers' relationships with students.
9. Grades spoil students' relationships with each other.[3]

All nine of these effects were found in my class. I was no longer emphasizing relationships. I wasn't inspiring. Letter grades and points became a shortcut—a way to avoid the hard work of getting to know my students on a personal level, working with them when they struggled, finding creative ways to encourage and instill wonder. I was avoiding the "actual work" to which Carl was referring.

I came across the work of Ruth Butler. In 1988 she published "Enhancing and Undermining Intrinsic Motivation."[4] Butler studied the effects of only comments, comments and grades, and only grades on student performance. She found that students who received only comments consistently outperformed the other two groups. Ironically, students who received both comments and grades performed about the same as (and sometimes worse than) those who received grades only.

I learned that comments, comments and grades, and grades impacted the ways students saw themselves. Butler suggested those who received comments only were more engaged in the task and viewed *the work* as either a success or failure. This meant that the work had problems that could be corrected, and the student had the power to make these revisions. However, when students received grades, they were more ego driven and saw success and failure as a reflection of *themselves.* Thus when I would put a letter or a number on student work, I was passing judgment on the student.

It bothered me that my students saw themselves as either successes or failures and that this attitude diminished their desire to try more challenging tasks. If students saw themselves as successes, they would be less likely to attempt tasks that could make others see them as failures. Conversely if my students perceived themselves as failures, they'd be less likely to put themselves into situations that reinforce this feeling. Butler's work forced me to look in the mirror and consider how my grading practices affected my students.

Ultimately I wanted my students to see learning as a process of ongoing trial and error rather than as a judgment of who they are. If my students did not fail, they did not learn. How often had I heard students say, "I suck at math," or "I just can't write," or even "I'm a C student"? If my students were going to learn and be challenged, then judgment needed to be eliminated. I had to take action.

THE WAY OUT

I was easily convinced I had to eliminate grades. However, this meant I couldn't use them to make my students work. So could I engage students without points and letters? Once again Carl hit the hammer on the head. This is the actual work of a teacher.

It became more apparent to me that students need to find value in what they learn. There has to be substance in school. In his book *The Schools Our Children Deserve,* Alfie Kohn challenges teachers to consider the value of the curriculum. At one point he questions the purpose of children knowing how to find the square root of a given number. What is the square root of ninety-three? Kohn's answer is, essentially, "Who cares?" [5] He suggests that if children cannot use the information in their daily lives, then there is no value in the curriculum. However, if it is important for children to know how to solve for the square root of a given number, then there needs to be a reason. This could be said about anything teachers expect kids to study in school from the US Constitution to *Beowulf.* Why do students need to know these things?

They need to know these things because they are going to be citizens of the world, and part of being a citizen means to have an understanding of culture, history, and the ideas that are the foundation of our nation. I latched on to the ideas found in Daniel Pink's book *Drive*. He suggests three things that motivate someone to learn: autonomy (the desire to be self-directed), mastery (the urge to get better at something), and purpose (the idea that what is being done has meaning).[6]

I wanted to tap into my students' drive and inspire them to achieve greatness. In order to do this, I had to start with the students' interests. I had to open conversations and get to know my students. I needed to provide choice and allow them to ask questions they found important and encourage them to seek out the answers. I had to give them control over their learning.

I started to look at school as an opportunity to expose students to learning. I started to implement more student voice and choice. I began to adopt project-based, problem-based, and inquiry-based learning.

Instead of reading *The Odyssey* and asking students to write an argumentative, five-paragraph essay on the book, I challenge my ninth-grade students to go deeper into the story. We use project-based learning and transform my classroom into a courtroom. We put Odysseus on trial for breaking and entering and assault with a deadly weapon for his actions in the cyclops's cave. Telemachus faces justice for multiple counts of first-degree murder. Penelope is tried for falsifying information and obstruction of justice. Students play the roles of lawyers, witnesses, defendants, and the jury and grapple with difficult questions around justice. To grade this work would be ridiculous. My students know whether their efforts were effective because they will either win their case or lose. They will feel prepared during the trial or get obliterated by the opposition. Someone is declared guilty or not guilty.

My senior English class is challenged through problem-based learning when they are asked, "What problems need to be resolved in our school?" I challenge my students to research these problems globally to discover how these problems affect students beyond our four walls. They research the problems locally by performing interviews and surveys. Ultimately they research and come up with solutions that can create positive change in our school and present these solutions to an audience with the power to help them bring about change, such as our building leadership team, the school board, or the administration team. During this time, students are reading, writing, and having critical discussions.

My students make a difference. One group addressed issues of sexual assault in school by developing curriculum to inform their peers about consent and the ongoing, lifelong impact sexual assault has on the survivor. Another group challenged the school by making a variety of menstrual hygiene products available for free, as many young women cannot use one-size-fits-all products or do not carry the cash to purchase them.

My seniors do not need me to give them grades to know whether they did a good job. Rather, they feel the satisfaction of learning that they have the ability to develop solutions to issues they feel passionate about. This sense of satisfaction—knowing that they have the ability to make a difference and be heard—transcends any grade I might put on their work. They develop the skills that help them become engaged citizens who will face the challenges of an ever-changing, complex world, which they will soon inherit.

I placed the students in the center of the classroom and made them the focus of the class. In order to make learning relevant to them, I had to listen to them.

THE CHALLENGE

Because there are factors beyond our control, students will not be engaged 100 percent of the time. Kids struggle with all sorts of challenges, such as exhaustion, poverty, abuse, divorce, and trauma. And because there are certain essential things for kids to understand in order to be responsible members of society, it is the teacher's call to build relationships, challenge students, and let them know we care enough about them that we will not accept anything less than their full potential, because our students are worth it.

One of my favorite movie teachers of all time is Mr. Hand from *Fast Times at Ridgemont High*. Mr. Hand is able to reach Jeff Spicoli despite his attempts to avoid, disengage, and frustrate his teacher.[7]

At the end of the film, Spicoli is getting ready to go out and celebrate

Figure 2.2. Mr. Hand and Jeff Spicoli from *Fast Times at Ridgemont High*.

the end of the school year. However, Mr. Hand shows up at Jeff's home, sits down with him, and begins discussing the American Revolution. Mr. Hand does not accept any excuses from Jeff. When Jeff claims he left his book in the locker at school, Mr. Hand pulls out a copy and settles for nothing less than for Spicoli to take the time to read and explain his analysis of the text. Ultimately Spicoli demonstrates understanding and expresses a sense of pride in his accomplishment.

Mr. Hand holds Spicoli accountable to demonstrate an understanding of the Revolutionary War—and he does this *with* Spicoli. The greatest lesson Mr. Hand teaches, and Spicoli understands this, is that no one is beyond hope. Every student, no matter how much they may challenge us, is worth our effort.

Learning is something done alongside others, not something imposed on them. If the learning is essential, then students need to be pushed until they get it. What makes teaching difficult is that it requires the teacher to care for the student and see value in the student. Because what is truly important is the child, and this is the lesson that must be learned.

Assigning grades was the easy way out of doing the actual work of teaching. They made it easy for me to avoid building relationships and meeting the needs of the individual student. Eliminating grades tested my creativity and patience. I was forced to rethink what went on in my class. Students had to take ownership of the class.[8] I had to incorporate individualized learning and lots of voice and choice.[9] I had to replace worksheets, tests, and quizzes with better forms of assessment.[10] I had to make sure students were engaged and wanted to learn. I had to do the work *with* them.[11]

I still have students who challenge my patience and push me to my limits. However, I do not look at them as a problem, but rather as an opportunity to become a better teacher. They are a reminder to tap into my inner Mr. Hand, sit down beside them, and do the learning *with* them. I do this because they remind me of the person I want to be—a teacher who cares for each and every student independently of what they do in class. I do this because they are worth the effort.

NOTES

1. Hughes 1985.
2. Blackwelder 2017a.
3. Kohn 2016.
4. Butler 1988.
5. Kohn [1999] 2003.
6. Pink 2009.
7. Heckerling 1982.
8. Blackwelder 2017b.
9. For individualized learning, see Blackwelder 2017d. For voice and choice, see Blackwelder 2017c.
10. Blackwelder 2017e.
11. Blackwelder 2018.

SOURCES

Blackwelder, Aaron. 2017a. "Changing the Guard." Thinking 101. October 21. https://mrblackwelder.wordpress.com/2017/07/03/changing-the-guard/.

Blackwelder, Aaron. 2017b. "How I Facilitate Student-led Class Discussions." Thinking 101. December 2. https://mrblackwelder.wordpress.com/2017/02/16/how-to-facilitate-student-led-class-discussions/.

Blackwelder, Aaron. 2017c. "How My Class Went from a Dictatorship to a Democracy." Thinking 101. February 18. https://mrblackwelder.wordpress.com/2017/02/18/dictatorship-to-democracy/.

Blackwelder, Aaron. 2017d. "Passion Projects: Engage Your Child This Summer."

Thinking 101. July 4. https://mrblackwelder.wordpress.com/2017/06/28/passion-projects/.

Blackwelder, Aaron. 2017e. "Rethinking Assessment." Thinking 101. July 2. https://mrblackwelder.wordpress.com/2017/04/08/rethinking-assessments/.

Blackwelder, Aaron. 2018. "How to Value Personal Time While Providing Great Feedback." Teachers Going Gradeless. August 24. https://teachersgoinggradeless.com/2018/01/06/time-feedback/.

Butler, Ruth. 1988. "Enhancing and Undermining Intrinsic Motivation: The Effects of Task-Involving and Ego-Involving Evaluation on Interest and Performance." *British Journal of Educational Psychology* 58(1): 1–14. https://doi.org/10.1111/j.2044-8279.1988.tb00874.x.

Heckerling, Amy, dir. 1982. *Fast Times at Ridgemont High*. Refugee Films. Film.

Hughes, John, dir. 1985. *The Breakfast Club*. Universal Pictures. Film.

Kohn, Alfie. [1999] 2003. *The Schools Our Children Deserve: Moving beyond Traditional Classrooms and "Tougher Standards."* Reprint, Boston: Houghton Mifflin.

Kohn, Alfie. 2016. "From Degrading to De-Grading." February 23. http://www.alfiekohn.org/article/degrading-de-grading/.

Pink, Daniel H. 2009. *Drive: The Surprising Truth about What Motivates Us*. New York: Riverhead Books.

Chapter 3

———

JUST ONE CHANGE (JUST KIDDING): UNGRADING AND ITS NECESSARY ACCOMPANIMENTS

Susan D. Blum

———

For the last decade and a half, I've engaged in anthropological research on higher education, learning about the serious mismatches between what we know about learning "in real life" and learning in college that help account for poor outcomes in many educational settings. In my most recent book, *"I Love Learning; I Hate School": An Anthropology of College*, I identified a number of ways that formal education has led to a *lack* of learning especially through what I (and others) call "the game of school."[1] Colleges promote credentials, obedience, and the sorting of haves and have-nots, but not necessarily learning.[2] I hypothesized that if I could make the learning in the classroom more resemble the natural ways people learn outside the classroom[3]—"in the wild"—it would be both more effective and more enjoyable for everyone.

People kept pushing me to provide solutions. When asked what I would do if I could make just *one* change—not everyone embraces my more revolutionary suggestions—I answered that I would get rid of grades.[4]

Of course in some ways this is a trick answer, because everything is connected; you can't make just one change. But getting rid of grades is a critical focus of mine, and it has been both harder and more successful than I expected.

I'd been making some efforts in that direction for a long time, such as not putting grades on essays or projects unless students were too panicked and felt they needed to know what I was secretly recording (none did; many spoke of the relief of not focusing on grades). They got plenty of comments, after they also assessed their own writing. Self-assessment had entered my classroom at least as early as 2012 and possibly earlier. But I had retained a grading policy, with points and relative weights for various heterogenous components (attendance, participation, writing, sometimes quizzes). Very traditional.

Still, I fretted over how to make my pedagogy align with my theoretical understanding of how people learn. *Fretted* may be too light a term: I wondered whether I could keep teaching if I didn't believe in the enterprise, a teacher-centered sorting-fixated enterprise where learning seems to be a *means* toward the end, which is the grade, rather than a grade as a means to the end, which is *learning* (and to which grades don't contribute).

In August 2016, as I prepared my classes, deeply immersed in the thinking that had led to *I Love Learning*, I decided I would go all the way and get rid of grades. Or at least get rid of them as much as I could—right up to the end of the semester, when I was required to submit them.

I had read many accounts of individual faculty members and whole colleges that were grade-free, but in mid-August of that year, I discovered Starr Sackstein's book *Hacking Assessment: 10 Ways to Go Gradeless in a Traditional Grades School*, which gave me both courage and some cover in case students or administrators challenged my decision.[5]

My reasons for wanting to get rid of grades were numerous: I felt as if students were fixated on grades above all else. In fact, as I reported in my book, students told the research team that "the purpose of college is to get good grades." Most faculty conversations with students include some discussions of grades: *What do you want? What do I have to do to get an A? How can I improve my grade? What are the criteria for grades?* And the professor takes on the role of judge rather than coach, acting as all-controlling widget producer instead of companion on the road of learning. The shorthand is *sage on the stage* as opposed to *guide on the side.* It felt like there was no space for adventure, zest, risk—or even for genuine learning. Everything focused on pleasing the professor. And in my research on learning and education, I had learned a lot about grades, such as:

- **Grading requires uniformity.** It assumes uniform input, uniform process, and uniform output. I've stopped believing that is a useful way to approach student learning. Students don't start out the same. They don't have the same life experiences— or even academic experiences—during our semester together. They don't go to the same places afterward. They have different goals. ("Learning outcomes" assume uniformity, in the factory model of schooling.)

- **Grades don't provide adequate information.** If the purpose of grades is to convey a student's adequacy, excellence, compliance, effort, or gain in learning, then they fail. Is a student who enters already knowing a lot, continues to demonstrate knowledge at a high level, misses an assignment because of a roommate's attempted suicide, and ends up with a B+ the same as someone who begins knowing nothing, works really hard, follows all the rules, does quite well, and ends up with a B+? What information is conveyed? What about someone who loves biology and excels in those classes, but who loathes history, bombs in history classes, and ends up with a 3.0 GPA? Compared to someone who muddles through every class and ends up with a similar GPA, yet with no passion, excellence, or highs or lows? A highly knowledgeable but independently minded student who can't be bothered to come to class? What do we learn from the GPA? What does a course grade mean?

- **Grades don't truly motivate students.** Educational psychologists distinguish different types of motivation: (a) intrinsic, or doing things for their own sake, and (b) extrinsic, or doing things for external benefits not inherently part of the activities themselves.[6] I would also add fear and avoidance as big motivators, or doing something to avoid negative consequences. Extrinsic motivators often reduce intrinsic motivation.

Grades are the quintessential form of extrinsic motivation: they reward for accomplishment. But they are also threats: if you don't comply in every way, no matter how you feel about anything, you will be dethroned. Yet the fact is most people are motivated by interest or need, not by arbitrary mandates. Research from multiple fields shows that people (and all mammals and birds . . .) are consumed with curiosity and joy when they learn new things.[7] Sometimes it is hard and sometimes it is needed (as for a workplace that changes), but learning happens all around us all the time—TED talks, podcasts, *Nova*, adult ed, learning from WikiHow, lectures at libraries, church study groups, knitting circles, work challenges.[8] And all without being graded.

Further, extrinsic motivation leads to the minimax principle. If the only thing you care about is something beyond the activity itself—an extrinsic reward such as the grade—it is sensible to do as little as possible to procure the highest possible reward (grade), which Arie Kruglanski, Chana Stein, and Aviah Riter, following a century of game theory, referred to in 1977 as the "minimax strategy" in instrumental behavior.[9] Cheating, shortcuts, cramming—all those make sense if the only goal is points or winning.

Ultimately this focus on points leads students to treat college as a game.[10] Games are fun, but if the goal is amassing points and winning at any price, then a game is the wrong model for college—at least if learning, not just winning, is the goal. Of course, games can also be absorbing and done for their own sake—playing *Words with Friends* or *Grand Theft Auto* or the fabulous *Reacting to the Past*[11]—so those types of games are fine. The problem is when college is seen *only* as a survival course.

An additional problem with grades is that students see the rules as arbitrary and inconsistent. Different professors have different scoring—participation, homework, teamwork or no teams, tests, showing your work, partial credit—all of which appear to be plucked out of thin air and make no sense, as I found in my research on plagiarism.[12] Citation? Sharing? Page length? Number of quotes? Consult notes or closed book? Students have to figure out in each case what the professor wants. It all seems arbitrary, and therefore unconnected with anything meaningful or real.[13]

In fact, grades *are* arbitrary, even if they appear scientific, objective. Faculty vary considerably in how they weight various dimensions of the class experience, or even on exams what percentage is represented by any given question. Arbitrariness has several defects. It is uninformative, and it is alienating: it keeps students nervous and off-kilter, on edge.[14] Just because there is a number doesn't mean it is objective. That is simply scientism.[15]

Throughout their years in school, students are taught to focus on schooling rather than learning. Is the goal of school, including college, primarily achievement, success, accomplishment?[16] Compliance? Is the focus on learning the actual skills people will need or want outside college? Discovering the mysterious workings of the world? Learning something new about themselves?[17] Rare is it that someone asks students, "What are you learning?" instead of "How are you doing?" or "What'd you get?"[18] Much more common is students' mutual assistance in locating "easy A" classes. Yes, it's practical—but surely this isn't anyone's idea of what higher education should be for.

A final problem is that grades encourage a fear of risk-taking. Grades seem so consequential that students believe they can't take a chance on anything unproven. In most college classes, a mistake is punished by a lower grade, which is then averaged into the other grades, even if the student completely masters it after that initial try. Yet mistakes are information and contribute to learning. In tasks like riding a bicycle or submitting an article for publication, feedback about shortcomings is information that helps with improving.

SOLUTIONS

I have tried to address these problems with solutions. Some of the tactics, which are all intertwined, that I have used in my own classes include the following.

- **Decenter grading.** We don't talk about the point breakdown because I don't have one in my classes anymore. We talk about what the goals are for everything we do: for reading, writing, discussion, research, and projects.

- **Emphasize the entire portfolio.** A semester is a nice, long, luxurious time for a lot of activities, reflection, conversation, writing, and wondering. At the end we can assess the entire experience, rather than students worrying about how an early misstep is going to mean lack of success.[19] In appendix 3.1 you see how I walk students through a review of their entire journey, as they note where they began, what activities they did, how they might regard them months later, and how they think about their total experience. (Review is built in, but not for a conventional exam—for a self-examination instead!)
- **Have students develop an individual plan.** I developed this myself on the model of an individualized education program (usually used in special education), though I have since discovered two similar models: Universal Design for Learning and Individual Development Plan.[20] The idea is to have students figure out how a class fits with their own lives, course of study, and interests. Even if it is required, I want them to articulate some value for themselves. I try to meet with every student early in the semester and again midway through to talk about how prepared they are, what they are eager to learn or do, and what causes apprehension or even dread. I encourage them to try something scary, not just to stick with what is comfortable and reliable at producing a good grade. In appendix 3.2 you see the template that begins their reflection, including defining some of their own short-term and longer-term goals, whether or not they have anything to do with this particular class.
- **Build a practice of self-assessment.** If the genuine goal of college is to prepare students for life, then it is vital that they develop their own standards. Even when standards are set by professions, workers aren't generally monitored for every single task. And a conscience is required to ensure that superiors' demands are ethical and just. So rather than ask students to submit work with the hope that *I'll* think it's excellent, I encourage them to develop honest standards and self-scrutiny.

This also contributes to that desirable skill of metacognition, or thinking about thinking.[21] Every assignment is accompanied by students' written self-assessments of their work. What were they trying to get out of the assignment? What did they learn? What was successful? What was less successful? Why? What might they do differently? What would they like help with? That should serve them better in life than hoping that mediocrity will be seen as fabulous. Sometimes things aren't perfect—and that's okay. But it is useful for them to understand and even articulate the reasons. (*I didn't give myself enough time. I started too late. I didn't understand this. I couldn't really get into this subject. I've never tried this before.*) Throughout our lives beyond college, we won't excel at and plunge enthusiastically into every single thing we do all day, and we certainly won't be proficient at things we attempt the first time. Forcing students to pretend enthusiasm—for the "attitude" grade—is a kind of violence, akin to the emotional labor detailed by Hochschild in her amazing book *The Managed Heart*.[22]

- **Conduct portfolio conferences.** In addition to earlier meetings, I end each semester with brief—five-minute—portfolio conferences with every student. (I do this now for all my classes, during the final exam period; typically my classes are below thirty students.) I give them a document to complete prior to our meeting and instruct them to look back through all their work. The goal is to show them their learning, by comparing their early and later understanding, and to help them feel pride for their body of work. It also forces them to review the material, which research shows fosters retention.[23] Students suggest their grade, which I can accept or not. No, not every student suggests an A.

OUTCOMES

I have now been using this approach exclusively, in every class, at every level, for seven semesters.

I enjoy my relationship with my students much more. I love the atmosphere of the classroom. I don't dread "grading"—having conversations with—student work nearly as much as I used to, though the time involved is not less (see chapter 13, Warner). I believe the encouragement of learning and even risk-taking in the service of growth has been successful.

Students reflect that it allows them to relax and focus on learning, perhaps for the first time. One student wrote in a reflection on one of my classes that used ungrading, "I honestly enjoyed writing for me, instead of necessarily for a professor or an outside source. I felt I had more freedom to express what I wanted to say, and I feel like I wasn't focused too much on making claims that could get me points." In fall 2019 one student reported in our midsemester conference that, to their pleasure, "my stress decreased but my motivation didn't."

I am confident that at least some of the students are sincere in generating their own adventure in learning.

COMMENTS TO SKEPTICS

I know this seems idealistic and, for many classes and many professors, impossible. Here are my thoughts on that:

Going gradeless to some extent can be done in a class of any size and of any type, though students may find it alarming and unfamiliar. Some faculty use something called "contract grading," which still uses a traditional scale but puts some of the control in students' hands. (See chapter 7, Katopodis and Davidson.)

You can provide opportunities for students to make choices, which allows them to find at least a tiny bit of intrinsic motivation even in the most conventional of courses.[24] (I had a student write recently about the most conventional writing all semester in my Food and Culture class, in which I had given them options, "I loved this assignment! Keep it for future classes. I had so much fun.")

Some assignments—maybe small ones—can still be risk-free and contribute to intrinsic motivation by being utterly fascinating, completely useful, or fun. (There's a social and emotional component to all learning.)[25]

You can always offer low-stakes exercises that are perceived as enjoyable and not trivial, in any course.

And even if your supervisors are skeptical, as long as the process serves the central goal of contributing to student learning, they shouldn't object. This book may help. (Don't risk your entire career, however.)

Here is one piece of evidence from a student who really trusted the process and responded honestly to the question, What assignment(s) pushed you to learn the most? "While it ended up being one of my weaker pieces, I felt that my [project] was my most personally informative piece. I read so many different sources on the [topic] and really took a deep dive to explore the reasons why the [people do what] they do."

Isn't that a beautiful, honest analysis of learning? I want students to believe that this education is for them, not for me.

I can never go back!

CODA: REAL TALK

It is hard, though.

The very hardest dimension is not merely the time required for the conversations, the conferences, the comments on the work. The hardest work for me has been relinquishing control, following students' needs (which I try to predict, but predictions don't always match particular groups), and—I know this is shocking—trusting students.[26]

Also students may voice objections. In the past years, I've had one hostile graduate student and one fairly oppositional first-year student who both seemed to think I was abdicating my responsibility. This hurts, and is frustrating, but it reminds me that students come from a conventional system where my class is one of four, five, even six or seven, they are taking, after twelve or sixteen or eighteen years in conventional systems. The onus is really on me to explain, to meet them where they are, not to fantasize about students who have dreamt of a liberatory pedagogical experience. It has forced me to develop explanations, to work on the timing for explaining it—not early in the semester, only after students begin to see the ways the class works—and to provide evidence for the benefits of this approach.

Some students—say, pre-med—may decide that their "hard" classes deserve more time than the apparently easy one without points, grades, scores. Here is where I take a step back and remind myself that the student in my class is also in other classes, has personal challenges, work obligations, and many other things that they juggle, just as I and others do. If I am treating students as adults, then recognizing that my course may not be central has to be acceptable.

Conversations with the contributors to this book have helped me feel less isolated.[27] My hope is that it can help others expand this conversation.

NOTES

This chapter is a modification of an article originally published as "Ungrading" in *Inside Higher Ed*, November 14, 2017, https://www.insidehighered.com/advice /2017/11/14/significant-learning-benefits-getting-rid-grades-essay.

1. Blum 2016; Blum 2015; Kirschenbaum, Simon, and Napier 1971; Labaree 2010.
2. For credentialing, see Caplan 2018; Collins 1979. For sorting of haves and have-nots, see Labaree 2010. For the lack of promotion of learning, see Bok 2006.
3. Paradise 1998.
4. For disagreement with my revolutionary suggestions, see Eyler 2018: 221–22. For getting rid of grades, see Blum 2017; Kohn 2011; Kohn [1993] 2018.
5. Sackstein 2015; see also chapter 4 of this book. For accounts of grade-free schools, see Jaschik 2010; Lash 2017.
6. Deci 1971; Kohn [1993] 2018; Ryan and Deci 2000.
7. Livio 2017; Panksepp and Biven 2012.
8. Lave 2009.
9. Kruglanski, Stein, and Riter 1977.
10. Blum 2015.
11. Reacting Consortium, Reacting to the Past, https://reacting.barnard.edu/.
12. Blum 2009.
13. Gatto [1992] 2005.
14. The alienation is a huge and central problem, one I'm deeply concerned about but can't explore here. See Fromm 1955; Laing 1969.
15. Muller 2018.
16. Pope 2001; Demerath 2009; Holtgreive 2016.
17. Deresiewicz 2014. All but the most elite students largely see college as too expensive for these highfalutin goals nowadays. See Goldrick-Rab 2016.
18. Kirschenbaum, Simon, and Napier 1971.

19. This is not the purchasable e-portfolio being marketed by several corporations. This is just assembling students' work, as an artist does.
20. UDL Center, Universal Design for Learning, http://www.udlcenter.org/; Graduate School, University of Wisconsin Madison, "Individual Development Plan," https://grad.wisc.edu/pd/idp/.
21. Brown, Roediger, and McDaniel 2014.
22. Hochschild 2012.
23. Brown, Roediger, and McDaniel 2014.
24. Pink 2009.
25. Cavanagh 2016.
26. That has led to abandoning my three-decade-long attendance policy, with great trepidation, encouraging students to become part of a community of learners that benefits from everyone's presence. See Bain 2004; chapter 13, Warner, of this book.
27. Foley, Morris, Gounari, and Agostinone-Wilson 2015.

SOURCES AND FURTHER READING

Bain, Ken. 2004. *What the Best College Teachers Do*. Cambridge, MA: Harvard University Press.

Becker, Howard S., Blanche Geer, and Everett C. Hughes. 1968. *Making the Grade: The Academic Side of College Life*. New York: Wiley.

Blum, Susan D. 2009. *My Word! Plagiarism and College Culture*. Ithaca, NY: Cornell University Press.

Blum, Susan D. 2015. "The Game of School." *Peeps Magazine* 1: 22–29. https://www.academia.edu/19672842/The_Game_of_School.

Blum, Susan D. 2016. *"I Love Learning; I Hate School": An Anthropology of College*. Ithaca, NY: Cornell University Press.

Blum, Susan D. 2017. "Ungrading." *Inside Higher Ed*. November 14. https://www.insidehighered.com/advice/2017/11/14/significant-learning-benefits-getting-rid-grades-essay.

Bok, Derek. 2006. *Our Underachieving Colleges: A Candid Look at How Much Students Learn and Why They Should Be Learning More*. Princeton, NJ: Princeton University Press.

Brown, Peter C., Henry L. Roediger III, and Mark A. McDaniel. 2014. *Make It Stick: The Science of Successful Learning*. Cambridge, MA: Harvard University Press.

Caplan, Bryan S. 2018. *The Case against Education: Why the Education System Is a Waste of Time and Money*. Princeton, NJ: Princeton University Press.

Cappel, Constance. 1999. *Utopian Colleges*. New York: Peter Lang.

Cavanagh, Sarah Rose. 2016. *The Spark of Learning: Energizing the College Classroom with the Science of Emotion*. Morgantown: West Virginia University Press.

Collins, Randall. 1979. *Credential Society: A Historical Sociology of Education and Stratification*. New York: Columbia University Press.

Deci, Edward L. 1971. "Effects of Externally Mediated Rewards on Intrinsic Motivation." *Journal of Personality and Social Psychology* 18: 105–15.

Demerath, Peter. 2009. *Producing Success: The Culture of Personal Advancement in an American High School*. Chicago: University of Chicago Press.

Deresiewicz, William. 2014. *Excellent Sheep: The Miseducation of the American Elite*. New York: Simon & Schuster.

Eyler, Joshua R. 2018. *How Humans Learn: The Science and Stories behind Effective College Teaching*. Morgantown: West Virginia University Press.

Foley, Jean Ann, Doug Morris, Panayota Gounari, and Faith Agostinone-Wilson. 2015. "Critical Education, Critical Pedagogies, Marxist Education in the United States." *Journal for Critical Education Policy Studies* 13(3): 110–44.

Fromm, Erich. 1955. *The Sane Society*. New York: Henry Holt.

Gatto, John Taylor. [1992] 2005. *Dumbing Us Down: The Hidden Curriculum of Compulsory Schooling*. Reprint, Gabriola Island, BC: New Society Publishers.

Goldrick-Rab, Sara. 2016. *Paying the Price: College Costs, Financial Aid, and the Betrayal of the American Dream*. Chicago: University of Chicago Press.

Hochschild, Arlie. 2012. *The Managed Heart: Commercialization of Human Feeling*. Updated ed. Berkeley: University of California Press.

Holtgreive, Joseph. 2016. "Too Smart to Fail? When Students Focus Their Attention on Grades and How They Are Performing, Learning May Not Result." *Inside Higher Ed*. August 16. https://www.insidehighered.com/views/2016/08/16/students-focus-too-much-grades-detriment-learning-essay.

Jaschik, Scott. 2010. "No Grading, More Learning." *Inside Higher Ed*. May 3. https://www.insidehighered.com/news/2010/05/03/no-grading-more-learning.

Kirschenbaum, Howard, Sidney B. Simon, and Rodney W. Napier. 1971. *Wad-ja-get? The Grading Game in American Education*. New York: Hart Publishing Co.

Kohn, Alfie. 2002. "The Dangerous Myth of Grade Inflation." *The Chronicle of Higher Education*. November 8, p. B7.

Kohn, Alfie. 2011. "The Case against Grades." November. https://www.alfiekohn.org/article/case-grades/.

Kohn, Alfie. [1993] 2018. *Punished by Rewards: The Trouble with Gold Stars, Incentive Plans, A's, Praise, and Other Bribes*. 25th anniversary ed. Boston: Houghton Mifflin.

Kruglanski, Arie, Chana Stein, and Aviah Riter. 1977. "Contingencies of Exogenous Reward and Task Performance: On the 'Minimax' Strategy in Instrumental Behavior." *Journal of Applied Social Psychology* 7(2): 141–48.

Labaree, David F. 1997. *How to Succeed in School without Really Learning: The Credentials Race in American Education*. New Haven, CT: Yale University Press.

Labaree, David F. 2010. *Someone Has to Fail: The Zero-Sum Game of Public Schooling*. Cambridge, MA: Harvard University Press.

Laing, R. D. 1969. *The Divided Self*. New York: Pantheon.

Lang, James. 2016. *Small Teaching: Everyday Lessons from the Science of Learning*. San Francisco: Jossey-Bass.

Lash, Jonathan. 2017. "De-Grading: Why Do Schools Use Grades That Teach Nothing?" *Huffington Post*. September 25. https://www.huffingtonpost.com/jonathan-lash/degrading-why-do-schools-_b_12123164.html.

Lave, Jean. 2009. *Cognition in Practice: Mind, Mathematics, and Culture in Everyday Life*. Cambridge: Cambridge University Press.

Livio, Mario. 2017. *Why? What Makes Us Curious*. New York: Simon & Schuster.

Milton, Ohmer, Howard R. Pollio, and James A. Eison. 1986. *Making Sense of College Grades*. San Francisco: Jossey-Bass.

Muller, Jerry Z. 2018. *The Tyranny of Metrics*. Princeton, NJ: Princeton University Press.

Nespor, Jan. 1990. "Grades and Knowledge in Undergraduate Education." *Journal of Curriculum Studies* 22(6): 545–56.

Panksepp, Jaak, and Lucy Biven. 2012. *The Archaeology of Mind: Neuroevolutionary Origins of Human Emotion*. New York: Norton.

Paradise, Ruth. 1998. "What's Different about Learning in Schools as Compared to Family and Community Settings?" *Human Development* 41: 270–78. https://doi.org/10.1159/000022587.

Pink, Daniel H. 2009. *Drive: The Surprising Truth about What Motivates Us*. New York: Riverhead Books.

Pope, Denise Clark. 2001. *"Doing School": How We Are Creating a Generation of Stressed Out, Materialistic, and Miseducated Students*. New Haven, CT: Yale University Press.

Rogoff, Barbara. 2001. "Why a Nonconventional College Decided to Add Grades." *The Chronicle of Higher Education*. September 14, p. B17.

Rose, Nikolas. 1999. *Governing the Soul: The Shaping of the Private Self*. London: Free Association.

Ryan, Richard M., and Edward L. Deci. 2000. "Intrinsic and Extrinsic Motivations: Classic Definitions and New Directions." *Contemporary Educational Psychology* 25: 54–67.

Sackstein, Starr. 2015. *Hacking Assessment: 10 Ways to Go Gradeless in a Traditional Grades School*. Cleveland, OH: Times 10 Publications.

Varenne, Hervé. 1974. "From Grading and Freedom of Choice to Ranking and Segregation in an American High School." *Anthropology & Education Quarterly* 5(2): 9–15.

APPENDIX 3.I: LingAnth FALL 2019 END-OF-SEMESTER REFLECTIONS

December 18, 2019

These meetings will occur in the classroom!

YOUR TIME: [   ]

Arrive 10 minutes before Your Time: [   ]

We will have only 5 minutes each for our discussion.

Most of the work is done in your own self-reflection—which I will read carefully, and discuss with [TA].

Copy and paste this document into your own document and answer the questions there.

Please bring a hard copy to our meeting.

***

We have shared a long and involved journey this semester. We began by generating questions, some of them soul-burning and some of them factual (and many of them about logistics).

We read about linguistic diversity, about language and thought, about indexicality. We considered questions connected to social issues, and wondered how language began—and what, after all, it is! You read things, did things, talked. Your fellow students brought our course to link to the world, IRL.

We thought about—through reading, class discussion, projects, writing—a lot of topics:

- Wonder
- Your Linguistic Autobiography
- The Ethnography of Speaking/Communication
- The Functions of Language
- Interaction, Conversation, Joint Action
- Semiotics
- Modalities, New Media, Technology, Writing, Social Media
- Variation
  - Language and Thought
  - Introducing a Language
  - Class/Region/Race/Nationality/Ethnicity/Gender/ Sexuality/Age/Ideology
- The Nature of Language
  - Language Socialization and Education
  - Language Origins
  - Social Issues

This activity is designed to have you review and reflect on what you have learned and done this semester.

Your Name:

What is the key question you would like to answer here?
Ask the question, and answer it:

I. Scavenger Hunt

1. Please find and look at the program for the semester.
2. Collect all your daily cards; read at least some of them.
3. Collect all your writing for the course, including posts and assignments, and class worksheets or notes.
4. Open Slack.
5. Open Google Drive.
6. Get some coffee, tea, or water. Or your favorite beverage. Just don't spill it on your keyboard. ;)

All this constitutes your "portfolio" for the semester.

***

II. Looking at Specifics

a. Daily Cards / Slack

i. Choose 3 of your favorite or best or most fabulous questions and type them in here. Why did you choose these?

ii. Choose 3 of your favorite quotations and type them in. Why did you choose them?

b. Your Linguistic Autobiography

   i. Read it, again.
   ii. Has your thinking changed about this since your mid-semester review?

c. Ethnography of Speaking

   i. Read it.
   ii. What do you remember about this experience?

d. Conversation Analysis

   i. Now that this is a bit far in the past, how do you feel about your work?
   ii. What do you remember?

e. Modalities

   i. One-minute statement
   ii. "The New Rules of Language are Fine": Debate 1
   iii. What do you think about the nature of social media? Are they good, bad, neutral? Should they be regulated? For whom? By whom? On what basis?

f. Variation

   i. Language and Thought

      1. What do you think people should know about linguistic relativity?

   ii. Introducing a Language

      1. Read it and one other group's.
      2. What have you learned?
      3. What would you want people to know about this—say, your roommate, or your cool aunt/uncle?

   iii. Class/Region/Race/Nationality/Ethnicity/Gender/Sexuality/Age/Ideology

      1. What's indexicality?
      2. How does this intersect with ideologies?

3. Did you change your mind about any groups' linguistic behavior?
4. Is there anything people should know about these topics? What?

g. The Nature of Language
  i. Language Socialization and Education
     1. We didn't spend a lot of time on this, but has anything stuck with you about this topic? What?
  ii. Language Origins
     1. Why is this such a hard topic?
     2. Do you have a theory about it?
     3. What do you think is the most important aspect of language? Why?

h. Social Issues
  i. What issues regarding language are especially important for citizens to understand?

***

III. General Reflections

a. What do you know now that you did not know in August?
b. What work was challenging? What was fun? What was useful? What didn't seem useful?
c. Did you learn anything unexpected?
d. Did you expect to learn something that you didn't learn?
e. Did you develop some new questions?
f. Did you change your mind about anything?
g. If you were going to write a language myth—something people generally believe, but which is false—what would it be? And why?
h. What is linguistic anthropology?
i. What do you wonder about? What soul-burning question(s) do you currently have? What questions would you like to investigate? When? How?

j. What's one random fact you learned this semester? Where did you learn it?

k. What's a profound insight you've gained?

***

IV. Some Feedback

a. Did you ever talk about this outside class? Often / occasionally / rarely

b. Were there any memorable readings?

c. Did you become curious about anything new?

d. Did this class connect with any other courses?

e. What was your initial reaction to the lack of focus on grades? How do you feel about it now?

f. Did you make a new friend?

g. What do you think you'll remember in 5 years?

h. Have you thought about the ways you learn? Have you observed anything that you might take forward with you?

***

V. Numbers

a. Approximately how many classes did you miss?

b. How many daily cards do you have?

c. In terms of participation in class and posting on Slack, how engaged and mentally present were you in the class?

_____ there and ready to go all the time

_____ sometimes engaged and sometimes texting or surfing or doing work for other classes

_____ pretty remote

d. Approximately how much of the reading did you do?

_____ 90–100%

_____ 75–89%

_____ 50–74%

_____ less than 50%

Do you have any comments about . . . ?

a. The reading itself
b. Your reading of "the reading"

***

VI. Give yourself a check / zero for each activity and assignment.

_____ Linguistic Autobiography

_____ Language IRL

_____ Daily Cards / Slack

_____ Ethnography of Speaking

_____ Conversation Analysis

_____ Introducing a Language

_____ One-Minute Statement

_____ Debate 1—Modalities

_____ Debate 2—Social Issues

_____ Your "job" (Daily Card team, snack team, social team, tech team, wild card team)

(include a check mark if you did it)

***

VII. Please suggest a grade for yourself, with comments.

Grade: ....

Explain how you arrived at this grade.

***

VIII. Do you have any other comments?

Have a wonderful winter break! Keep in touch!

APPENDIX 3.2: FOOD AND CULTURE SPRING 2019 MID-SEMESTER REFLECTION

Yes, I know it is not quite halfway, but it is still MID(-ish). The goal of this exercise is to take stock, request feedback or assistance, and see if there are any things that should be applauded or altered before the semester ends.

Please assemble your writing for the semester so far.

1. What were your goals for this course?
2. What are your goals for college, in general?
3. What are some of the main things you've learned so far?
4. Is there any reading that you especially enjoyed? What? Why?
5. If you could use any format and address any audience to talk about what you're learning, what format, what audience, and what content would you choose? (You can dream beyond this course, and beyond school . . .)
6. How do you feel about the writing exercises in our class so far?
7. How many of the writing assignments have you completed?
8. How many of the self-assessments have you completed?
9. Is there anything still remaining to complete? If so, please list here.

   i. Item(s)
   ii. Anticipated date(s) of completion

10. Your overall assessment of your writing

   i. For learning
   ii. For demonstration of learning
   iii. For general craft

11. How many contributions have you made to discussions on Google Docs or Slack?
12. Do you read your classmates' contributions? Do you have any comments about them?

13. Approximately how much of the assigned reading do you usually do?

_____ 76–100%

_____ 51–75%

_____ 26–50%

_____ 25% or less

14. How do you feel about your participation during class? Explain.
15. Do you ever talk about this class outside class?

_____ never or rarely

_____ sometimes

_____ frequently

16. Are there things you'd like clarified? Elaborated?
17. What do you hope to get out of the remainder of the semester?
18. Are there things that you expect to carry with you after the semester ends? What? Why?
19. Are there things you would like to do?
20. Are there things you would like me to help with?
21. If you were going to give yourself a grade right now, what would it be? Why?

Other comments . . . [from you, the student]

Chapter 4

———

SHIFTING THE GRADING MINDSET

Starr Sackstein

———

Language matters. It's that simple. What we say and how we say it has a big impact on how students and other stakeholders respond to our choices. Even the tone of our voices conveys meaning around our diction that can have subtle but significant ramifications.

Students are always waiting for a variety of cues from their teachers and peers to determine what and how much they are learning. So rather than perpetuate issues around grading—like subjective and/or vague feedback, or labeling students—by using the same language we've always used, it's time to deliberately shift away from judgmental language that hinders learning to vocabulary that helps to neutralize, as we change our assessment practices.

Getting rid of grades is a big and challenging step to make, but it *can* be done and even if you aren't ready to go all in, there are ways to adjust small things in the classroom that will lead to important growth for students.

So many of our experiences with grades are tied up in schemas created by the system and the folks who have perpetuated long-term beliefs about the need to label learning in a particular, seemingly universal language. However, even those letters and numbers that we all assume people understand don't always mean what they say.

Numbers and letters can be deceiving, especially when we factor in averages, other nonspecific learning assignments or additions for extra credit, and deductions for late work or other often nondisclosed reasons that add to or detract from communication of learning. For this reason we must figure out how to communicate learning in a way that precisely demonstrates what kids know and can do, so that all people involved can understand.

If we start with the words we use when communicating learning (e.g., "good job" or "this is wrong"), we can begin to develop appropriate language that doesn't judge but instead aligns with actual performance in a way everyone can truly understand. This way we leave nothing to assumption and misunderstanding; we instead ensure that what we say is what we mean and that the person receiving the information (student, parent, colleague, etc.) knows what learning we are referring to.

Additionally, when we move away from more traditional words associated with grading, we have an opportunity to shift the way students feel about their own learning and they, too, have a new vocabulary for discussing what they know and can do. These practices align particularly well with systems that employ portfolio assessment and reflection.

Look at table 4.1 from *Hacking Assessment*. The traditional grading language is passive and judgmental. Subconsciously, by using this language, we put the focus on the wrong things. The emphasis here is compliance, and too much onus is on the teacher and not enough on the learner. This shift away from traditional grading seeks to make learning

Table 4.1. Shift from grades vocabulary to neutral vocabulary of assessment

Grades Vocabulary	No-Grades Vocabulary
grading	assessing
score	assess
"What did I get?"	"What did I learn?"
"This is wrong."	"Try another way."
problem	challenge, opportunity
judgment or criticism	feedback
get good grades	achieve proficiency or mastery

Source: Sackstein 2015b

and assessment an active experience that promotes a culture of seeking deeper meaning rather than of playing school.

When we say to each other or to kids that we are grading, it diminishes the work we are trying to do. What we are actually doing is assessing growth and understanding, and by doing so, we can better improve instruction for the learners we work with and determine what is working and what is not. Assessing student learning is all about checking where students are against standards and learning targets we have created and making sure students understand these concepts and can speak to them as well.

Grading, conversely, speaks to the act of a teacher reading through student work and assigning a score to it, sometimes with narrative or constructive feedback, sometimes without. The teacher does the heavy lifting, and often the student doesn't take the time to read through the important information (the feedback) but rather skips directly to the meaningless number or letter.

Some may say that narrative feedback is appropriate for formative assessment, but that grades are needed, even essential, with summative assessment, which is an end point. This kind of thinking, however, still falls short of helping students understand what they know and can do. Summative assessments often don't allow students to show the true depth of their ability, which is why reflection is so essential to filling in the gaps. Ultimately if schools must put grades on report cards, then teachers can confer with students with a portfolio of work and decide on a grade together. This way the student voice can be represented and no arbitrary grade will surprise the learner.

Scoring is another term that means essentially the same thing as grading, except perhaps no feedback is given besides the score. This is suggestive of multiple-choice tests and holistically scored writing samples for summative work that won't be revised. Rather than *scoring*, we should again use the more active term *assessing* because we are trying to see what students know and can do. When we start to adjust what we call what we are doing, students will do the same.

The ultimate goal is to deemphasize the talk of grades and play up the discussion of learning. After assessments, this is an opportunity to give students more of a voice in the process. If we take the time to let students reflect, to share with us what the assessment may have missed, then we get a fuller picture of the students in a way that might make more sense for them.

At some point in elementary school—or some may argue when systems start to test—the shift away from sheer curiosity to an obsession with knowing the numbers begins. Whether it is the parental influence, the teacher control, or the student's drive to be perfect, students seek the elusive perfect score as it is the only way they can feel successful. So it is natural for these students to demand to know the results of a test or other assessment, almost immediately after it concludes.

"What grade did I get?" or some other variation like "What did I get?" is a question most teachers don't enjoy having to answer. But imagine if we could get students to think instead, "What did I learn?" This question has the opportunity to lead to a rich conversation. Encourage parents to fight the urge to ask their children, "What did you get on the test?" and instead ask, "What did you learn in school today?" Open up the pathway to explore a deeper understanding of what it is to question, to seek knowledge and value—not the labels a system has created, but the purpose behind what was being assessed in the first place. Our *why* exists in the process of exploration as we develop into higher thinking selves.

Because grades are such an embedded part of the way we think about school, it will take an effort by all involved: the administration, the teachers, the students, and the parents. We all need to work together to elevate learning beyond the scores placed on exams and report cards. All students should be able to speak to their learning against decided-upon standards and skills, and be able to articulate what they know and can do, as well as areas of challenge yet to be mastered.

One way schools can bring parents on board is to offer informational sessions at the beginning of the year to help them understand why the changes are happening, explain how things will look different, and elicit ways parents feel they can contribute at home. It will be necessary to have an open dialogue about their concerns and remind them that they can ask questions at any time to better support their children. Additionally, schools can create YouTube channels that provide more information about how to read online portals and give an inside look at the classroom and what has shifted. Each year in my classroom, I would send a letter home to parents, and then speak to them at Back to School Night. If the turnout wasn't good, I started adding short videos to my YouTube page to help them be on board. We also had student-led conferences in lieu of traditional parent-teacher conferences, which put students in charge of sharing their portfolios. Often the students weren't in my classes but were in my advisory group. This ensured that parents couldn't come to me just about grades, but had to explore the learning with their child or children by appointment.

School systems and educators have an obligation to transparently share with students of all ages what and why they are learning so that students can internalize this purpose and make it real and important for themselves. Once we make a concerted effort to drive the emphasis away from scores and labels and back to feedback and learning, students can actualize as thoughtful learners, equipped to progress beyond being compliant players of the game of school. Compliance can't be what motivates learning. Compliance simply cannot be what school is all about. It sends the wrong message about what we value and stifles creativity and curiosity.

When students see a red x on their papers or we tell them they are wrong, we are shutting them down and ending potential learning experiences. Grades do this too. Even high grades end the learning process, as placing a label on learning is an act of completion. It is a judgment that says the work is done enough to be scored. If we want students to keep pushing, revising, learning, we must continue to provide feedback without a particular grade.

In lieu of scoring, why not say to a student "You aren't there yet" or "Try another way" to encourage them to keep going? When we say "try another way," we want to make sure we are filling students' toolboxes with strategies, so they learn to use what they have in a variety of ways. Educators can't assume that students know what is wrong, how to fix it, or how to improve it. It is our job to ensure that they first recognize the error or weakness, offer a few strategies for them to try, and then provide more feedback as to which ones worked the best and why. Ultimately we want students to be able to make choices about the strategies they employ based on their own perception of what needs improvement. This can be done by first asking students to collect their feedback and strategies in one place with a feedback log.

After we spend time teaching students how to collect their feedback and the appropriate strategies to use for different kinds of revisions or problems, they have a written repository of strategies associated with specific challenges to use. One example of how this can work is when giving feedback on student writing: the teacher first puts feedback in their documents, and then students can transfer their feedback into the log.

Since learning is so nuanced, we must find ways to foster understanding and develop tools for synthesis and application beyond mere identification. With teachers' use of more instructive, and concrete, feedback, students will be able to review what they have learned, use the feedback, and then practice applying it first in similar settings and then to alternative ones across content areas. Teaching students to maintain their feedback, reflect on the learning, and then self-assess in an ongoing fashion will help them transfer learning more effectively and efficiently. It also helps when we use the same language to provide the feedback.

There are simple ways students can log their feedback, whether in a notebook or a Google Doc: students can track the areas they are consistently getting feedback on and then set specific goals for improving those areas. This is also a helpful way for teachers to start providing more individualized instruction through the work in context. For example, if a student writes a reflection after completing an essay speaking to areas they have been working on and their perception of personal growth, the teacher can read the reflection and tailor feedback appropriately for that particular learner.

If we know a student is working on cohesion in their writing, they might express through their reflection the specific areas of the essay where they employed strategies taught in class on that subject. As the teacher reads the essay with cohesion in mind, the teacher can identify where the student has successfully grown and where areas of need continue to exist. Perhaps there is a level of mastery that has been developed. This can be celebrated in the feedback, and then a new area can be addressed. Since we never want to overwhelm students with the feedback we give, targeting the specific areas in this way helps keep the learning in focus, a few goals at a time.

One major mistake many educators make is trying to identify and address every error or challenge a student has in a paper. They spend so much time reading and providing feedback that the paper or assignment looks diseased when it is finished. When a student sees this much feedback on a paper, it can have a negative impact. Students may shut down and not learn anything, only feeling defeated and like failures. If we spend time targeting the feedback around a particular topic we are working on or around student goals, we are better able to make sure students grow where they need to grow and they will be more inclined to take the time to read and internalize the feedback they have received. This is far more productive for both the student and the teacher.

As we start to shift our words, the behaviors will follow both for the teacher and for the learner. And once all these things are in sync with each other, then changing the way we assess in class becomes the next logical step. Of course building the routines and the language will take time, especially if it is not a systemic choice. When teachers work alone to accomplish this feat (as I did), students often get mixed messages. These messages can undermine the work we are doing and will insist we take time as needed to have the learning conversation again. It is incumbent on the teacher to shift the conversation as many times as needed until the students stop asking about grades. It is also important to have conversations with colleagues and administrators so they understand the undertaking. It is preferable to have everyone working together, sending the same message and promoting a similar ideal. If we truly want this shift to happen and make its way into the way we do things, then it needs to be something decided on as a group.

Of course it is likely that a whole department, school, or system may not be ready to make the shift at the same time. The best way to combat this obstacle is to, at the very least, help them understand the purpose. Provide resources for them to read. Engage in conversations where both sides can be explored and ask for their help in not undermining your efforts to make this change. People will talk, especially if they don't understand. So help them understand.

Once the expectations are clear and students are comfortable in the new environment, only then will the real growth happen. In the traditional system, learning often happens in spite of our practices, but not always for everyone. Too often we assume that because things were a certain way when we were in school, they must remain that way. But the world changes. Kids change. Learning tools change. We would be remiss if we just kept doing the same thing because it is how we have always done it. And since grades have never made sense, why would we want to perpetuate a practice that only hurts kids?

Education should be equipped with an endless feedback loop rather than a terminal grade. Start the loop of communication by changing the words you use in conversations about learning, and then learning will become about mastery instead of the bottom line on a report card.

Think about the words you use in class and the ones you use when students aren't directly involved. How do you speak about learning with your colleagues, parents, administrators? Which ways of speaking can have potentially negative connotations, and how can they be adjusted for a growth mindset? Remember, words matter. We must be cognizant of the way we feel about learning, because we convey many messages with our words and our disposition around it.

How can you shift the way you talk about learning in your space to affect the growth of your students?

FURTHER READING

Barnes, Mark. 2013. *Role Reversal: Achieving Uncommonly Excellent Results in the Student-Centered Classroom.* Alexandria, VA: ASCD.

Barnes, Mark D. 2015. *Assessment 3.0: Throw Out Your Grade Book and Inspire Learning.* Thousand Oaks, CA: Corwin.

O'Connor, Ken. 2016. *A Repair Kit for Grading Plus DVD Plus Seven Strategies of Assessment for Learning: 15 Fixes for Broken Grades.* Upper Saddle River, NJ: Prentice Hall.

Sackstein, Starr. 2015a. *Hacking Assessment: 10 Ways to Go Gradeless in a Traditional Grades School.* Cleveland, OH: Times 10 Publications.

Sackstein, Starr. 2015b. *Teaching Students to Self-Assess: How Do I Help Students Reflect and Grow as Learners?* Alexandria, VA: ASCD.

Sackstein, Starr, and Jill Berkowicz. 2017. *Peer Feedback in the Classroom: Empowering Students to Be the Experts.* Alexandria, VA: ASCD.

Sackstein, Starr, and Connie Hamilton. 2016. *Hacking Homework: 10 Strategies That Inspire Learning outside the Classroom.* Cleveland, OH: Times 10 Publications.

Wormeli, Rick. 2018. *Fair Isn't Always Equal: Assessment and Grading in the Differentiated Classroom.* 2nd ed. Portland, ME: Stenhouse.

Chapter 5

———

GRADES STIFLE STUDENT LEARNING. CAN WE LEARN TO TEACH WITHOUT GRADES?

Arthur Chiaravalli

———

Several years ago I encountered the work of Dylan Wiliam, who researched the effect of teacher feedback on student improvement. In his book *Embedded Formative Assessment*, he cites a study by Ruth Butler wherein she examines the three types of feedback teachers give: grades alone, both grades and comments, and comments alone.[1]

The results of Butler's research might seem counterintuitive: the students who showed the most growth were those who received comments alone. Even grades paired with comments—which at face value would seem to be the richest form of feedback—were just as ineffective as giving grades alone.[2]

Wiliam concludes: "That most students virtually ignore . . . painstaking correction, advice, and praise is one of public education's best-kept secrets."[3]

Not only do grades not encourage growth, they inhibit it. Grades take the focus off feedback.

As a teacher of English language arts who prides himself on providing quality feedback, I find this result particularly disturbing. But it didn't surprise me: frequently a student who receives an assignment back glances at the letter grade and then stows or throws it away without ever reading the comments. This remains true even though, for most of my career, I have allowed students to revise and improve their scores on assessments.

Something about the letter grade causes learning to stop.

Finally, after much more reading, reflection, and deliberation, I made the decision to use *feedback and revisions only*, without entering a letter grade until the end of each term. It just made sense.

Much of Butler's and Wiliam's research confirms the findings of other researchers like Carol Dweck, whose book *Mindset* introduced the world to growth mindset, and Daniel Pink, whose book *Drive* argued that extrinsic rewards and punishments stifle creativity, higher-order thinking, and intrinsic motivation.[4]

In short, the grade becomes a false currency that, over time, seems to override students' intrinsic desire for mastery and personal sense of purpose. Students find themselves trapped in the Sisyphean task of continually laboring for a letter or number. And as Camus put it in his *The Myth of Sisyphus*, "There is no more dreadful punishment than futile and hopeless labor."[5]

One might argue that these letters and numbers still represent something. But due to grade inflation and idiosyncratic grading policies, that "something" has no consistent or reliable meaning. As Robert Marzano writes, "grades are so imprecise, they are almost meaningless."[6]

Furthermore, like printed currency no longer moored to the gold standard, scores, grades, GPA, and class rankings decreasingly possess any guaranteed *exchange* value. Students may still be able to exchange these currencies for college admission, scholarships, and in turn well-paying jobs, but these are no longer foregone conclusions. Laszlo Bock, formerly of Google, asserts, "One of the things we've seen from all our data crunching is that G.P.A.'s are worthless as a criteria for hiring, and test scores are worthless . . . We found that they don't predict anything."[7]

Getting into college is not enough. In order to avoid an adulthood driven by debt on a par with indentured servitude, students almost always need major scholarship help.[8] Society has to be concerned when generations of graduates will need to adopt a near-mercenary mindset to pay back crippling debt. Who will be our teachers, social workers, musicians, poets, dancers?

For students the question arises: will I truly be able to exchange this letter grade, this GPA, or this class rank for anything of value? Perhaps at one time students could, regardless of the underlying quality of the education. But the answer is increasingly no, that these empty distinctions guarantee you little if anything in life, as the book of Isaiah puts it,

Why spend your money for what is not bread;
your wages for what does not satisfy?[9]

Since the significance and value of grades have steadily declined, it makes even less sense to let grades do us a double disservice by hobbling learning in the classroom. And since I hope to engender dispositions of growth mindset and intrinsic motivation in my students, I want to eliminate any practices and policies that prevent these perspectives from flourishing.

That includes letter grades.

Now in my classes, students only receive written and verbal feedback about what they did well and what they can improve. Using an online portfolio platform (I use Seesaw), it is relatively easy to document student progress toward meeting learning targets. While I do still usually give a mainstream assignment through which students can demonstrate those targets, students can also suggest other ways to show the same learning. For example, to show their recognition of how ancient poets use the characteristics of oral literature to convey meaning, I might ask students to write a short analysis of an ancient text, identifying the presence of those characteristics and how they parallel meaning. But students could also write and perform a poem or rap that uses the same ancient methods to support the message and emotion they want to express. With Seesaw, students can upload documents, pictures, videos, and links to work they've done elsewhere. Additionally I frequently have students draw on, highlight, annotate, and comment on their own artifacts, instilling a habit of regular self-assessment. Seesaw has built-in drawing, labeling, and commenting features that facilitate this kind of reflection.

Throughout the term students evaluate their own and other students' work, make improvements in response to feedback from their teacher and peers, and elicit and receive new feedback—all of which has been shown to aid students in becoming more engaged and effective learners.[10] This feedback cycle is not unlike the process used by coaches to prepare players for an upcoming game or meet. Coaches don't put a score on the scoreboard during practices; that only happens during the game. Up until that moment of truth, coaches do everything they can to develop players in the skills and concepts they will need to succeed. To grade or rate them sends the subtle message that their current achievement is fixed. This is the exact opposite of the mentality needed to sustain growth and improvement. The goal is to keep the conversation going as long as possible.

As we continue that conversation, I do still use our traditional online gradebook to more or less tally students' submission of artifacts. A 1/1 in the gradebook indicates that an artifact has been completed at an adequate level; a 0/1 indicates that the work has not been submitted or has not yet demonstrated the skill. I weight these tallies as 0 percent, so they have no effect on the cumulative grade, which I base on a preliminary grade students identify at the beginning of the term. If a student has too many missing artifacts, I will override this grade with an I, or Incomplete. I use the comment field for each assignment to direct students and parents away from the gradebook and toward our portfolio platform, where more detailed feedback is available. We have trained students and parents to look to reductive numbers to judge students' current status; weaning them from this habit won't happen overnight. In my communications with students and parents, I continually emphasize the merits of providing comments alone in promoting growth.

At the end of each term, I ask students to submit artifacts that demonstrate their mastery of our learning targets. They use a simple Google Form (fig. 5.1) that features links to any exemplary work or full-class feedback I have shared with students throughout the term. Students also review any verbal or written feedback they received individually and point out areas where they showed growth in response to that feedback, either through revisions or improvements on subsequent attempts.

Ultimately students select and support a final term grade, using wording from my descriptive grading criteria, which describe the levels

Term 4 Grade Evaluation - AP Lit

Dear Students,

Please use the following form to reflect on your work this term. It will lead you through the four statements on the Descriptive Grading Criteria (https://goo.gl/tPM5cu). You should make sure to have your Seesaw portfolio up (https://app.seesaw.me) while you do this so you can review work and include SHARE LINKS as evidence.

As you reflect on what you demonstrated this term, please make sure to check your work against the exemplary work shared throughout the term. Before going on to the next section, jot down the letter grade you chose for each statement.

As always, please honor the exemplary effort and work of your peers by rating yourself honestly and accurately for each of the four bullet points on the Descriptive Grading Criteria. I wish you all the best to you as you begin the exciting next chapter in your life. Do NOT be a stranger!

Sincerely,

Mr. Chiaravalli

Figure 5.1. Term 4 grade evaluation for Advanced Placement Literature.

of achievement and growth associated with an A, a B, and a C grade (fig. 5.2). I don't go lower than a C, because to me that indicates the student has not demonstrated mastery or understanding of one or more skills or concepts. In those cases, I ask students either to revise or redo the assessment, or demonstrate the skills elsewhere. Rather than give students a low grade and rubber-stamp them onto the next level, I give students time to revisit and demonstrate mastery of those targets.

Emphasis is always placed on more recent levels of performance, rather than on earlier attempts where students were still learning the skill or concept. I use Form Publisher—a Google Forms add-on—to publish and peruse these student grade evaluations in Google Docs, and use in-text comments to reply to their self-evaluation. I usually agree with these determinations. Sometimes I argue they earned something higher. If I don't agree and enter a lower grade, I always give them the opportunity to follow up on the specific areas holding them back.

I've found that this approach, while not perfect, allows students to

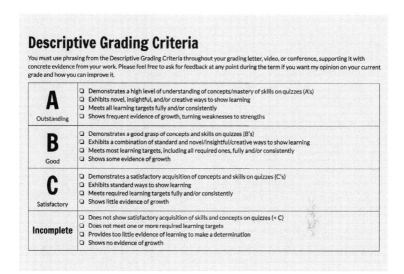

Descriptive Grading Criteria

You must use phrasing from the Descriptive Grading Criteria throughout your grading letter, video, or conference, supporting it with concrete evidence from your work. Please feel free to ask for feedback at any point during the term if you want my opinion on your current grade and how you can improve it.

A Outstanding	❏ Demonstrates a high level of understanding of concepts/mastery of skills on quizzes (A's) ❏ Exhibits novel, insightful, and/or creative ways to show learning ❏ Meets all learning targets fully and/or consistently ❏ Shows frequent evidence of growth, turning weaknesses to strengths
B Good	❏ Demonstrates a good grasp of concepts and skills on quizzes (B's) ❏ Exhibits a combination of standard and novel/insightful/creative ways to show learning ❏ Meets most learning targets, including all required ones, fully and/or consistently ❏ Shows some evidence of growth
C Satisfactory	❏ Demonstrates a satisfactory acquisition of concepts and skills on quizzes (C's) ❏ Exhibits standard ways to show learning ❏ Meets required learning targets fully and/or consistently ❏ Shows little evidence of growth
Incomplete	❏ Does not show satisfactory acquisition of skills and concepts on quizzes (< C) ❏ Does not meet one or more required learning targets ❏ Provides too little evidence of learning to make a determination ❏ Shows no evidence of growth

Figure 5.2. Descriptive grading criteria.

have greater awareness and ownership of their learning. They know what they need to improve and how to improve it. They are no longer numbed by numbers.

Now is the time we shift the focus of schools from grades back to learning, creating an environment in which our students can thrive and grow.

NOTES

1. Wiliam 2018. See also Butler 1987.
2. Butler 1988.
3. Wiliam 2014.
4. Dweck 2008; Pink 2009.
5. Camus and O'Brien 2018: 119.
6. Marzano 2000: 1.
7. Bryant 2018.
8. Konczal 2009.
9. Isaiah 55:2.
10. Boaler 1998.

SOURCES

Boaler, Jo. 1998. "Open and Closed Mathematics: Student Experiences and Understandings." *Journal for Research in Mathematics Education* 29(1): 41. https://doi.org/10.2307/749717.

Bryant, Adam. 2018. "In Head-Hunting, Big Data May Not Be Such a Big Deal." *The New York Times.* October 19. https://www.nytimes.com/2013/06/20/business/in-head-hunting-big-data-may-not-be-such-a-big-deal.html.

Butler, Ruth. 1987. "Task-Involving and Ego-Involving Properties of Evaluation: Effects of Different Feedback Conditions on Motivational Perceptions, Interest, and Performance." *Journal of Educational Psychology* 79(4): 474–82.

Butler, Ruth. 1988. "Enhancing and Undermining Intrinsic Motivation: The Effects of Task-Involving and Ego-Involving Evaluation on Interest and Performance." *British Journal of Educational Psychology* 58(1): 1–14. https://doi.org/10.1111/j.2044-8279.1988.tb00874.x.

Camus, Albert, and Justin O'Brien. 2018. *The Myth of Sisyphus.* New York: Vintage.

Dweck, Carol S. 2008. *Mindset: The New Psychology of Success.* New York: Ballantine Books.

Konczal, Mike. 2009. "Student Loans Are the New Indentured Servitude." *The Atlantic.* October 12. https://www.theatlantic.com/business/archive/2009/10/student-loans-are-the-new-indentured-servitude/28235/.

Marzano, R. J. 2000. *Transforming Classroom Grading.* Alexandria, VA: Association for Supervision and Curriculum Development.

Pink, Daniel H. 2009. *Drive: The Surprising Truth about What Motivates Us.* New York: Riverhead Books.

Wiliam, Dylan. 2014. "Is the Feedback You're Giving Students Helping or Hindering?" Learning Sciences International. Dylan Wiliam Center. November 29. https://www.dylanwiliamcenter.com/is-the-feedback-you-are-giving-students-helping-or-hindering/.

Wiliam, Dylan. 2018. *Embedded Formative Assessment.* Bloomington, IN: Solution Tree.

Part II

———

PRACTICES

Chapter 6

———

LET'S TALK ABOUT GRADING

Laura Gibbs

———

GETTING RID OF GRADES

Given that you're reading this book, I'm going to assume you have some kind of dissatisfaction with your current grading practices, something that has you thinking about alternatives. I'm excited to share my ungrading practice here; it works great for me, but will it work for you? It might help to start by thinking about the dissatisfaction that brought you to this book.

STARTING WITH DISSATISFACTION

My own ungrading practices evolved from a long history of dissatisfaction with grading, both as a student and as a teacher. And so I'd like to suggest you do a quick study of your own dissatisfaction: try jotting down ten memories that come to mind when you think about grading, any memories at all. A few memories will come quickly, experiences that have crystallized and probably already guided your grading practices. If you delve deeper, though, you might find some memories that are rawer, less routinized, and thus offering new insight into your grading dissatisfaction. So take a minute to do that before you continue reading. (I've shared my list in appendix 6.1 at the end of this chapter.)

ALL-FEEDBACK-NO-GRADES

Just as there are many different ways to assign grades, there are many different ways to ungrade. I call my approach *all-feedback-no-grades*, which is to say that I put no grades on student work; instead, I give my students feedback, lots of feedback. In describing my approach below, I will try to generalize so that the approach could apply to all kinds of classes, but every teaching context has its own possibilities and its own constraints. For the record here's my teaching context (deep breath to say it all in one go): I'm a full-time adjunct instructor of fully online, upper-division, general education, writing-intensive Western and non-Western humanities courses at a large public university in the United States. I teach in the open, so for more information, you can visit my website, MythFolklore.net.

Now, briefly, this is how I implement an all-feedback-no-grades approach in my classes:

- **Individual Feedback:** I put no grades on student work. Instead I provide individual feedback to help the students improve their work from week to week. And their work does improve, sometimes dramatically. That is, for me, the most important measure of success. You can check out my students' writing projects at Storybooks.MythFolklore.net.
- **Culture of Feedback:** I explicitly teach the students about giving and receiving feedback so that they can give each other helpful feedback and also make good use of the feedback they receive. As part of that process, I teach students about growth mindset and the positive value of learning from mistakes. You can check out our class feedback resources at Mindset.MythFolklore.net.
- **Gradebook Declarations:** When they complete an assignment, students record their work in the learning management system (LMS), using a "declaration" quiz, which is just a quiz with a true-false question containing a checklist of the requirements for that assignment. When students click *true* as the answer, the assignment points go into the gradebook. Each assignment

is worth just a few points; there are no high-stakes assignments or tests. (I've used this system in three different LMSes over the years: first Blackboard, then D2L, and now Canvas.)

- **A-B-C Letter Grades:** I am required to turn in an A-B-C letter grade at the end of the semester, and that grade is based on the total points in the gradebook. All points in the gradebook come from the students' declaration quizzes; it has nothing to do with any action on my part. Students can chart their own progress from week to week to make sure they are on track for the grade they want.
- **Pass/Not-Pass.** While the students pay attention to their letter grades, I do not. My only goal is that every student pass the class. Each week I sort the total points in the gradebook from low to high, looking only at the very lowest totals. If there is anyone at risk of not passing the class based on their progress so far, I send them an encouraging email.

As you can see, it's not a complicated system, and I think that's important. Anything having to do with grades is emotionally charged for students, and I don't want to overwhelm them with something complex or confusing. Students do the work, they record the work they do, and they move on to the next assignment. It's a simple system, and I am pleased to say that students embrace the system enthusiastically.

WHAT STUDENTS SAY

My university collects end-of-semester course evaluations from students, and that process went digital in fall 2010, so we now receive those student comments in searchable PDF form. That makes it easy to keep track of comments that mention grades or grading. I've collected all the student comments related to grading since fall 2010, and you can see that document at Evals.MythFolklore.net. I would encourage you to take a look to see what the students say. If I were to receive negative feedback from students about the grading system, I would change my approach, but the only feedback I get is positive. In fact, it is extremely positive. Here are some typical comments:

There was an emphasis on learning the course material rather than worrying about grades.

The grading system encourages students to write for the sake of writing and not for the sake of a grade.

This is one of the best classes I have taken at the University of Oklahoma. I learned so much and never had to stress about my grade. I always knew where I stood in the course, the organization made me feel comfortable by the first week.

It was very fun and I learned a lot! I really liked that I had the freedom to write just to write rather than for a grade.

The self-grading was definitely a nice feature. This class afforded me freedoms that I was not granted in any other class. I felt like I was being treated like an adult for once.

I really liked it. It was fun and was all about learning not just a grade.

I really liked how there were a lot of assignments and grades were given based on participation. I felt that I learned much more this way because the emphasis was on learning and creativity rather than a test.

You put a lot of time into the course but you get out what you put in. I also liked that you basically decided what grade you got based on how much work you wanted to do. You knew that as long as you did the work, you would get a 100. This doesn't mean it was easy though!!

This unique format gave me the ability to learn and express my understanding in a way that didn't come along with anxiety about grades. This is the first time I have ever taken a course and was not stressed about grades so I purely learned the material. It was amazing and I think I learned more in this course than I have in any other in a long time.

I loved being able to write what I wanted and not be graded subjectively. It made it easy for me to be creative!

I could go on, but suffice to say that all the comments about the grading—*all* the comments—are positive, with one exception: "The self grading bit was really strange." I'm not sure that is a negative comment, but it's the closest thing to a negative comment about grading in the hundreds of course evaluations I've received in the past ten years.

So, now that I've described some of the practical features of my approach, along with the students' reactions, I want to move on to some philosophical aspects of ungrading and the benefits of ungrading for both teachers and students.

UNGRADING AND MY PHILOSOPHY OF TEACHING

Before I describe my own philosophical assumptions about teaching, I'd like to suggest a little experiment like the one I suggested above: pause and take some time to write down your basic assumptions about teaching and learning. Then you'll be able to see just how much our assumptions overlap. A lot of overlap might indicate that some of my practical approaches could work for you too.

My philosophy of teaching comes down to just one word: freedom. Freedom is the idea that guides all my course design choices, and there are two ideas about freedom that are relevant to ungrading. First, learners need the freedom to grow and learn in their own ways, and second, they need the freedom to make mistakes without being punished.

Learners need freedom to grow and learn in their own ways, and they need feedback to support them in that learning.

While grades aspire to be a form of feedback, the main function of grading is coercion, the opposite of freedom. We use grades to make students do things that we want them to do. We may have good intentions with our students' interests in mind, but that does not change the fact that we are using grades as a form of control. Schools coerce students in other ways too, of course, like how most students enroll in my classes because the classes are required for graduation. I cannot change the fact that students are forced to take general education classes in order to graduate, but I can choose not to compound that coercion with the further coercion of grading.

Removing grades gives students the space they need to explore in order to discover what is meaningful and valuable to them. Instead of defining the learning objectives in advance, with the same objectives for all students, I can give the students the freedom to choose their own learning goals, and it then becomes my job to help them get there. As I shift the balance from grading to supportive feedback, I am showing the students that I really care about their learning and that I want to help them learn about the things that are important to them.

When teachers give feedback together with a grade, the students see the feedback as justification for the grade, but if there is feedback without a grade, then students can see the feedback for its own sake and act on it (see chapter 2, Blackwelder). So if you've ever asked why students don't read or use your feedback, try not giving grades and see what happens. Grades tell students that the grade is what matters. When you get rid of grades, you can show the students it is their work that matters instead, and by giving them feedback to improve their work, you show them that their work matters to you too.

Students also feel more free to give each other honest feedback in the absence of grades. Grades are about judging, but feedback is about helping, and in my experience, students are eager to help one another. In addition, as they examine each other's work, they get ideas that can expand their own awareness and understanding, and by coaching others, they develop skills that are useful beyond the classroom.

Yes, it takes time and effort on the teacher's part to help students learn how to give each other useful feedback, but I have found that this is time well spent. Helping your students to develop their own feedback skills allows you then to focus on the kind of feedback only you can provide. Just how that division of labor works in any class depends on the subject matter and the students' backgrounds, but in any classroom, you can enlist your students' help in maximizing both the quantity and quality of feedback, and everyone wins when students are helping each other to learn.

Learners need the freedom to make mistakes in order to learn from those mistakes; they should not be punished for making mistakes.
When I tell people I am against grading, what I really mean is that I am against punitive grading, any process that punishes students for making mistakes. Those punitive grading systems teach students to avoid mistakes at all costs, rather than encouraging them to use mistakes for feedback and further learning.

Sure, we might tell students they need to learn from their mistakes, and we might even give them feedback intended to help them learn from their mistakes, but the grade tells a different story: the grade punishes them for any mistakes they make, large or small. As such, those grades are always an occasion for regret and remorse, looking backward instead of forward. With letter grades an A is often the only grade that comes with no remorse—or, worse, maybe only an A+ will do. Percentages are even more unforgiving: anything less than one hundred means you failed somehow. You made mistakes. You left things out. Somehow or other you did something wrong. And no matter how well you do next time, the less-than-perfect grade is going to remind you that you did something wrong. This specter of perfectionism, I would argue, is the most dangerous side effect of punitive grading, something that causes harm to every learner, both those at risk of failing and those at risk of getting one hundred.

Learning, after all, is not about being perfect and never making mistakes; instead learning is about being able to understand your mistakes and act on them. Are your mistakes the result of a lack of skills? You need to practice those skills. Are your mistakes the result of a lack of sleep? Then you need to get more sleep. The variety of mistakes and reasons we make them is enormous, which is why so much effort is required from both learners and their teachers. The grade on a report card or a transcript does not allow anyone—not students, not teachers, and not parents or potential employers—to tell the difference between a student who is short on skills and a student who is short on sleep.

The most powerful feedback feeds into a revision process so that students can see their work improve over time, iterating and reiterating as needed. As such, revision should be a positive element in any learning process, but traditional grading undermines the value of revision work. At best, students see revision as a way to raise their grade. At worst, revision becomes a form of punishment inflicted on students for a poor grade: you did a bad job, so you have to revise.

Students thus learn to avoid revision, seeing it as a negative feedback signal: you didn't get a good enough grade, so you're going to have to revise. But when you get rid of grades, revision is no longer a reward, and it is no longer a punishment; it's just what you do in order to improve and learn more. There is always more to learn, so there is always more revising to do. All students revise their writing in my classes: the students who are already highly skilled writers, along with the students who are novices. Everybody needs to revise their work and to do so repeatedly (teachers too!) because there are always new experiments to try and new skills to practice.

BENEFITS OF GOING GRADELESS

I have seen nothing but benefits to going gradeless, both for myself and for the students. If I had some doubts or if I had observed any drawbacks, I would include those observations here, but there have been no downsides, at least not in my experience. In addition to the benefits I've already mentioned above, such as combating perfectionism, here are some more benefits I've seen.

- **Ungrading reduces stress.** Are your students stressed about grades? Ask them, and they will tell you. My students feel a lot of stress about grades, and I am glad about any effort I can make to reduce that level of stress. When students comment on the grading system in my classes, they often mention the benefits of learning without the stress of grades. Stress about grades is harmful for learning, and it is harmful for the students' well-being overall. That goes for teachers too: if you feel stressed out because you have to grade student work, then you might experience less stress if you stop grading (see chapter 13, Warner).

- **Ungrading helps form new learning habits.** Students learn a lot of bad habits as a result of grading, and those habits are hard to change. Probably the most universal habit taught by traditional grading is "do what it takes to gets an A." Don't ask questions, don't look for meaning; just do what you are told to do and focus on the grade. An even more harmful form of that habit is "do the minimum it takes to get an A." The single biggest challenge I face as a teacher is helping students to free themselves from that habit of doing the minimum. And here is the worst-case scenario: the habit of doing whatever it takes to get an A, no matter what, is how students can justify cheating on an assignment. Yes, students all know it is wrong to cheat, but if a student believes getting a bad grade is the worst possible thing that can happen, then that justifies the cheating: cheating is the lesser of those two evils. When you replace grades with feedback, you obviate that equation, so students can focus on learning instead.

- **Ungrading makes room for creative work.** Students do creative writing for my classes, which is often something completely new for them, and like anything new, it can be frightening. Not putting grades on their work is the key to encouraging them to take that risk and try something new. If you want your students to do creative, open-ended assignments, or any kind of project-based learning, then try going without grades to see what happens.

- **Ungrading promotes better communication.** Insofar as grades are a form of communication, they are Tarzanesque: the vocabulary of ABCDF does not say much. With the addition of pluses and minuses, you end up with a vocabulary of eleven words. Clearly we need better ways to communicate. By shifting from grades to feedback, you are able to communicate more fully and more honestly with your students, and that then encourages them to do the same with you.

- **Ungrading opens up new course design possibilities.** Do you have graded assignments in your classes simply to generate grades? Eliminating grades gives you a chance to consider the real purpose of the assignment, and you might find that you are able to create more meaningful assignments as a result. Instead of graded assignments, I far prefer assignments that have a long-lasting purpose, assignments that the students themselves can use later in the semester, and assignments that have an even more lasting value. My archive of past student projects is the most valuable content in my classes. Instead of inspiring students to get an A, I would like to inspire them to create a project they would be proud to put in the archive when the semester is over, something to inspire students in future semesters just as they were inspired by the work of past students in the class.

CONCLUSION: AN UNGRADING WISH LIST

By offering a wish list here as my conclusion, I don't want to create the impression that I am unhappy with my current practice: it works nicely, allowing me to do my job with joy and enthusiasm. At the same time, you never know when you might meet a kindly magical fairy who offers to grant you three wishes. So if the ungrading fairy were to grant me three wishes, I'm ready with my list. What would you ask for? These would be my three wishes:

- **No more letter grades.** If there were only a pass/not-pass record at the end of the course, I think I could do an even better job of helping my students in their learning. So I would like to get rid of the meaningless ABCDF for an even simpler P/NP system, where the only courses appearing on a student's transcript would be the courses they passed.
- **No more GPA.** If the fairy says my first wish is going to take a long time to implement, then I would ask that, in the meantime, we stop averaging those meaningless letter grades into the even more meaningless GPA. That way the consequences of students choosing to take a less-than-perfect grade in a

given class would not persist in the form of the GPA and its faux decimal-point precision.

- **Support for ungrading.** Even by magical standards, those first two wishes are big asks, but my third wish is easy: administrators should give teachers the support they need in their ungrading experiments. When I first began ungrading, I had to fly under the radar, especially as an adjunct instructor with no tenure protection. That climate of fear benefits no one; every teacher, tenured or not, must have the freedom to experiment, with grades and with everything else, in order to find what works best for them and for their students. Experiment, and then share what you learn! That's the real magic.

ACKNOWLEDGMENTS

There are many people who have inspired me in my teaching adventures over the years, and I am not going to try to name them all, but instead I will just say: thank you. Most of all I am grateful to my students; they inspire me every day.

There is, however, one person in particular whom I would like to single out because there is a singular story I would like to tell about him, and that is professor John Hurst of the education school at the University of California, Berkeley. John joined the UC Berkeley faculty in 1961, and he went on to establish the peace and conflict studies program there and also Democratic Education at Cal (DECal). The DECal program, based on the work of Dewey and Freire, was a way for Berkeley students to organize independent study groups for credit, creating courses that were otherwise not available. I was a student course facilitator for DECal during the 1980s, and it forever changed my understanding of what education can and should be. The only type of grading for DECal courses was P/NP, and this is a story that DECal course facilitators used to tell about John Hurst and P/NP grades:

John was teaching in the ed school back in the day, but he loathed grades and grading, so his solution was just to give every student a grade of A. No matter what. This system was working just fine until one term when one of his students passed away in a tragic accident shortly after the term had started. When John filled out the final grade report at the end of the term, he gave that student an A. The department chair noticed this anomaly and asked John about it. John explained that he gave every student a grade of A, no matter what. The chair said he wasn't sure whether that was an acceptable grading policy, so he would have to check with the dean. The dean said he wasn't sure either, so he would have to check with the faculty senate. The faculty senate said that was not okay at all, and they stripped John of the right to give traditional letter grades. Henceforth, he would only be allowed to give P/NP grades, no matter what kind of class he was teaching. Thus John Hurst became the only faculty member at Berkeley forbidden to use letter grades. And nothing could have suited him better.

This story was told to me in different ways by different people, and I have often repeated the story too, but I don't know whether it's true. It was such a good story that I didn't want to ask John to confirm or deny it. As the reporter says in *The Man Who Shot Liberty Valance*, "When the legend becomes fact, print the legend." John Hurst died in 2016 at the age of eighty-six. He was a professor both of peace and of courage, and I know he would have enjoyed reading this book; I hope he would approve of the anecdote.

FURTHER READING

Brown, Brené. 2010. *The Gifts of Imperfection: Let Go of Who You Think You're Supposed to Be and Embrace Who You Are.* Center City, MN: Hazelden Publishing.

Dweck, Carol. 2006. *Mindset: The New Psychology of Success: How We Can Learn to Fulfill Our Potential.* New York: Random House.

Eodice, Michele, Anne Ellen Geller, and Neal Lerner. 2017. *The Meaningful Writing Project: Learning, Teaching, and Writing in Higher Education.* Logan: Utah State University Press.

Faber, Adele, and Elaine Mazlish. 1996. *How to Talk So Kids Can Learn.* New York: Charles Scribner's.

Kohn, Alfie. [1993] 2018. *Punished by Rewards: The Trouble with Gold Stars, Incentive*

Plans, A's, Praise, and Other Bribes. 25th anniversary ed. New York: Houghton Mifflin Harcourt.

Lang, James. 2013. *Cheating Lessons: Learning from Academic Dishonesty*. Cambridge, MA: Harvard University Press.

Sackstein, Starr. 2015. *Hacking Assessment: Ten Ways to Go Gradeless in a Traditional Grades School*. Cleveland, OH: Times 10 Publications.

Schulz, Kathryn. 2011. *Being Wrong: Adventures in the Margin of Error*. London: Granta Books.

Socol, Ira, Pam Moran, and Chad Ratliff. 2018. *Timeless Learning: How Imagination, Observation, and Zero-Based Thinking Change Schools*. San Francisco: Jossey-Bass.

Warner, John. 2018. *Why They Can't Write: Killing the Five-Paragraph Essay and Other Necessities*. Baltimore: Johns Hopkins University Press.

APPENDIX 6.1: MY TEN GRADING MEMORIES IN CHRONOLOGICAL ORDER

My earliest grading memory is of my mother comparing report cards with another mother in first grade. The other girl had Es for excellent, but I just had Ss for satisfactory and some Us too. I can still hear the embarrassment in my mother's voice.

I went to an experimental school in fourth grade where we picked what we did every day and didn't get grades. I loved it. When we had to do the state assessment test at year's end, I colored in the multiple-choice bubbles to make pictures. My mother was worried about my poor scores, but my teacher laughed when I told him what I had done.

When I was in seventh grade, my science teacher gave me an F on a quiz because supposedly I had let my friend copy my answers. He told me I had to hunch down more and wrap my arms around the answer sheet . . . "or else." I decided he was the problem, not me or my friend.

My eighth-grade science teacher had us study memory. We memorized a vocabulary list until we got 100 percent on the quiz. Then one month later, we took the quiz again. In general people didn't remember anything. So much for getting 100 percent on a vocabulary quiz.

One of my high school teachers used Scantrons for quizzes and ran the Scantron machine right there in the class, saying each person's name as he ran the sheet. The machine beeped for every mistake,

APPENDIX 6.1

which was embarrassing, and it was also embarrassing when it didn't beep because it meant you were making other people look bad.

I got an A+ in one of my classes during my first semester of college. It made me obsess about getting at least one A+ every semester after that.

In all my college classes, I would put at least one howling error in each paper I turned in to see if someone was actually paying attention to what I wrote.

I worked as a grader when I was an undergraduate, and I could not decipher a lot of the handwriting in the hastily scribbled blue books. The professor just told me to do my best and not worry about the fact that I couldn't read the writing.

When I was a graduate student teaching an introductory language course, a student came to me and asked me to give her a B. Her parents were paying her $500 to get a B her first semester of college so she would not get stuck in the trap of maintaining a 4.0 GPA. She wanted to do all the work to get an A, but she needed me to please record it as a B at the end of the semester.

In my first semester of college teaching, I had fifty students in a mythology class. I did not think I could put detailed comments on that many papers, so I asked the class who would like detailed comments to use in order to revise their papers. The revision would not change the grade; it would just be a chance to get help on improving their work. I expected maybe half the class would want comments, but only one student did. (That was the semester I decided to quit grading and find a better approach.)

Chapter 7

CONTRACT GRADING AND PEER REVIEW

Christina Katopodis and Cathy N. Davidson

A new batch of students sits in your classroom on the first day of the semester, quietly reading over your syllabus while you talk them through it. They are wondering, "How do I get an A in this class?" This is the first-day-of-school ritual we all have repeated, year after year. It's what we knew when we were sitting in those desks long ago, when we were students. It's what our students now expect from a college class.[1]

Now imagine a different scenario: you begin by looking students in the eyes, and you ask them, "What is success in this class for you? And how can I help you achieve it?" By asking these questions at the start of the class, an instructor offers students an opportunity to think about why they are taking a course and what constitutes success. Students may not know how to answer these questions at first because in all likelihood they have never been asked such questions *before* a class begins—or ever. We front-load our courses with a commitment to student success, as students define success for themselves, rather than asking too late, "How can I help?"

Questions like these, asked at the outset, shatter old habits and expectations, turn the future into a blank canvas, and give students autonomy within the safe structure of a classroom. Students *need* to practice and exercise autonomy in higher education before they enter a significantly less structured world outside the academy. Asking students to determine success for themselves, and to carefully review and agree to a contract as members of a community, affords them an opportunity to practice self-determination—one of the most important qualities a self-reliant adult needs in any career path or community.

Our purpose in discussing our ungrading and peer review methods is to offer others step-by-step advice about the thinking, methods, assumptions, and practical choices that go into redesigning classroom assessment inspired by equality, not oppression (to use Paulo Freire's famous terminology).[2] A pedagogy of equality aims to support and inspire the greatest possible student success, creativity, individuality, and achievement, rather than more traditional hierarchies organized around a priori standards of selectivity, credentialing, standardization, ranking, and the status quo.

That, of course, is the most binary way of framing the redesigned student-centered classroom. However, in the real world in which most students live, if they are paying tuition, they also want something more concrete than a sense of their own learning: they want some formal, institutional recognition of the effort they have invested in their learning. (Otherwise, why not just learn from a friend or from a book or online?)

That is where contract grading and peer evaluation come in. To us they are expansive alternatives to conventional grading, while still offering students a meaningful, documentable, and responsible credentialed form of credit for learning attainments. Thus contract grading is both an idealistic, student-centered way of writing one's own learning goals and a better alternative to conventional grading and credentialing. By adding the peer review component, contract grading is also an act of community.

INSTITUTIONAL MATTERS

Our first rule for contract grading: talk to your registrar's office first. Some colleges and universities do not allow it. Always make sure what you are doing meets the formal rules of your institution. Institutions are "mobilizing networks."[3] They offer places of organization, activism, networking, and support. They also come with their own restrictions and rules, and you have to learn to work around and with them. There's no right way to implement contract grading and peer evaluation—both can take on many forms in classrooms with varying student bodies and teaching styles, which is why we offer more than one adaptable example and template at the end of this chapter.

Institution and level don't matter, in our experience. We believe contract grading, combined with peer review, works well at any kind of institution and with any level of course. We've observed it used exceptionally well in a highly diverse middle school class with a number of students with learning and attention issues, for example.[4] Cathy Davidson has used it in classes primarily at Duke University, and Christina Katopodis has used it in classes from first-year writing to advanced English courses for majors in her experience teaching across three very different campuses, at Tallahassee Community College, New Jersey City University, and Hunter College, CUNY.

Size *may* matter: we don't personally know whether it does, but it may. We have never used contract grading in a course where we have had more than thirty students.

WHY—AGAIN. NEVER FORGET THE WHY.

Problems that arise are not with the level of students or the kinds of institutions but with institutional requirements. We have found that students respond to the challenge of taking their own learning seriously if they believe the instructor takes that challenge seriously, consistently, and for a reason: always explaining why is hugely important when you are changing the status quo.

One why is to prevent alienating students from their own education. In the words of Ira Shor, "Alienation in school is the number one learning problem, depressing academic performance and elevating student resistance."[5] Another why is to educate as a practice of freedom. According to bell hooks, "To teach in a manner that respects and cares for the souls of our students is essential if we are to provide the necessary conditions where learning can most deeply and intimately begin."[6]

Once you know your why, the next step is incorporating the most important part of learning into your curriculum: metacognitive reflections about the activities themselves. *Metacognition* is the professional term for thinking about how we think—and we know that metacognition, like group and peer learning, helps students to learn better. It gives them the tools for and a sense of control over their own learning. Students need to hear how a lesson or skill set applies elsewhere; they need us to pull up the drapes and show the scaffolding at work in our lesson plans. The scaffolding behind an activity is not readily visible, not even to experienced pedagogues, without holding the blueprints in hand to understand *why* something works. Knowing an activity's purpose is crucial to learning its biggest takeaways.

TWO MODELS OF UNGRADING

Model I. Contract Grading for Twenty-First-Century Literacies

Rather than a hypothetical contract grade, below you will find an actual contract for A, B, C, D, and F grades that Davidson used in a course called Twenty-First Century Literacies. She hesitated even to write in a failure clause but in the end did so, reverting to professorial judgment since failure is a breach of contract, in essence.

Students contracted for A, B, and C grades in the course. The C student explained that he was competing in a major athletic competition and had a leading role in a play that semester; he said he didn't need a higher grade for his GPA, and yet very much wanted to be in the course. Contracting for the lowest grade he had ever earned allowed him to take a class that, unfortunately, our institution had not allowed to be offered as pass-fail. This was an advantage of contract grading that was surprising, and yet another benefit.

Giving students more autonomy is *not* about cutting corners—not for us, not for them. Equality must be thoughtfully structured into a classroom.[7] Experiment with the model below as a template to start with, and then take some time to make it your own. That is, after all, some of what we mean by peer-to-peer learning, acknowledging that none of us is ever entirely independent in our thinking, however original we may think ourselves to be.

A Note on the Badging Method for Judging Satisfactory Work

Before you read the model below, the peer evaluation methods used in this specific course need some contextualization and elaboration.[8] While contract grading sets up how much work one wants to do, peer evaluation establishes parameters for what might constitute satisfactory work and gives students responsibility for determining what does or does not constitute the satisfactory completion of a contract. The terms for peer evaluation should be structured as carefully as contract grading. The first step is for students themselves to determine the categories for judging. One such method is peer badging, a system of recognition for satisfactory work originally developed by open-source computer coders in the 1990s, who often worked together anonymously online yet needed a way of evaluating and praising one another in order to facilitate collaborations, including with new partners. Now badging is more commonplace—for example, it is used in systems such as Lyft or Uber where passengers can commend drivers for such attributes as good navigation, friendliness, a clean car, or fun conversation. In a classroom, students might discuss what they consider to be most important in a project and then define categories for evaluation accordingly, such as depth of research, originality of thesis or argument, persuasiveness, clarity of the writing, examples, application, and the significance of the project. Students know in advance that they will be reading work by their peers with these categories in mind and that their own work will be read in the same way.

An important feature of badging is that students are not required to give negative grades; they simply award a badge when they admire someone's work in that category. One effective way of badging is for, say, three students to read the same paper or project independently and award badges. Then the writer sees the aggregated results. If, for example, three peers have awarded them badges for depth of research but none for examples, the student very clearly sees they need to add examples, and so forth. This method works for individuals and also for teams. In group or team projects, badges might be awarded for such contributions to the group as leadership, implementation, creativity, and other characterological and management practices essential for good collaboration.[9]

In the model below, you will see that students determined whether their peers' work was Satisfactory, earning them full credit for the assignment, or Unsatisfactory, meaning that students believed the work required substantial revision in order to obtain credit. A badge system offers more detailed feedback to supplement this ungrading method and allows students to communicate to one another what's working and what needs improvement. It is at this point that, in Davidson's classes (as in the model below), the instructor uses the badges as well as discussion among peers (those who evaluate the project and the person who wrote it) to devise suggestions for how to improve the paper and bring it up to the "acceptable" standards of the group. Evaluation is a complex process and a life skill, yet it is almost never taught in higher education, even in management programs where giving and receiving feedback and taking a project to the next iteration are essential.

Twenty-First-Century Literacies: Syllabus Description of the Course's Contract Grading

You determine your grade for this course by fulfilling a contract that spells out in advance the requirements as well as the penalties for not fulfilling the terms of your contract. Peer evaluation comes in when students charged with leading a unit assess (as Satisfactory or Unsatisfactory) how well their classmates fulfill the assignments.

Peer leaders for the given unit will work with the other students in this class, giving feedback to each student and working to achieve an S grade. If a student fails to submit an assignment or does not submit a satisfactory revision after receiving careful feedback, the peer leader will record a U grade for that assignment. (The same method will work on assignments graded by the professor.) Every student will be in a position of peer grader (working with two students at a time) once during this semester. Learning together, giving and receiving feedback, is a subject we will discuss in depth. *It is the single most valuable life skill you can take away from this course.*

CONTRACT GRADING

The advantage of contract grading is that you, the student, decide how much work you wish to do this semester. If you complete your work on time and satisfactorily, you will receive the grade for which you contracted. This means planning ahead, thinking about all of your obligations and responsibilities this semester, and also determining what grade you want or need in this course.

The advantage of contract grading to the professor is no whining, no special pleading, on the student's part. If you complete the work you contracted for, you get the grade. Done. I respect the student who only needs a C, who has other obligations that preclude doing all of the requirements to earn an A in the course, and who contracts for the C and carries out the contract perfectly. *(This is another one of those major life skills: taking responsibility for your own project management and workflow.)*

GRADE CALCULATING

At our second class session, each student will sign, with a classmate as a witness, a contract for a grade. I will countersign, and we will each keep a copy of your contract. In addition, you will be given an individualized online and physical grade reporting sheet. You will be responsible for maintaining these in an accurate way.

There are only two grades for any assignment: Satisfactory and Unsatisfactory. Satisfactory is full credit. Unsatisfactory (poor quality, late, or not submitted) is no credit. At the end of the course, we tally. If you fail to do a contracted assignment or your peers do not deem your work satisfactory, you will receive the appropriate grade as spelled out in the contract.

Peers (details below) who are in charge of leading a class unit will determine if the blogs or other assignments posted each week are satisfactory. If not, they will give extensive and thoughtful feedback for improvement with the aim of collaborating toward satisfactory work. The goal is for everyone to produce satisfactory work (no matter what quantity one has contracted for). Our peer leaders will work with students to achieve that goal.

Basically the contract specifies the *quantity* of satisfactory work a student promises to complete during the term. *Quality* is determined by one's peers—with the goal that peers offer feedback to ensure that every assignment eventually meets the *quality* goal of a satisfactory assignment.

REQUIREMENTS FOR A GRADE OF A

(1) Class Attendance/Participation

Class attendance is required. If you contract for an A in the course, you may miss two classes (and the corresponding blog posts) without an official (doctor or preapproved) excuse. Penalty: If you have more than two unexcused absences, your grade for the entire class will automatically drop 0.5. If you miss four classes, it will drop 1.0, and so on.

If you are missing for a nonmedical/emergency reason, you have to have approval in advance and, at that time, state your plan for making up the missed work. You are still responsible for the readings and filing the weekly blog.

(2) Weekly Blog or Equivalent Writing or Other Media Assignment (400–500 words)

Think of this as an evolving research paper. It has the same importance, weight, and seriousness. It will be on our class WordPress site, visible to all the other students and the instructor but not to the general public. There will be a comments section where you will receive feedback from the instructor, the other students, and the two or three students (*peer reviewers*) leading and assessing that particular unit.

Blogs must be completed by midnight the night before the class session. All students are required to read the blogs by their classmates before class and are encouraged to comment in writing as well as in class discussion. Blogs are substantive, should use secondary sources where appropriate, and can use video, sound, images, and animation as well as text.

Penalty: If you are late and/or miss more than two blogs over the course of the semester, your grade will automatically drop by 0.5. If you miss or are late for four, it will drop by 1.0, and so on.

These blogs will not be visible beyond our class. Students may choose to reblog their work in a public place or on their own blogs (optional).

(3) Collaborative, Peer-led Unit on a Selected Literacy

Students will work in teams of two (or, in some cases, three) and will be responsible for a literacy, a unit of work that will occupy us for two or sometimes (when there is a visitor or an event) three class sessions. Typically students will make a presentation, guide a reading, or conduct a field trip one class and then will do follow-up, with the help of the instructor, in the second class. *No talking heads please!* Think of ways to make your presentation as interactive, engaged, thoughtful, and inspiring as possible.

(4) Public Contribution(s) to Knowledge

Each student is required to make two substantive contributions to a significant public resource such as Wikipedia. One contribution can be a detailed comment on a *New York Times* article or another major media outlet, including a significant blog post on the HASTAC site.

Penalty: Failure to make these two public contributions will result in an automatic 0.5 deduction from the total course grade.

(5) Midterm Contribution to a Collaborative, Wiki-Based Midterm

In lieu of a traditional midterm exam, the class will, collectively and using a wiki, create a concise blog post tying together key lessons and insights about twenty-first-century literacies studied in the first half of the class, will post the finished blog on the www.HASTAC.org website, and then will work on a social media campaign to draw attention to the blog through your own various social networks. The instructor will open the wiki with the challenge topic: What are twenty-first-century literacies? Students are invited to change the topic in the course of the online discussion. At the specified due date, the blog must be ready to be posted to www.HASTAC.org.

This is an exercise in collective thinking, leadership, and project management. Everyone must contribute, but remember our method in this course is "collaboration by difference," the HASTAC methodology based on open web development that we all have something in which we are excellent, and we do best by learning how to pool resources wisely. At the end of the assignment, you will need to let the instructor know what and how you contributed.

(6) Final Collaborative Three-Minute Public Literacy Video

You will turn your work on your peer-led literacy unit into a video that will be hosted on the HASTAC YouTube channel and will be open to the public at large. The rough cuts will be viewed during the last week of class as a recap of the entire class and will receive feedback from the class, and then final versions must be submitted for uploading to the YouTube channel by final exam day.

CONTRACT FOR A GRADE OF A

By signing this contract for an A in this class, I agree to all of the terms above.

CONTRACT FOR A GRADE OF B

I wish to earn a grade of B in this class. To fulfill my contract for a grade of B, I will complete satisfactorily #1, 2, 3, 4, and 6 above. I will not miss more than four classes. If I do, I understand that my grade for the entire class will drop by 0.5 for each absence beyond that.

CONTRACT FOR A GRADE OF C

I wish to earn a grade of C in this class. To fulfill my contract for a grade of C, I will complete satisfactorily #1, 2, 3, and 6 above. I will not miss more than six classes. If I do, I understand that my grade for the entire class will drop by 0.5 for each absence beyond that.

1. Your Contract Grade: _____
2. Your Name: _____
3. Signature: _____
4. Date: _____
5. Witness Name: _____
6. Witness Signature: _____
7. Date: _____
8. Co-signed by Instructor: _____
9. Date: _____

A NOTE ON D AND F GRADES

The instructor reserves the right to award a grade of D or F to anyone who fails to meet a contractual obligation in a systematic way. A D grade denotes some minimal fulfilling of the contract. An F is absence of enough satisfactory work, as contracted, to warrant passing of the course. Both a D and F denote a breakdown of the contractual relationship implied by signing any of the contracts above.

Epilogue

This story of contract grading has a surprise ending. Instead of a collaborative, public midterm and a three-minute digital literacy video, the students in Twenty-First-Century Literacies took charge of the class during a class period when the professor was out of town. When she returned, they produced a full table of contents for a book and a new contract, insisting that all but one of the students would work for an A and an A meant a perfect, proofread, satisfactory, publishable chapter in a book that the students, collectively, would copyedit, design, and publish on HASTAC.org, on GitHub, and as a physical book available on Amazon.com. What was a progressive pedagogue to do? She threw out the original contract and, after many warnings that this was incredibly ambitious, allowed the students to write *Field Notes to Twenty-First Century Literacies: A Guide to New Theories, Methods and Practices for Open Peer Teaching and Learning.*[10] The landing page for this book has had nearly twenty thousand unique visitors. The introduction to the volume has had over ten thousand.

So that is the lesson of ungrading: once you create a structure where students can imagine themselves as large, authoritative, creative, and confident, be prepared—they may just take you seriously enough to achieve that optimistic and idealistic goal.

***

Model II. Collaborative Peer Evaluation

An American Literature: Origins to the Civil War course that Katopodis taught at Hunter College in fall 2018 was based on a wide variety of peer learning, colearning, and participatory practices. Students cocreated a syllabus, voting on how attendance should be taken, on a fair and just participation policy, and on learning outcomes based on their own goals for the semester. They also chose to receive feedback instead of grades on their reading reflections so they could focus on personal development, especially in critical thinking and clear writing, throughout the semester.

Another aspect of ungrading in this course was an exercise in self-evaluation before peer evaluation at the end of the semester. Although these evaluations were eventually used to inform students' individual and group participation grades, the grades were the least important part of the process. The evaluations guided students through thinking about assessment in sophisticated ways that allowed them to understand what it means to judge and to be judged and how evaluation can lead to excellence and confidence, not mortification and humiliation.

To move toward this deeper understanding of ungrading, Katopodis offered students a list of thought topics for their consideration in the forms below. These topics focus on student preparedness, group leadership, volunteerism, good listening, and other service qualities students can apply and improve on in the future.

A Note on Static Groups

Throughout the semester, students worked in static groups (the same five to six students per group) during and outside of class time. Static groups operate more like teams: students learn one another's names, each student finds their role in the group based on their strengths, students help each other catch up on missed work, and absences impact group performance in class. The time spent with the same five to six students throughout the semester enables peers to give more detailed qualitative feedback in their evaluations. Another advantage to keeping students in consistent teams throughout the semester is that students are given more flexibility (one bad week is not enough to condemn a student when a good week can offset the bad); however, this model can also work for rotating groups if evaluations are given at the end of all projects. At the end of the semester in this particular class, students determined, through self- and peer evaluations, a recommended grade for themselves as well as for each of their group members—but only after they provided detailed, qualitative assessments of their work according to the forms below.

Self- and Peer-Evaluation Form for American Literature: Origins to the Civil War

Take a moment to think about how you worked with your peers and how they worked with you this semester. Working in groups helps us practice listening and leadership skills as we organize different points of view through effective communication to achieve common goals.

SELF-EVALUATION

1. How prepared were you to work in groups? Did you complete the readings every time, most of the time, some of the time, or rarely?
2. Were you a good listener? Did you take your peers' opinions into account all of the time, most of the time, some of the time, or did you most often dominate the conversation?
3. Were you a good volunteer? Did you volunteer contributions to the conversation, take notes, or speak on behalf of your group to give the class a recap of what you talked about?
4. What else would you like to share about your participation? Feel free to share any of your reflections on your skills (what you feel strong about, what you would like to keep working on in the future) or notes about what happened this semester that may have prevented you from being an ideal group member. (Keep in mind that no one is perfect! We are all working on things and always getting better at what we set out to do!)
5. What grade do you think you earned for your participation in group work? (And if you feel that group work wasn't your strength, but you shared your notes in the collaborative notes Google Docs fairly frequently, take that valuable contribution into consideration too.)

These are the questions students answered for and about themselves. The form guides students in disassociating participation from talking to think instead about participation as both *service* and *leadership* within a democratic community. In the final and most complex evaluative action of the semester, students used these deep self-evaluations as a way of then evaluating one another. This process of self-scrutiny and self-discovery helped students to realize that judgment and feedback are not criticisms but the beginning of really learning. In addition, these insights about themselves helped prepare students for evaluating their peers thoughtfully, generously, and fairly.

To aid students in evaluating one another (a task that takes real courage), Katopodis offered an abbreviated template that mimics the process above to help students present their evaluations of their peers in a pointed, succinct way. This template also affords students a structure within the classroom to help depersonalize their evaluations and make them part of the collective learning process of the class, even on the level of the method, format, and instrument through which it was presented.

Here is what that peer-evaluation template looked like.

PEER EVALUATION

My peer, _____,

1. Was mostly PRESENT for class, 50/50, or mostly ABSENT? (circle one)
2. Read EVERY TIME, MOST TIMES, SOMETIMES, or RARELY? (circle one)
3. Was a good listener ALWAYS, MOSTLY, SOMETIMES, or NEVER? (circle one)
4. Was a good volunteer ALWAYS, MOSTLY, SOMETIMES, or NEVER? (circle one)
5. What else would you like to share about this group member's participation?
6. What grade do you think your peer earned for participation in group work?

Epilogue

What the class discovered through this careful evaluation of their own evaluation practices confirms the research and scholarship on ungrading as a practice: conventional grading can be an obstacle to real learning as well as to developing one's own intellectual voice. Conversely, structured, responsible peer evaluation opens doors not just to learning but to self-discovery, community building, and collective action and change. Scholars such as Peter Elbow, Asao B. Inoue, Alfie Kohn, Jeffrey Schinske, Jesse Stommel, and Kimberly Tanner have studied these practices extensively.[11]

However, the scholarly voice with which we will end this essay is that of the students themselves: "I received your class comments regarding our group work. I thought they were a supremely deft touch that shows your commitment to a democratic and connected classroom. I've never seen that sort of feedback before and think that every class should include introspection and positive critique of a student's ability to work together with others." Significant here is the student's commenting evaluatively on evaluation itself.

Similarly another student writes: "Thank you so much for your response and advice—I've never received such detailed advice from any professor/educator . . . before, so I wanted you to know I really appreciate it." This is the opposite of grade grubbing, of cringing and becoming defensive about feedback. The student has clearly come to understand response and advice not as criticism but as something powerful, helpful, and, sadly, unique.

In the end the students' evaluations of one another were so constructively and sensitively framed, serious, and sophisticated that the instructor, with permission, shared peer feedback anonymously with each student. Rather than ungrading being an exercise in teacherlessness (as its detractors so glibly assert), everyone in the course became a teacher, a coteacher and a colearner. Everyone in this course became, in the end, in the words of one student, "a real educator, not just a teacher."

NOTES

1. Throughout this essay, the authors refer to themselves by both first and last names or last names only. This is strategic since research shows that female scholars (and professors) are typically referred to by their given names and male scholars by their family names. Like all of the seemingly arbitrary or simple aspects of teaching, there are values embedded in these practices. For a fuller discussion, see Savonick and Davidson [2015] 2018.
2. See Freire 1972.
3. Davidson and Goldberg 2010: 145.
4. Davidson 2012.

5. Shor 1987: 13.
6. hooks 1994: 13.
7. See Graduate Center Learning Collective 2017.
8. See Davidson 2019.
9. For further discussion, see Grant 2014.
10. The 21st Century Collective 2013.
11. See Elbow 1994; Inoue 2019; Kohn 2006; Schinske and Tanner 2014; Stommel 2018.

SOURCES

Davidson, Cathy N. 2012. *Now You See It: How Technology and Brain Science Will Transform Schools and Businesses for the 21st Century*. New York: Penguin.

Davidson, Cathy N. 2013. "Essential Tool Kit for Peer Learning and Peer Teaching." HASTAC. June 4. https://www.hastac.org/blogs/cathy-davidson /2013/06/04/essential-tool-kit-peer-learning-and-peer-teaching.

Davidson, Cathy N., and David Theo Goldberg. 2010. *The Future of Thinking: Learning Institutions in a Digital Age*. Cambridge, MA: MIT Press.

Elbow, Peter. 1994. "Ranking, Evaluating, Liking: Sorting Out Three Forms of Judgment." *College English* 12. https://scholarworks.umass.edu/cgi/view content.cgi?referer=&httpsredir=1&article=1011&context=eng_faculty _pubs.

Freire, Paulo. 1972. *Pedagogy of the Oppressed*. New York: Herder and Herder.

Graduate Center Learning Collective. 2017. *Structuring Equality: A Handbook for Student-Centered Learning and Teaching Practices*. Edited by Hilarie Ashton. HASTAC. https://www.hastac.org/collections/structuring-equality-handbook -student-centered-learning-and-teaching-practices.

Grant, Sheryl. 2014. "What Counts as Learning: *Open Digital Badges for New Opportunities*." DMLResearch Hub. August 31. https://dmlhub.net/wp-content /uploads/files/WhatCountsAsLearning_Grant.pdf.

hooks, bell. 1994. *Teaching to Transgress: Education as the Practice of Freedom*. New York: Routledge.

Inoue, Asao B. 2019. *Labor-Based Grading Contracts: Building Equity and Inclusion in the Compassionate Writing Classroom*. Fort Collins, CO: WAC Clearinghouse and University Press of Colorado. https://wac.colostate.edu/books/perspectives /labor/.

Kohn, Alfie. 2006. "The Trouble with Rubrics." *English Journal* 95(4). https://www .alfiekohn.org/article/trouble-rubrics/.

Savonick, Danica, and Cathy N. Davidson. [2015] 2018. "Gender Bias in Academe." January 26, 2015; updated May 1, 2018. https://www.hastac.org /blogs/superadmin/2015/01/26/gender-bias-academe-annotated-bibliography -important-recent-studies.

Schinske, Jeffrey, and Kimberly Tanner. 2014. "Teaching More by Grading Less (or Differently)." *CBE—Life Sciences Education* 13(2): 159–66. https://doi.org /10.1187/cbe.CBE-14-03-0054.

Shor, Ira. 1987. "Educating the Educators: A Freirean Approach to the Crisis in Teacher Education." In *Freire for the Classroom: A Sourcebook for Liberatory*

Teaching, edited by Ira Shor, pp. 7–32. Portsmouth, NH: Boynton/Cook Publishers.

Stommel, Jesse. 2018. "How to Ungrade." March 11. https://www.jessestommel .com/how-to-ungrade/.

The 21st Century Collective. 2013. *Field Notes to Twenty-First Century Literacies: A Guide to New Theories, Methods and Practices for Open Peer Teaching and Learning*. https://www.hastac.org/collections/field-notes-21st-century -literacies.

Chapter 8

CRITIQUE-DRIVEN LEARNING AND ASSESSMENT

Christopher Riesbeck

The divide between teaching and learning and traditional assessment is real. Many of us think about the relationships we could develop and the authentic learning students could engage in if only we could remove grades from the conversation.[1]

Twenty years ago I did just that. In an intermediate-level programming course I teach at Northwestern University, I replaced grading with critiquing. I replaced weekly (or longer) one-and-done assignments with a continuous *do-review-redo* submission process.

I subsequently adapted this critique-driven approach to similar technically intensive courses and, with mixed results, to other courses with an emphasis on the writing of texts, and have explored automated assistance in the critiquing process.[2]

If and when grades are needed, the critique-driven approach provides both narrative detail and a helpful, easily read quantitative view of each student's progress, accomplishments, strengths, and weaknesses. Compared to typical portfolio-based solutions for going gradeless, mapping a term's worth of submissions and critiques to a final grade is more transparent, granular, and scalable.

This approach also demonstrates that going gradeless is not somehow only for topics such as writing. If anything, I believe critique-driven learning and assessment makes more sense in highly technical and "objective" subject areas.

A CRITIQUE-DRIVEN GRADELESS COURSE

One of the courses I teach at Northwestern University is Introduction to Artificial Intelligence Programming. It is a 300-level course, open to all students, but intended primarily for juniors, seniors, and graduate students. The course focuses on programming techniques central to the development of symbolic reasoning systems—that is, systems that infer facts, given a set of known facts and a set of implication rules.

The course requires students to master some basic computer science ideas that are typically underemphasized in introductory courses, such as functional programming, recursion, and search algorithms. It also introduces a new programming language (Lisp) and some new concepts, such as symbolic knowledge representations.

The course page, addressed to students, explains how the course works, as follows.

- You (the student) select an exercise and send me a working solution.
- I (the instructor) critique your solution and return it to you.
- You revise and resubmit your solution.
- We repeat this cycle until I have no more critiques.
- You repeat this process with another exercise until the course ends.

I never grade your solutions. Either a solution is fine, or it needs more work.

At the end of the term, your grade is based on three factors:

- **Progress:** How far did you get? How many different kinds of problems did you do? How difficult were these problems? How many different topics and skills did you explore?
- **Quality:** How good is your code by the end of the course? What level of critiques are you getting?

- **Effort:** How often and how steadily did you submit, including revisions? How hard did you push yourself from your personal starting point?[3]

The course FAQ sets an expectation for effort: "Do at least three new submissions per week, plus fixing and resubmitting previous entries. That typically means about thirty exercises plus their resubmissions in our ten-week quarter."

To help self-assess, there is a class statistics page, described later.

This critique-driven learning and assessment has been my solution for how to go gradeless since 1997. It's the model for my programming courses at Northwestern, and for several online courses in software development I have designed and piloted for Socratic Arts Inc.

I warn my students to expect critiques on almost all submissions. If something were easy to do perfectly, I wouldn't assign it as worth reviewing.

I warn them that sometimes there will be more critiques than code (see fig. 8.1).

```
(defun bfs (end path-queue node-seen net)
You shouldn't need a visited parameter since each path so far
contains the nodes you need to avoid.
  (if (null path-queue)
For testing, you need to use empty-queue-p. Otherwise, your code
may be queueing solutions rather than returning immediately. See
the instructions.
      nil
      (let* ((path (car path-queue)) (node (car path)))
        (catch 'end-is-found
          (when (eql node end) (throw 'end-is-found (reverse
path)))
A recursive function with catch/throw doesn't do anything
useful. Each recursive call stacks a catch, so the throw goes
only one step up, just like normal return.
          (cond ((member node node-seen)
                  (bfs end (cdr path-queue) node-seen net))
                (t
                  (multiple-value-setq (path-queue node-seen)
                                        (update-accumulators path
node net path-queue node-seen))
                  (bfs end path-queue node-seen net)))))))
Keep the simple code Graham. Find a better place to put the
abort BEFORE a path that goes to the end is added to the queue.
Find a place to put the catch so that it doesn't get stacked
more than once.
```

Figure 8.1. Example of student submission with feedback.

Twenty years without handing out and arguing about grades. How has this turned out for me and my students?

FOR MY STUDENTS . . .

It's no big deal. This continues to surprise me. This is unlike any other course they take at Northwestern, and yet no student has said the class should switch back to the traditional graded model. No one has complained about lack of transparency in grading. What they (correctly) tell other students about is the importance of continuous resubmissions. For my students, one and done is never enough.

One reason for the relative smoothness of the transition is that *gradeless* here doesn't mean being in the dark about progress or the eventual final grade that Northwestern requires. My students care about those grades. They complain about teachers who are slow to return graded quizzes and homework assignments. How do I get around this problem? Technology! I developed a web application to store submissions and critiques. At any time students can view a summary of what they've done so far: what they've submitted, what's been completed, and how long since their last submission (fig. 8.2). They can also see how their statistics compare with the rest of the class.

Students no longer send me "How am I doing?" emails because they know where they stand. I do get questions of the form, "What should I focus on next?" That's a question I'm happy to answer.

FOR ME . . .

My interactions with students are now about the content of the course. Students never argue about how many points a submission just received, and I never worry about assigning such points. Any discussion students and I have is about the feedback. For that reason I no longer feel like I am throwing feedback into the wind.

My class lectures have evolved. I am now free to spend more time on interactive explorations of challenging concepts. The many details for specific programming tasks occur just-in-time in the form of miniature lectures in the critiquing. Students who grasped those concepts from the

Student Statistics

Total Submitted	Exercises Finished	Exercises Unfinished	Days Since Last Submission / New Exercise
44	20	2	7 / 7
39	19	2	6 / 6
42	18	1	7 / 7
29	18	1	8 / 8
45	16	2	6 / 8
37	16	2	6 / 6
38	15	3	8 / 8
37	15	3	6 / 6
47	14	6	6 / 6
46	**14**	**5**	**6 / 6**
38	13	2	8 / 8
36	13	4	6 / 7
43	12	3	7 / 11

Figure 8.2. Student summary view of submissions, relative to classmates.

reading never need to see those lectures. Those who do need them see them in the context of a specific problem they are working on.

I have a more accurate and complete grasp of what my students do and do not understand. When I first began this process, I wrote down a dozen critiques I expected I would need, based on years of prior experience teaching this course. These critiques focused on general standards for good code, such as clarity of names, modularity, most appropriate choice of language constructs, and so on. But once I started critiquing actual submissions, I immediately began creating a very different library of critiques. The themes were the same, and reuse was very high, but the critiques that worked best were much shorter—a sentence to a paragraph—and specific to subcategories of my original themes. Over the years, this library has evolved. As of fall 2016, approximately five hundred distinct critiques are in active use.

Until the end of the term, I don't think about grades at all. When it comes time for grades, thanks to technology, I have a complete history of all submissions and feedback. I know who has submitted what, the number of topics each student covered, and the summaries each critique received (fig. 8.3).

With this mix of details and summaries, grading is fast and fair. Assigning grades takes approximately an hour, even with eighty students and several thousand submissions. The process seems more equitable than traditional grades, and students seem to agree. I receive, at most, two to three postcourse grade queries from students. During the most recent two terms, I received no questions about final grades at all.

IMPLEMENTATION AND TECHNOLOGICAL SUPPORT

Implementing reusable critiques is the easy part. A number of tools provide reusable feedback functionality, such as Turnitin, QuickMark, and eMarking Assistant. Teachers have made clever use of Google Keep and similar tools to store text clippings.[4]

When I began twenty years ago, I used email for submissions and responses, and a Window text clipboard utility to keep my reusable critiques. The downside was that the library of critiques was stored on one machine. I then created a simple web application into which I could paste the student's submission and insert critiques. I still used email for submissions, but now I could critique from the office or home.

The final important change was expanding the critiquing application to include storage of the student submissions and my responses, replacing the use of email. This became known as the Code Critic, which over eighteen hundred students have used in various courses since 2006.

This last step was essential in making critiquing scalable in an environment where final grades are still required. Reviewing hundreds

Summary for .....

Total Submissions: 47 **Total Exercises Finished:** 17 **Total Topics** 12 **Total Undone** 4

Topic History: *(The lists show the number of submissions for each completed exercise for each topic)*
chap2 (3) chap3 (3) chap5 (1 3) chap6 (5) chap7 (2) chap8 (2) chap9 (2 3:2 2) chap10 (1:0 1 2) lisp-ex (2) web (2) files (2) input output (2)

Repeated Critiques: *(The first number says how often a critique was given, the second says how many submissions since last use of critique)*
otherwise ok: 4 (3); otherwise fine: 2 (24); mixed case: 5 (16); bad indentation: 5 (14); too complicated: 2 (3); test can't be false: 2 (3); negative point: 2 (3); le 11 list generated: 2 (44); if or: 2 (3); JS arrow return: 2 (35); 95 solve called: 2 (18);

Show texts of all submissions and critiques (may be very long)

Submissions from

Exercise	Submitted	Status	Comment	Critique(s)
Lisp #11: map-range, find-range, every-range, reduce-range	Oct 9, 2019 12:09:07 AM	Not done yet		(list) for nil; defun nested; if not; le 11 list generated; map list function; mixed case;
Lisp 1: has-number-p	Oct 9, 2019 12:09:47 AM	Almost done		atom consp listp; comments inline; le1 3 branch cond; mixed case;
Lisp #11: map-range, find-range, every-range, reduce-range	Oct 11, 2019 3:02:50 PM	Not done yet	better -- but can be simpler and better yet!	le 11 list generated; recursion vs iteration;
Lisp 1: has-number-p	Oct 11, 2019 3:06:31 PM	Done		listp for consp; otherwise ok;
Graham 2: Basic Lisp	Oct 11, 2019 4:45:25 PM	Not done yet		bad indentation; comment not needed; critic not run; mixed case; nested cond;
Lisp #11: map-range, find-range, every-range, reduce-range	Oct 15, 2019 10:42:29 AM	Not done yet		le 11 duplicate DOs; loop feature not used;

Figure 8.3. Instructor summary view of student submissions and feedback.

of emails from every student and boiling them down into a final assessment was slow and effortful. It was not hard to skim and get a big picture view of any specific student's effort and progress, but comparing students for those inevitable B versus B+ distinctions was challenging and overly subjective.

Centralizing the submissions into a database that could organize by exercise, tabulate completed versus almost completed solutions, and display the critique history for each student enabled a level of rapid, objective, and continuous analysis that email review could never provide. Even the most basic tally of number of exercises done versus almost done was valuable, given the do-review-redo framework. The next level up was to characterize critiques and exercises along several dimensions and tally those. For example:

- Level (i.e., basic, intermediate, advanced)
  - Exercises can be characterized by their level of challenge.
  - Critiques can be characterized by the level of mistake they address.
- Content
  - Small exercises can be characterized by the skills they focus on (e.g., in coding, use of functions, use of iterative forms, etc.).
  - Critiques can be characterized by the skills where problems are identified.

CRITIQUING VERSUS PORTFOLIOS

I believe that critique-driven learning and assessment, which includes do-review-redo, offers several advantages over holistic portfolio-based assessments.[5] Student portfolios were to replace information-poor numeric grades with a rich multiperspective record of a student's effort and progress. What better way to judge a student's ability to write or design than to see their writings and designs?

The challenge of course is how to summarize portfolios usefully and efficiently. The richer and more in depth a portfolio is the more time-consuming and frustrating it is to reduce to a final grade; the more challenging it is to reframe as a narrative for parents that can answer the frequent question, "But how is she doing compared to the class?"; and the more challenging it is for the students to interpret and evaluate.

With critique-driven learning and assessment, it is possible to develop more easily quantified proxies for effort, progress, and accomplishment. Effort, in terms of submissions and resubmissions, is easy, of course, as is progress, in terms of tasks done. If tasks are categorized by skills and content areas, finer-grained assessment of progress is possible, as well as clear guidance on what the student still needs to tackle.

Tallies of work done, though, say little about the quality of work or the ability of students to do similar work without substantial guidance from the teacher. This is where categorization and tallying of critiques received play an important role. Tallying critiques provides a gauge on quality and independence:

- Are basic critiques still being applied late in the course, or has the student moved beyond those?
- Was a "well done" received quickly, with few critiques and revisions, or only after a number of submissions?

To make this work, it's important to categorize exercises and critiques by the associated microskills and content elements. I have found that doing so is in turn a valuable way for me to assess the quality of my exercise pool. Early on I realized that sometimes I had only one exercise that required a specific microskill of interest to me. Ideally any important skill should be reflected in three or more warm-up exercises and in at least one challenge exercise.

CRITIQUES VERSUS RUBRICS

Rubrics are a common method to provide explicit criteria for evaluation of a student artifact or performance. Analytic rubrics in particular apply such criteria to different aspects of the work, like quality of writing, quality of argument, quality of references, and so on. There are many examples of rubrics for evaluating programming assignments, such as table 8.1.[6]

Analytic rubrics have some intuitive value. They make explicit the various dimensions an instructor considers important to a particular type of work, such as clarity of presentation and solidity of analysis. They also try to make clear how to recognize quality along each dimension.

Such rubrics are used by instructors and teaching assistants to justify the grades given to students and, ideally, suggest how students can improve. They are also often used to enable consistent and fair peer evaluation.

But rubrics do not address any of the major problems with grading. The example rubric (table 8.1) used semantic column labels, but students and instructors know that "unsatisfactory" will be interpreted as 0, "amateur" as 1, "acceptable" as 2, and "exceptional" as 3. Every row will be reduced to a number, even though the boundaries between columns will be blurry, given terms such as *most* and *some* and subjective criteria such as "fairly easy to read." These hard-to-justify individual numbers

Table 8.1. Example computer programming rubric

Trait	Exceptional	Acceptable	Amateur	Unsatisfactory
Specifications	The program works and meets all the specifications.	The program works and produces the correct results and displays them correctly. It also meets most of the other specifications.	The program produces correct results but does not display them correctly.	The program is producing incorrect results.
Readability	The code is exceptionally well organized and very easy to follow.	The code is fairly easy to read.	The code is readable only by someone who knows what it is supposed to be doing.	The code is poorly organized and very difficult to read.
Reusability	The code could be reused as a whole or each routine could be reused.	Most of the code could be reused in other programs.	Some parts of the code could be reused in other programs.	The code is not organized for reusability.
...				

are then summed to create an even less-well-justified total. There is no difference in the end between "a program is exceptional on meeting specifications," and "unsatisfactory on readability," and vice versa, even though one works and the other doesn't. Anything not listed in a rubric row doesn't count, such as using a creative approach to the solution. Finally rubrics identify issues but are weak on remedy.

Single-point rubrics are a popular way to deal with many of these weaknesses of analytic rubrics. For each row the only fixed content is the criteria for acceptance. The only scores are 1 (done) or 0 (not done). When not done, comments specific to the work are written to identify what needs to change. Similarly comments specific to the work are written to note aspects that go above and beyond what is required (see table 8.2).

Table 8.2. Single-point programming rubric

Trait	Areas Needing Work	Criteria for Acceptance	Evidence of Exceeding Standards
Specifications		The program works and meets all the specifications.	
Readability		The code is fairly easy to read.	
Reusability		The code could be reused in other programs.	
...			

Single-point rubrics share several characteristics with critique-driven learning. Both emphasize mastery. In both approaches a solution is either done (i.e., has no significant defects) or needs revision. Both emphasize the need for specific feedback when there are defects and provide opportunity for praise when exceptional work is submitted.

This second aspect, however, has been seen as a challenge for the use of single-point rubrics: "The main disadvantage of single-point rubrics is that using them requires more writing on the teacher's part. If a student has fallen short in many areas, completing that left-hand column will take more time than simply highlighting a pre-written analytic rubric." [7]

This is exactly where critiques shine. Take for example a student program that fails to meet the rubric criteria "The code could be reused in other programs." I have observed that general critiques such as this evolve over time into more finely tuned versions, such as "This function is not reusable because it communicates with other functions using global variables" or "This function is less reusable than it could be because it contains a literal numeric constant."

When attached to a specific piece of code, this provides the student with a concrete example of the issue at hand, with an explanation, without requiring additional writing. Building a library of specific reusable critiques leads not only to faster feedback but to more uniform feedback and a better understanding of the subject matter that can be shared with other instructors, teaching assistants, and students.

CHALLENGES, LIMITATIONS, AND DESIGN CONSIDERATIONS

I would never go back to my old graded-assignment approach to teaching programming. But critique-driven learning and assessment is by no means without challenges and occasional failures.

The biggest challenge for students with critique-driven learning is the lack of specific due dates in the do-review-redo process. Students master exercises at different rates, and choose somewhat different paths through the pool of exercises and topics, based on interests and need for practice. While there are standards for effort and progress, there are no due dates. Very few students fail the AI Programming course, but those that do always do so because they do not submit anything until the course is almost over. Reminders help and this could be automated better, but the nagging need to do another exercise "soon" often loses when students face looming deadlines for assignments in other courses.

The biggest challenge and ongoing disappointment for me is the need to deal with plagiarism. A substantial part of the materials development for my AI Programming course is the curated pool of several hundred exercises, organized by the specific skills involved and level of difficulty. With any pool of repeatedly assigned programming exercises, there will be solution sets online. Many are placed by students on sites such as GitHub, as a standard part of their normal programming practice. Some students are unaware that their answers are indexed and easily found with web search. The problem has worsened as enrollments in the course have tripled from thirty to ninety or more, either because some of the additional students are less prepared or because there is a perceived safety from discovery in a large class.

To deal with this, I now have to use the Moss tool every term to scan for possible cases of plagiarism (though human memory alone is surprisingly good at recognizing recurring patterns during the critiquing process).[8] In turn, since plagiarism is hard to prove with shorter solutions to simpler problems, I have had to increase the weight in my final tallies on the challenge exercises.

GOING GRADELESS: PART OF A BIGGER CHANGE

Roger Schank has often said, "There are only two things wrong with education: what we teach, and how we teach it."[9] Getting rid of grades is an important part of fixing the *how*, but it's important not to lose sight of the *what*.

I was fortunate in that programming is a good *what*. It's a skill. It's something students want to learn. It's almost always taught using learning by doing. It's important to get the details right—what skills to focus on, what types of problems to assign—but the basic framework for learning programming is in good shape. Other subjects in similarly good shape are design, sports, art (creation), and music (performance). The critique-driven approach worked quite well, for example, in a pilot course I was involved with a decade ago teaching business writing (memos, emails, meeting summaries, and such) to English as a Second Language learners. The goals, authenticity, and relevance of the skills being learned were clear to the students.

But most subjects that students encounter, such as math, English, and history, lack those characteristics. I encountered this failure when I tried getting my students to learn to do agile retrospectives. This is a process where teams identify and causally analyze development issues, make simple changes in practice, and track whether the changes help. The analysis turns out to be surprisingly hard to do and takes much practice and feedback. It seemed ideal for a critique-driven approach, so I had all students submit weekly analyses for feedback and revision. I failed to get any significant learning, over half a dozen offerings of the course, with many different attempts to structure the analyses. Even as objective a critique as "your root cause analysis needs more than one causal" failed to lead most students to develop longer causal chains. Eventually I realized the core problem was that they didn't see the need for improvement. Without motivation, getting to done becomes a learning-free activity just as much as getting a better grade.

Critique-driven learning's emphasis on mastery only works if students want to master the skills involved. To make that happen, students must see clear value gained for effort invested. This value may be in becoming able to do some desired task, such as playing a tough guitar riff or mastering a difficult video game level. It may be learning a coding skill that will enhance job prospects. But often the only value gained in a course is a credential, not the skill. You need several years of algebra to get a high school diploma, and you need a diploma to get a job, but students know exactly how often their parents and other adults have had to factor polynomials.

Most of my computer science students saw no clear value to improving their development processes—that is, how they subdivide and prioritize work, how they collaborate with team members, how they assess the quality of the code before delivery, and so on. The book *Peopleware*, first published in 1987, noted, "The average software developer, for example, doesn't own a single book on the subject of his or her work, and hasn't ever read one."[10] Programmers did own many books, at that time, but they were about programming languages, such as C and C++ and Java, and libraries for game programming and 3D graphics. What they didn't own were books on becoming a better, more professional developer. My students didn't perceive any problems with their development processes. They saw it as unavoidable and acceptable that a serious programming project would involve many mistakes, increasingly messy code, and bugs. Requiring them to master agile retrospectives involved great effort for little perceived personal value.

Appeal to authority had no effect. I pointed students to numerous blog posts from developers on how retrospectives and continuous improvement were the single most important agile practice. This had as much effect as nutritional experts telling them to eat more vegetables. The students received no inherent reward in doing retrospective analyses, nor did they expect to be tested on that skill in any job interview. Therefore, they saw no value in mastering this skill.

In contrast I did succeed in changing student practice in another area. Most students learn programming as a solitary activity. One person types away at one computer. Even if this is happening in a room with other developers, there is little conversation or interaction. Agile software development, though, recommends a practice called *pair programming*. Two developers work on one computer developing code. One developer drives (i.e., types the code) and the other developer navigates (i.e., plans and dictates the code). The driver takes care of the details, making microdecisions and asking questions about specific choices. The navigator worries about the bigger picture, where the code is going, how it might be tested, and so on. In situations where one developer is more skilled than the other, the less skilled developer drives. This leads to just-in-time learning. The driver learns while contributing to the project. The navigator learns how to explain new coding concepts and software design patterns.

When I first tried to get students to pair program, they hated it. They would do it once or twice, then go back to solo programming. Other faculty reported similar resistance.[11] Then I tried a different agile practice: *swarming*. Swarming is when the entire team works in one room, usually in pairs, on related parts of a common task. The goal of swarming is to increase throughput—getting one thing completely done rather than several things partly done—and keep the entire team on the same page as to what's been built and how it works. Swarming was a group activity that teams enjoyed once they tried it. Teams did it with little pressure from me. As the term progressed, and schedules made swarming difficult at times, some teams would revert to coding solo. Within a week they almost always noticed missed tasks, duplication of work, and code conflicts. Most teams returned to swarming as soon as possible, with pair programming as the next best option. The teams saw clear value—programming as a social activity—and eventually additional values, such as more efficient development.

SUMMARY

Critique-driven learning and assessment is a fine-grained semi-quantitative approach for mastery learning that is gradeless, but fits comfortably in environments requiring final grades. It is appropriate when student deliverables are the primary focus for feedback and skill development.

NOTES

1. Kohn [1993] 2018.
2. Qiu and Riesbeck 2008.
3. Chris Riesbeck, "How This Course Works," CS 325 AI Programming, accessed February 27, 2019, http://www.cs.northwestern.edu/academics/courses/325 /admin/grading.php.
4. Eric Curts, "Using Google Keep for Grading Comments in Docs," *Control Alt Achieve*, March 4, 2017, https://www.controlaltachieve.com/2017/03/keep -grading-comments.html.
5. Kajfez, Mohammadi-Aragh, Brown, et al. 2013; O'Connor and Lessing 2017.
6. Florida International University, "Computer Programming Grading Rubric," Rubrics and Curriculum Maps, accessed February 27, 2019, https:// assessment.fiu.edu/resources/rubrics-and-curriculum-maps/index.html.
7. Gonzalez 2014.
8. Schleimer, Wilkerson, and Aiken 2003.
9. Shaughnessy, Fulgham, and Schank 2011: 31.
10. DeMarco and Lister 1999: 11.
11. Williams, Kessler, Cunningham, and Jeffries 2000.

SOURCES

DeMarco, Tom, and Timothy Lister. 1999. *Peopleware: Productive Projects and Teams*. 2nd ed. New York: Dorset House Publishing.

Gonzalez, Jennifer. 2014. "Know Your Terms: Holistic, Analytic, and Single-Point Rubrics." *Cult of Pedagogy*. May 1. https://www.cultofpedagogy.com /holistic-analytic-single-point-rubrics/.

Kajfez, Rachael L., Mahnas J. Mohammadi-Aragh, Philip R. Brown, Katharine A. Mann, Cheryl A. Carrico, Kelly J. Cross, John A. Janeski, and Lisa D. McNair. 2013. "Assessing Graduate Engineering Programs with ePortfolios: A Comprehensive Design Process." *Advances in Engineering Education* 3(3).

Kohn, Alfie. [1993] 2018. *Punished by Rewards: The Trouble with Gold Stars, Incentive Plans, A's, Praise, and Other Bribes.* 25th anniversary ed. Boston: Mariner Books.

O'Connor, John S., and Avi D. Lessing. 2017. "What We Talk about When We Don't Talk about Grades." *Schools: Studies in Education* 14(2): 303–18.

Qiu, Lin, and Christopher K. Riesbeck. 2008. "An Incremental Model for Developing Educational Critiquing Systems: Experiences with the Java Critiquer." *Journal of Interactive Learning Research* 19(1): 119–45.

Schleimer, Saul, Daniel Shawcross Wilkerson, and Alexander Aiken. 2003. "Winnowing: Local Algorithms for Document Fingerprinting." In *Proceedings of the 2003 ACM SIGMOD International Conference on Management of Data*, June, pp. 76–85. ACM Press. https://dl.acm.org/doi/10.1145/872757.872770.

Shaughnessy, Michael F., Susan M. Fulgham, and Roger Schank. 2011. "Interview with Roger Schank." *Educational Technology* 51(1): 30–39. www.jstor.org /stable/44429892.

Williams, Laurie, Robert R. Kessler, Ward Cunningham, and Ron Jeffries. 2000. "Strengthening the Case for Pair Programming." *IEEE Software* 17(4): 19–25.

Chapter 9

———

A STEM UNGRADING CASE STUDY: A REFLECTION ON FIRST-TIME IMPLEMENTATION IN ORGANIC CHEMISTRY II

Clarissa Sorensen-Unruh

———

UNGRADING: GENESIS AND EVOLUTION

Ungrading, a term that suggests the opposite of grading, has long been associated with the idea of purposefully eliminating or minimizing the use of points or letters to assess student work. Schinske and Tanner have provided "evidence that accuracy-based grading [i.e., grading based on correct answers for simple fact-based questions] may, in fact, de-motivate students and impede learning."[1] The current grading system, as we know it, may be doing more harm than good for our students.

My journey began with a blog post and a fundamental dismantling of my assumptions, courtesy of a friend on Twitter, Jesse Stommel: "Just published a new piece about ungrading and other alternative approaches to assessment. I continue to be disturbed by how many otherwise pro-ductive pedagogical conversations get sidetracked by the too easily internalized ubiquity of grades."[2]

Then it quickly progressed into a discussion about many of the current issues with ungrading.[3] The discussion highlighted the difficulty many teachers found in the implementation of ungrading, particularly as it pertained to the tacit knowledge needed to implement ungrading effectively. Tacit knowledge transfers information through "sensed experiences, intuition, and implicit rules of thumb" and is not the same as explicit knowledge, or knowledge that transfers expertise through spoken and written language.[4]

I wanted to think through ungrading with colleagues who had already attempted it in their classrooms by tapping into their tacit knowledge on the subject. Ungrading started to emerge as a method to converse with my students about their performance, as opposed to merely assigning some number of points to try to communicate this instead. I could use ungrading to help students focus on feedback rather than a ranking system. This conversation started to answer some of my bigger concerns and questions: How was I going to make ungrading happen in my chemistry classrooms? Would I be able to convince my students to buy into ungrading?

So I did a bit more research into Alfie Kohn's important contributions to the topic. His assessment that "the more students are led to focus on *how well* they're doing, the less engaged they tend to be with *what* they're doing" was a striking insight.[5] I came to believe grading undermines learning daily by focusing student interest on achievement and not on learning.

I became convinced that ungrading was a good idea not just in terms of student agency but also in terms of social justice. Students deserved to be included in the discussion of grades. I set about deciding how I would implement ungrading.

First I needed to conduct a pilot project for a semester in one of my chemistry classrooms. Why only one? My health was such at the beginning of the semester that I could only foresee having enough energy for one class to accomplish ungrading in the way I desired.

The pilot class was my highest-level class offered during that semester—Organic Chemistry II. I chose my most advanced students because I've found in the tenure of my career that they are either the most flexible in thinking (due to their tenure as college students) or the most stringent (due to their tenure as college students). For this group, ungrading would either be an easy sell or a close-to-impossible sell.

In my Organic Chemistry II class, I would implement ungrading in both in-class exercises and in exams, which together made up 60 percent of the grade. Another 15 percent of the grade was devoted to learning journals, which were already graded using binary grading (100 percent for completion, 0 percent for missing work; sometimes if a student's work was *mostly* complete I would only take off 5–10 points). The final exam, which is mandatory and required by our department, made up the last 25 percent of the grade. In my estimation, the most important part of the ungrading scheme was the conversation regarding exams, because they both accounted for the largest percentage of the grade and represented the largest paradigm shift in my current grading scheme. Below is an excerpt from the syllabus used during the pilot semester.

ORGANIC CHEMISTRY II SYLLABUS EXCERPT

Learning Journal, Attendance, and @hypothes.is Articles (15%)

- In an effort to help students become digital citizens with appropriate professionalism online, five reflection papers detailing each student's learning journey (approximately one at the beginning and end of the semester and one for each exam) will be collected throughout the semester. Reflection papers will be in a blog format, with a minimum of four hundred words, and will be submitted through a free account on WordPress. Constructive and thoughtful comments on other students' blogs and/or answers for questions on the class social media can count for up to 5 percent of the in-class group work.
- Class attendance also counts within this percentage. If you miss class, please let me know. If you chronically miss class, please come talk to me during office hours or an individual appointment set up via email or Slack DM.

- In terms of the participation in any online discussion forums, including @hypothes.is articles, blog commentary, and the classroom social media site, you are expected to conduct yourself professionally as well as with respectful and thoughtful behavior. Quality counts! Your postings must have correct sentence structure and must be spell-checked. Learning journals and @hypothes.is articles are graded mostly on a participation basis; if you post or submit the journal with correct grammar and spelling on time and have discussed your learning journey in this class, then you will receive full credit for that posting or submission.

In-Class Exercises and Quizzes (15%)

- In-class exercises will be administered throughout the class. These exercises will be completed as homework as needed. The exercises may be completed individually or via group work.
- In-class exercises will be graded on a ternary scale based on feedback: 0 = Not submitted, 1 = Needs further work, 2 = Complete and correct!

NOTE: If an individual or a group receives a 1 on their work, they may resubmit their work for regrading ONE TIME within ONE WEEK of the original due date.

Examinations (45%)

- Three major in-class exams will be given throughout the semester during the class periods noted in the class schedule.
- We will be using a process called ungrading to incorporate feedback into the exam grading process. It's a fairly complex system, but the point is that I want to make exam grades more of a conversation between you (as the student) and me (as the instructor) than they are now. This progress involves a multitiered system of feedback:

- After the exams are completed and "graded," I will hand back the exams with only feedback (no scores). I will, however, use a spreadsheet for scores that I think each student earned for each exam question.
- Based on your work and the feedback given, you will write the number of points that you think you earned for each question. (Total points for each question are determined and shown before the exam is handed out initially.)
- I will then share the points that I think you earned from the spreadsheet.
- We will discuss any discrepancies. If my point total is higher than your point total, we'll typically count my point total. Generally, the final point total for each exam question will be an average of your score and my score.
- To keep students from artificially inflating their grade, if your overall score is within one standard deviation (1 SD = typically 8–15 points historically on my Organic II exams) of my overall score, then you will receive +5 bonus points. If your overall score is outside of three standard deviations of my overall score (that's somewhere between 24–45 points off of my score, folks), I will deduct 5–10 points off of your exam. The point here is that you need to evaluate yourself fairly based on how you think you did versus how I think you did (given that I have more historical expertise with this material and have access to the entire class's performance).

As I began to plan, I knew that this class counted for pre-med and most pre-health prerequisites, and I was afraid that if there weren't some kind of minimal alignment across the class in terms of grading, those programs would deny the credit for this class. It seems a bit ridiculous that they would, but our university down the street has denied classes as prereqs for less. Thus, the last bullet under Examinations was an essential piece of the puzzle for me.

I trust students. But I also think ungrading requires significantly different thinking about how grades are assessed and calculated. It requires students to have a great deal of metacognition about their learning compared with others in the class. It requires conversation about their performance with an expert in the field. It requires students to embrace their learning and their learning assessment in a *very* different way than they probably have in the past, and even if they fully embrace ungrading, there's still a possibility that students might dislike ungrading overall or find it too arduous, and therefore, the ungrading process might still create friction between the students and me.

I embraced this new journey with my students. I looked forward to the possibilities it might create in our learning discussions.

THE FIRST DAY: SELLING THE IDEA TO THE STUDENTS

I was prepared. I was ready for almost any student argument. I had thoroughly thought through how I would sell ungrading to my Organic Chemistry II students.

And then the first day happened. It was yet another reminder that we're never truly ready for new pedagogical implementations, no matter how ready we think we are.

The plan was to discuss career trajectories and how the skills learned in this class would help students move closer to the life goals they were attending college classes to achieve. Then relate how the skills they would build in ungrading would contribute to this life goal skill set. So I began with some discussion questions that the students would answer in pairs:

1. How important is it, to you, to develop skills in your coursework that will help you land a job when you graduate?
2. Can you pick the top five items in the following list that are considered most essential by employers?
3. Can you pick which items in the following list are most mismatched in terms of how students view their own abilities versus how employers view their abilities? *List: critical*

thinking/problem solving, oral/written communications, team-work/collaboration, leadership skills, digital technologies, professionalism/work ethic, career management, global/intercultural fluency[6]

Once they had answered the discussion questions in pairs and had written down their answers (so that they "owned" the outcome), we talked about what companies want (i.e., competencies) and how company managers perceive their recent college graduate new hires in terms of their proficiency in those competencies (table 9.1). The top five essential competencies (in descending order) were professionalism/work ethic (100 percent), critical thinking/problem solving (99.2 percent),

Table 9.1. Hiring companies' preferred competencies

Competency	Considered Essential*	Rated Proficient**
Teamwork/Collaboration	97.5%	77.0% in 2018 70.1% in 2019
Digital Technology	64.2%	65.8%
Critical Thinking/ Problem Solving	99.2%	55.8%
Professionalism/ Work Ethic	100.0%	42.5%
Oral/Written Communications	95.9%	41.6%
Leadership	68.6%	33.0%
Global/Intercultural Fluency	31.1%	20.7%
Career Management	47.1%	17.3%

* The percentages from all responding employers who, on a five-point scale, indicated that the respective competency was either "essential" (4) or "absolutely essential" (5) for college graduates to enter their workforce.

** The percentages from all responding employers who, on a five-point scale, rated recent graduates either "very" (4) or "extremely" (5) proficient in the respective competency.

Source: National Association of Colleges and Employers

teamwork/collaboration (97.5 percent), oral/written communications (95.9 percent), and leadership (68.6 percent).

And then I revealed the data for the third discussion question (table 9.2).

Table 9.2. Employers' ratings of recent college graduates

Competency	% of Employers Rating Recent College Graduates Proficient	% of Students Considering Themselves Proficient	Delta (Change between percentages)
Professionalism/Work Ethic (3)	42.5%	94.7%	52.2%
Oral/Written Communications (4)	41.6%	79.4%	37.8%
Critical Thinking/Problem Solving (1)	55.8%	93.8%*	38.0%
Teamwork/Collaboration (2)	70.1%*	90.9%*	20.8%
Leadership (5)	33.0%	70.5%	37.5%
Digital Technology (6)	65.8%	59.9%	5.9%
Career Management (7)	17.3%	40.9%	23.6%
Global/Intercultural Fluency (8)	20.7%	34.9%	14.2%

Source: Job Outlook 2018 (N = 201 employing organizations) or 2019 (indicated by asterisk *) and *The Class of 2017 Student Survey Report* (N = 4,213 graduating seniors) by the National Association of Colleges and Employers.

There are some interesting differences in opinion between how employers rate recent college graduates' proficiency in the competencies and how students consider themselves. The deltas (measures of difference) show those assessment differences, the largest of which exists for professionalism/work ethic (52.2 percent) and then for critical thinking/problem solving (38 percent), oral/written communications (37.8 percent), leadership (37.5 percent), and career management (23.6 percent).

So for four of the top five essential skills (as rated by employers), students rated themselves much higher in proficiency than their employers rated them. The closest rating between employers and students for the essential competencies was for teamwork/collaboration, which still had a delta of 20.8 percent. For all competencies, students consistently rated themselves much higher in proficiency than their employers did, with the one exception of digital technology, which happened to have the smallest delta as well.

Table 9.2 raises some interesting questions. Why are the deltas so large? And why did employers consistently rate their new hires lower than the new hires rated themselves, with the one exception of digital technology? And what skills could students build now so that the students could more accurately assess themselves and close the deltas?

I had set up the argument; it felt like an easy and slow pitch. Now I just needed my students to make the connection (*build* the self-assessment skills in class!). But my students had other ideas . . .

One of my students made the argument instead that this data only shows the bias of employers against new hires. And while he had a point, this was not the connection I was looking for. After a quick acknowledgment that his argument may be true for some (or even many) but probably not true for all (which he conceded), we were already off track.

So I was forced to refocus my efforts again. I asked my students whether they knew what they received on their last test in any class *before* they got it back. For those who worked full time, I asked my students whether they knew what their manager was going to say on their last performance review. And then I drew their laser-like focus back to the topic at hand by saying:

> I am tired of hearing from friends who were shocked by their latest performance review. I am tired of hearing from friends who had been fired when they didn't see it coming from a mile away. You should know exactly (or close to it) what your boss is going to tell you when you walk into your yearly performance review. And you should have a say in the review itself—otherwise it would be considered unfair. Why are grades any different?

Wow! Did that work like a charm. They got it. They knew why we were doing this ungrading thing. And they bought in. Whew!

THE FIRST EXAM: INVENTING A PROCESS I COULD USE REPEATEDLY

There's a major difference between wanting to accomplish something pedagogically and actually implementing it. I forget this important little fact every time I attempt something new. And every time, learning the tacit knowledge needed to implement my vision feels like re-creating the wheel. Ungrading was both the same and a different kind of experience than most pedagogical implementations (interventions?) I've initiated. Both more and less tacit knowledge was needed to implement ungrading. I'm not exactly sure why that was the case, but here's my explanation of the process.

Making the first exam was fun. I ended up embedding figure 9.1 next to each question to analyze confidence levels.

While the middle meh emoji was a bit unhappier than I would have liked, this set of emojis worked for the overall outcome. These emojis

Figure 9.1. Confidence levels as emojis. The emojis had the following designations: left happy face = "I knew the answer to that question"; middle meh face = "I'm not sure whether I got this question correct"; right sad face = "I don't know the answer for this question" or "I'm pretty sure I got this problem wrong." Students filled out their relative confidence in answering questions on the exam while the exam was in process.

weren't ideal or exactly what I envisioned. However, I let my students know what the emojis would be both in the syllabus and at the beginning of each exam, and that information helped them choose the right emoji for them on each question. And I was thrilled that I used emojis for the confidence levels (it was my wife's idea), as my students didn't need to spend too much time thinking about their confidence levels —it almost became second nature to them.

I also gave these instructions at the top of every page:

Confidence Levels (mostly in left margin): For each question (or part of a question), please mark your confidence level for your answer. CHOOSE ONLY one emoji per question/part.

The only trick with the confidence-level emojis was that space allotment started to get a little interesting when I asked multipart problems. Where did the confidence-level emojis go? Anywhere they could fit in (see fig. 9.2).

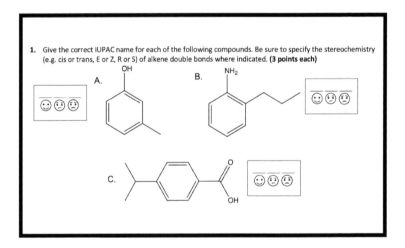

Figure 9.2. A multipart nomenclature question from my first exam. The confidence levels were a little confounding to place well but my students seemed to understand nonetheless.

Amazingly my students understood what was going on almost immediately with the confidence levels and answered all of them (i.e., I had 100 percent completion on the confidence levels throughout the entire semester).

It was almost intuitive . . .

For the grading of the exams, the most difficult aspect in the entire process was giving thoughtful feedback that was critical but helpful. I also included positive feedback, because that's what I have a great deal more practice doing. Having now practiced ungrading for more than one semester, I think this critical, yet helpful, feedback is the part of ungrading I would need to work on most. And in the midst of giving thoughtful feedback, I realized a major underlying assumption I've made throughout my grading life. I assumed my students would thoughtfully consider the points I'd taken off of each question as a stand-in for feedback. I made this assumption mainly because I thoughtfully took off those points, weighing exactly how much of the question had been missed and why it was necessary to take off the points. My major ungrading realization was that students did not get this message. At all. My students did not even recognize this kind of grading was something we regularly agonized over until they had to do it themselves. It was only when they graded their own papers for the first time that they realized taking off points had reasoning behind it and that the process of grading was muddy and difficult.

I returned the exams the first time with only feedback. The students had to submit an ungrading sheet with their returned exam in the next class session where they had detailed how many points they thought they earned on each question and why. Many students also submitted corrections of their work because we had voted as a class whether I should provide the answer key while they were assigning their own point totals and the vote had returned a negative result. In other words, my students wanted to figure out the key on their own while they were ungrading their own exams.

Sometimes it's shocking how much I love my students. Even when I didn't really care about the outcome, they made great choices that maximized their learning process *every time.*

Before I initially returned the exams, I made a grading template for myself where I filled in the points I thought they had earned on each question. An example of my beginning template is shown in table 9.3.

Table 9.3. Template for ungrading student exams

Point totals for each student are assigned for each exam question. This excel spreadsheet helps an overall grade consensus build between teacher and student.

The top row had the questions on the exam, and then the rows were divided in threes. The first row (in blue) of each triplet had the student name and my point totals for each question on the exam. The overall score column simply summed the points for each question across the row. The second row showed the student's evaluation of their own work. Their point totals were added to the sheet and, as you can see from Student 1, if they calculated their points differently, I accounted for that discrepancy. The last row in the triplet averaged my point totals and the student's point totals for each exam question.

Between my exam score and the averaged score, I took the higher of the two scores as the student's counted exam score (the second-to-last column on the right). I calculated basic statistics (mean, median, standard deviation, maximum grade [max], and minimum grade [min]) on each problem as well as the class set of exam scores for my own exam scores, the average exam scores, and the counted exam scores. If the student's overall exam score came within one standard deviation (calculated based on my exam scores) of my overall exam score for them, I awarded them five extra credit points on top of their final counted score for being metacognitive about their own performance on the exam versus their peers (an ideal I *hope* my exam score reflects).

On their exams (returned for the final time), I wrote four grades:

(1) YS (your score), the exam score the students gave themselves (reiterating their work on the sheet they had turned in); (2) MS (my score), the exam score I gave them before I handed the exam back with feedback only; (3) AS (average score), the averaged score of their score and my score; and (4) CS (counted score), the exam score I counted with the bonus points added, if applicable, for their metacognition.

Overall most students graded themselves more harshly than I graded them on the first exam. At times some students decided I was overly generous, and argued on their ungrading sheets that I should take off more points because they didn't know what they were doing.

Some students, of course, argued for more points. But those instances were rarer than I expected when I initially took ungrading on as a methodology I would implement in my classes.

The majority of my students received the five bonus points. They were very savvy about their performance on the exam versus their peers. Many of them, in fact, detailed why their performance was different from their peers on their ungrading sheets and how their relative confidence on specific questions factored into their performance.

Have I mentioned how much I love my students?

This first attempt went way better than I expected, and as the semester progressed, my students only learned more about what helped them most in terms of ungrading. Their ungrading sheets often became multipage essays, complete with citations and arguments, about their grading and why they gave themselves the points they did.

EXAMS 2 AND 3: REFRAMING THE EXPERIMENT AND REALIGNING EXPECTATIONS

Once one develops a system for implementing a pedagogical intervention, there's an underlying hope that it will work at least one more time.

Cue the crying laughter.

I thought once I had figured out the ungrading process, it could be used with every exam. What I forgot was the years of practice I've had simply taking off points without giving too much feedback. And that's where my awesome ungrading process derailed.

The class took exam 2 and filled out the confidence levels without a hitch. At the same time my Organic Chemistry II class was taking its exam, however, my General Chemistry II class was taking its exam 3. As the grading piles grew, I went into automatic pilot to grade them, including the exams I needed to ungrade.

I had completed about a third of the ungrading exams before I figured it out. And then the slew of colorful expletives explosively erupted.

I went back and gave as much feedback as I could while trying to white out the points taken off. But that made for some messy work that only partially solved the problem.

More importantly it put me behind schedule for giving feedback on their exams. So I failed to complete my spreadsheet in advance of returning the exams. To compensate for this failure, I scanned their exams (in their entirety) and vowed I would fill out the spreadsheet before they handed back their exams with their ungrading sheets. This scanning of exams without filling out the spreadsheet prior to handing them back, in fact, became my modus operandi for the second and third exams.

When I walked in with the exams, I admitted my mistake in taking off points on some questions and apologized. My students didn't seem to mind too much as a class. The ungrading process determined for exam 1 continued relatively unperturbed.

And then I received my students' ungrading sheets (which now more of my students used for corrections as well) for exam 2. While most of their ungrading sheets were fantastic and revealed beautiful and thoughtful work, a small handful of students decided to basically ignore my feedback and give themselves full credit on certain problems.

My students gave no argument, no reasoning, nor cited work discussing why. They just blatantly disregarded my feedback.

A conversation was needed to address this issue.

I walked into my Organic Chemistry II class with their now graded exams and explained what I had seen on a few students' ungrading sheets. After we briefly discussed the issue, here's (more or less) what I said:

> We all get feedback we don't agree with or, even worse, didn't want to hear. I usually get that kind of feedback on papers I've

submitted to peer-reviewed journals or on grants I've submitted to NSF. So I get it.

But when I want to disregard the feedback offered, I better have an excellent argument stating why I think I can disregard the feedback. I need to first thoughtfully lay out my argument in detail, then offer citations to provide evidence that my argument is valid.

So that's what we're going to do with the feedback I give on exams in this class. If there is feedback (that isn't totally positive) given for an answer you gave, then there was something wrong with that answer. If you disagree with this assessment of your work, then you need to lay out a thoughtful argument detailing why you disagree, and you need to justify your argument using at least two scholarly citations—your textbook can count as one of the two citations needed. If the point total you write down for the problem doesn't incorporate my feedback on the exam and no argument is given as to why, we will just count my grade as your grade.

Only one student argued a single problem thereafter, and they provided multiple scholarly citations for each answer in the multiple-choice problem as well as a thoughtful argument. So I gave them back the points I had taken off.

After this reframing of expectations, everything in exam 3 proceeded smoothly. Apparently we needed two iterations to frame and reframe the experiment in this particular classroom.

However, I will incorporate this reframing of expectations, and perhaps a fictional example of an excellent ungrading sheet, in future ungrading sections of my syllabi.

WRAPPING UP THE SEMESTER: TRANSFORMATION IN TEACHING AND LEARNING

For years I've provided problem/solution-type feedback on exams. I've tried to provide positive and constructive feedback that identifies student error patterns in real time. My feedback is both to groups of students, while we work on formative assessments, and to individuals on exams (i.e., summative assessment). And while the student groups pay more attention to the feedback and reiterate that same feedback to each other throughout the progression of formative assessment, the individual feedback has largely gone unnoticed along with grade point totals.

Let me state that last sentence one more time and in another way: the vast majority of my students have barely looked at their grades, let alone the feedback I provide them on an exam.

I decided to change that last pattern in spring 2019 and instead took on this grand experiment of ungrading. Instructional designs like the one I made for my ungrading experiment require constant honing until they work well. I know this honing process can take semesters or years. I tend to prize any process that stands the test of Occam's razor, and the Successive Approximation Model (SAM), with its emphasis on iteration and quick prototyping, is a clear process for design that stands this test. I used SAM in the case of ungrading because SAM is a model that allows for more spontaneity than most and requires a constant flow of creative input (see fig. 9.3).

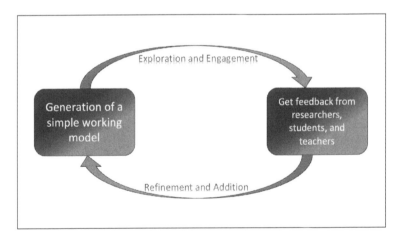

Figure 9.3. A simplified version of the Successive Approximation Model, based on Matuk, McElhaney, Chen, et al. 2016.

And yet every instructional design also requires a bit of love and a lot of luck. Ungrading requires mostly the opposite—a lot of love (or at least a sense that you are doing the right thing for your students) and a bit of luck. I'm also always looking for (a) ways to give better feedback that encourages and supports mastery levels of learning and (b) methods enabling students to take charge of their own learning, such that they can continue to excel even after my class ends. Ungrading was a process that accomplished both of these goals simultaneously.

Ungrading, for me, became a process within my exam grading that I used to focus student attention on individual feedback and that involved a conversation between the student and the instructor. I provided feedback to the students, and the students provided feedback to me about their answers and why they might have thought their answers were correct, even if I had provided feedback to the contrary. The conversation—both the written feedback and the oral conversation that happens once the written feedback process has ended—has illuminated what mastery learning entails. In addition, I learned a lot about how to scaffold my students' learning in future semesters.

My students often felt the same way in their blogged assessments of the ungrading process.

On Confidence Levels

So going into the first test, I thought it was helpful to first rate my level of confidence on the question while I came up with an answer. This allowed me to go back over my test and quickly identify questions I knew I needed to think more carefully about, and even use other questions I was sure about to help with questions I wasn't sure about.[7]

On Ungrading

In all honesty, I think that un-grading allows students to be able to look at their work and understand why they are getting the grade that they are. This gives the students the ability to look through their professor's perspective and see what their instructor's view is on their work. It also helps students to comprehend the thought process of their instructor. Lastly, un-grading gives students the opportunity to reflect on their own work after the exam has been taken instead of pushing it to the side and forgetting about it.[8]

I feel like it really assesses whether we understand the underlying concepts of the material because even if some small things are incorrect, we are given points based on our overall understanding. Here's an analogy: When editing one's (or someone else's) writing, you can focus on little details like errors in grammar or punctuation (lower level concerns), or you can focus on the overall argument/story the author is trying to create (higher level concerns). I feel like the ungrading focuses on the higher level concerns and therefore encourages a deeper understanding of the material, despite some potential issue with lower level ideas.[9]

The key is having the feedback on the exam from the instructor as it helps us to know what to look for in our mistakes. I did manage to get pretty close to the instructor's grade on each of my exams but again it was tough to decide how many points to give myself for each question.[10]

On the Conversation

I found the conversation aspect of ungrading helpful. The ability to have a conversation about one's thought process in answering the questions facilitates deeper understanding.[11]

Overall, I liked the idea of receiving constructive criticism from my instructor. Also, having the opportunity to discuss, with the instructor, any questions you had about the exam improved the learning experience for me as a student. Post exam discussions assured the student understood the content and where their answer went wrong.[12]

Seeing how this initial semester of ungrading affected me and my students showed me that ungrading is difficult and time-consuming.

Falling back into old patterns is relatively easy. But the agency given to the students for their own assessment in this process is unparalleled. I believe their learning was enhanced, and it is definitely worth the time and the steep learning curve.

NOTES

1. Schinske and Tanner 2014: 165.
2. Jesse Stommel (@Jessifer), March 11 2018, 11:08 a.m., https://twitter.com/Jessifer/status/972851876059336704.
3. Clarrissa Sorensen-Unruh (@RissaChem), January 1, 2019, 4:23 p.m., https://twitter.com/RissaChem/status/1080212845558550529.
4. Smith 2015: 11.
5. Kohn 2011 (italics in original).
6. National Association of Colleges and Employers, "Career Readiness Defined," https://www.naceweb.org/career-readiness/competencies/career-readiness-defined/.
7. Boyles 2019.
8. Vincent 2019.
9. Berggren 2019.
10. Aske 2019.
11. Berggren 2019.
12. Aguilar 2019.

SOURCES

Aguilar, K. 2019. "Ungrading." *Intro to Me*. April 17. https://introtome433270468.wordpress.com/2019/04/17/ungrading/.

Aske, J. 2019. "Thoughts on Ungrading." *Organic Chemistry Blog*. April 21. https://ochem2classblog.wordpress.com/2019/04/21/thoughts-on-un-grading/.

Berggren, K. 2019. "Ungrading." *Kiersten's Learning Journal*. April 14. https://kberggrenorganicchem2.wordpress.com/2019/04/14/ungrading/.

Boyles, S. 2019. "Ungrading Blog." *Sboylesochemblog*. April 25. https://sboylesochemblog.home.blog/2019/04/25/ungrading-blog/.

Kohn, Alfie. 2011. "The Case against Grades." November. https://www.alfiekohn.org/article/case-grades/.

Matuk, Camillia, Kevin W. McElhaney, Jennifer King Chen, Jonathan Lim-Breitbart, Douglas Kirkpatrick, and Marcia C. Linn. 2016. "Iteratively Refining a Science Explanation Tool through Classroom Implementation and Stakeholder Partnerships." *International Journal of Designs for Learning* 7(2). https://doi.org/10.14434/ijdl.v7i2.20203.

National Association of Colleges and Employers (NACE). 2017. "Employers Rate Career Competencies, New Hire Proficiency." December 11. https://www.naceweb.org/career-readiness/competencies/employers-rate-career-competencies-new-hire-proficiency/.

Schinske, Jeffrey, and Kimberly Tanner. 2014. "Teaching More by Grading Less (or Differently)." *CBE—Life Sciences Education* 13(2): 159–66. https://doi.org /10.1187/cbe.cbe-14-03-0054.

Smith, Gary A. 2015. "Why College Faculty Need to Know the Research about Learning." *InSight: A Journal of Scholarly Teaching* 10: 9–18. https://www.insight journal.net/wp-content/uploads/2020/01/Why-College-Faculty-Need-to-Know -the-Research-about-Learning.pdf.

Sorensen-Unruh, Clarissa. 2019. "Chem 2810 Exam 1 blank template." https://docs .google.com/spreadsheets/d/1lvRXPsRIOxH-3hACtDYWqCff4y1ZCFc4viEryXPP kA4/edit#gid=1383252286.

Vincent, G. 2019. "My Thoughts on the Un-Grading Process." April 25. *Grace's Organic Chemistry II Blog.* https://ochem2withgrace.home.blog/2019/04/25 /my-thoughts-on-the-un-grading-process/.

Chapter 10

———

THE POINT-LESS CLASSROOM: A MATH TEACHER'S IRONIC CHOICE IN NOT CALCULATING GRADES

Gary Chu

———

I am happy to see teachers reflecting on their practices, systems, and structures to focus on knowledge, not grades. There is an epistemological epidemic in the education system, and now is the time to change that.

—Maggie S., former student

Sixteen. She was sixteen when she wrote that reflection at the end of our first semester working together, which was one of the first semesters I swapped out points and percentages. Maggie knew there was something wrong with the way we, as educators teaching in a system that has stayed the course for decades, if not centuries, conducted ourselves. She saw school for what it was: a game. Like her peers, Maggie did what she needed to do to get to the next stage in her learning career, but unlike her peers, she saw education quite differently. She saw and understood what it meant to genuinely learn.

Growing up I was the prototypical good student, but I did not see things like Maggie did. I was beyond compliant, tested better than average, took courses teachers said would challenge me, and, most importantly, I did not question anything. I attribute a lot of that to my upbringing as a young Asian American with immigrant parents who quickly bought into many aspects and assumptions of White culture in the United States as a way to have their children assimilate to White American society.[1] Things like the Protestant work ethic, following every single rule out of fear, self-reliance, assuming control of my actions and environment, and not causing trouble all contributed to my going through the motions of the public American K–12 education system unscathed. Compound that with society's perception of and buy-in to the model minority myth, and I played the game to the best of my abilities.[2]

But seventh grade happened, and I will never forget it. Seventh grade was the first time I received anything lower than a B on my report card— and it was in reading. *Reading!* I was crushed. I still resent George for giving me that C. We are cool now though; he and I see each other on a regular basis, as he is a coach at the school I teach in.

Growing up Asian American, I felt the massive pressure of living up to the stereotypes associated with my race and ethnicity; I identify as Chinese American. I felt obligated to prove to my parents, teachers, peers, and society that I was a good student, and getting good grades was the proof. So I played the game and got good grades just because. I assumed my grades would paint this picture of me to colleges, but they did not do anything close to that. It was at the end of high school that I learned there was more to me, and college applications, than a pristine transcript.

See, grades today are not what they used to be. Way back in the day, I'm talking nineteenth century, grades were not distributed letters and numbers that marked how well students did in a particular subject area. They were, rather, verbal reports from the teacher to parents about what students knew and could do, as well as areas in which they could improve.[3] Verbal reports. Let that sink in for a moment. Teachers spent time discussing with each parent, guardian, home support how well, or not, their student was doing in class. Percentages, letter grades, and the 4.0 GPA entered the academic scene in the early twentieth century (thank you, Ivy Leagues), which is about the time that descriptive, verbal communication of what students knew left the conversation.

So without specific details about what a student knows, what purpose do grades serve?

In his book *Agency: The Teacher's Guide to Self-Directed Learning*, Larry Geni states that grading is part of an authoritarian system to reward and punish students.[4] They inhibit genuine learning and act as extrinsic motivators. Grades sort students along the bell curve (think college, and how professors determine cutoff grades using standard deviation). This idea of sorting is something many teachers might feel is a natural part of school: some students do really well, a large majority will do okay, and a handful do not. But what are the implications of sorting students?

Let's look at some facts:

- The National Assessment of Educational Progress data on achievement gaps shows there is a widening gap between White students and Black and Latinx students.[5]
- Socioeconomic status has a "substantial effect" on student grades.[6]
- For over three decades, girls have earned higher grades and grade point averages than boys in school.[7]
- Sixty to seventy percent of students with special education accommodations taking mainstream classes receive below-average grades in their general education classes, and more than half of all students have a GPA below 2.24, with 35 percent below 1.75.[8]

Grades, as educators have been reporting since the early twentieth century, have contributed to the ever-widening divide of learners based on race, socioeconomic status, sex, gender identity, ability, and more, granting even more access and opportunities to those who already had access and opportunity.

Think: Which groups have the most choice in courses? Who has access to earn college credit while in high school? Which students are placed in special education, remedial, and support classes? Who would benefit from a wider range of selection in their educational experiences and coursework?

Based on my experiences as both a student and a teacher in public education, students who identify racially as White and East Asian generally have the most choice in coursework. Those two groups also have access to Advanced Placement classes for college credit. Our African American, Afro Caribbean, Latinx, Indigenous, Southeast Asian, and Pacific Islander students are found in our special education, remedial, and support classes in disproportionate numbers.

Imagine a scenario where all students did well. What would that mean or how would that look? I can definitely hear some of my peers say the curriculum must be watered down, or that the class is too easy. Others might suggest grades are inflated.[9] But isn't the purpose of school supposed to be for all students to learn as much as possible? For all students to demonstrate a proficient understanding, with a goal of synthesizing the content? Optimistically, is it not feasible for all students to achieve at such high level?

Geni suggests that the de-emphasis of grades can lead to structural changes that are both necessary and important in developing genuine learning experiences for our students. The idea that "each student, regardless of background, should have equitable opportunities to demonstrate their mastery of course content and skills and be held to fair educational expectations" should be the basis for improved grading practices and improved learning.[10] Sounds good to me, Larry.

Am I suggesting that throwing out grades altogether is going to get all students from different backgrounds to the highest levels of understanding? No. But I am questioning how we, as educators, can address the issue of inequitable grading practices.

Peter Anderson suggests that developing structures deemphasizing grades changes everything while changing nothing at all.[11] Class may run as it has in the past, but what differs is the lack of leverage grades have on compliance and work completion. This forces the teacher to evaluate each piece of work they assign, questioning whether it will benefit student growth and learning.

Don't get me wrong. Going gradeless is scary. From what I gathered from my own unscientific poll, many teachers are unwilling to take this step into the unknown. Funny how that works: teachers are scared to take a risk, when they ask their students to do the same in their classes.

Perhaps the first step is to minimize grades, as Geni, Anderson, and Sarah Donovan suggest.[12] Perhaps students could evaluate the quality in their work in a way that mirrors teacher practices.[13] Perhaps students should be the ones providing evidence of their own learning in a student-led conference or portfolio.

There is no single, prescribed way to do this. It is important to find what works for the teacher and the students.

At the early stages of my philosophical and structural change, I leaned on Ken O'Connor's book *A Repair Kit for Grading: 15 Fixes for Broken Grades*. O'Connor provides many practical first steps for teachers trying to get their grades to reflect learning over compliance. For me the first few things taken out of grade calculation were things like effort, attendance, participation, zeros, and extra credit.[14] For a good deal of time, my gradebook consisted only of summative assessments, or in the eyes of my students, tests.

Still I was dissatisfied because students were unable to articulate what they knew and did not yet know. Instead they just knew they got an 83 percent on the unit 3 assessment, which consisted of four weeks of material. They still chased that elusive 100 percent, requesting reassessment opportunities to demonstrate their improved understanding; I happily invited any additional opportunities for students to show what they knew.

Enter *standards-based grading* (SBG). You have probably heard and read all sorts of things associated with this educational buzzword. You have probably heard and read about how people are "doing SBG" and how you can do it too.

It takes a lot of work to set up, and like many things, it can look different with each school, department, and even teacher. For me it was a combination of carefully written, student-friendly targets, and individualized descriptive feedback on student work. SBG transformed the way students and I engaged with respect to their progress toward understanding mathematics concepts. Instead of points and percentages, students would receive descriptive feedback on their pieces of evidence and a descriptor to denote where I viewed their understanding.

The change was drastic and proved to be something that took a lot more modeling and explaining than I anticipated. In the beginning, many were confused—students, parents, guardians, and home supports alike—and I found myself having to explain and justify what we were doing time and time again.

SBG became a regular structure in my classrooms and led me to what I quickly realized was more important than how to determine grades: getting students to understand and communicate their learning. The piece lacking in my practices was student metacognition.

And here I am today.

Daily structures in my classroom are not dramatically different compared to when I graded with points and percentages. We have our daily objective, whole-group discussion, collaborative practice, a quick formative check-in, and summary. The differences are my assessment and feedback practices.

In an effort to provide written individualized feedback to each student, we have daily openers and closers, as well as about one formative assessment per week. These formative assessments are relatively traditional: students work independently to show what they know about a given concept or demonstrate a skill. Prior to turning in their work for feedback, students write down their level of understanding for that concept or skill. They circle a number one through four, four being the highest level of understanding, and write down a justification for what they circled. Upon receiving feedback, typically provided within twenty-four hours, students have the opportunity to work with their peers to identify errors and misconceptions, correct any mistakes, and help each other out. After this feedback cycle is complete, I ask that students reevaluate their body of work having received feedback.

At the end of each unit, we assess all of the material. Some call this a summative assessment, though I still view it as formative, as I provide descriptive feedback on their work, and students still have opportunities to reassess *after* the end-of-unit assessment. The process of learning, and time required, is not prescribed, so students in my classes are allowed to assess previously learned content throughout our time together. For students in my classes, this is a norm, established early in the year. These end-of-unit assessments are mostly traditional, though the option for alternative assessments is always available for students (h/t Rick

Wormeli). Examples of alternative assessments I have done are one-on-one verbal assessments, video submissions, essays, and presentations. The ultimate goal is for students to demonstrate their understanding of the content, regardless of the medium.

This learning-assessment-feedback cycle is what we use throughout the year. It allows students the opportunity to process, demonstrate where they are with the content, receive individual feedback, and continue learning.

Because of the system in place, a letter grade must be issued at the end of each term. A combination of individualized descriptive feedback on the student's work, revisions and multiple attempts at demonstrating understanding, and one-on-one conferences with students throughout each semester leads us to determine an appropriate grade for the term. Yes, *us*. The thing that was missing was not whether things counted for points or the type of assessment. It was student input. Students making a case for a grade show such a high level of comprehension, digestion of the content, and metacognition. Through written reflection, vlogs, podcasts, and in-person conferences, students make the case for their grade—and I just listen.

Do we always agree on a letter grade? Absolutely not. There are always students with delusions of grandeur. But the conversation that follows always leads to understanding on both ends, with us always coming to an agreement. From my perspective, this removes the authoritarian status of the teacher that grades naturally add into the student-teacher dynamic.

You may be reading this thinking about how subjective this method of reporting is, but I encourage you to read "A Century of Grading Research: Meaning and Value in the Most Common Educational Measure" by Brookhart, Guskey, Bowers, McMillan, and Smith. I argue, with the support of one hundred years of research, that all grading and reporting is subjective. For me, it is a matter of developing a philosophy and creating structures to support a learning environment in which your students can thrive.

Unfortunately I am still required to issue letter grades by my school, district, higher education, society, you name it. But if I could have my cake and eat it, I would love to do what I am doing and not have to report a letter grade. Instead teachers would write a narrative of each student's progress throughout our time working together, and that portfolio would follow the student throughout their educational journey. It is not unheard of, as Alfie Kohn discusses in his *Educational Leadership* article "The Case against Grades." There are a number of elementary and high schools that produce narratives in lieu of report cards for their students.[15]

Yes, they get into college.

Yes, that includes highly selective institutions.

No, there is no reason it cannot be done.

"Because we've always done it this way" is not an excuse not to change. If we truly value learning, we must look at the ways we promote that in our environments. Grades continue to add pressure on our students, leading to increases in cheating, anxiety, stress, and mental health diagnoses.[16] We, as educators, must be willing to acknowledge there is a problem, to recognize we are limiting the extent to which we are creating lifelong learners, to look at our own practices, and to take the first steps in eliminating grades.

Is my way the right way? Nope. What I have found, and learned to accept, over the past few years is things change. Every fall there is a new batch of eager learners. As educators we adapt and do what is right for your and my students.

NOTES

1. Katz 1990.
2. Poon, Squire, Kodama, et al. 2016.
3. Brookhart, Bowers, Guskey, et al. 2016.
4. Geni 2018. See also Bradford 1976.
5. National Center for Education Statistics 2015; Hemphill, Vanneman, and Rahman 2011.
6. Johnson, McGue, and Iacono 2007.
7. Grasgreen 2013.
8. Munk and Bursuck 1997–1998.
9. Herron and Markovich 2016.
10. Geni 2018.
11. Anderson 2017.
12. Donovan 2017.
13. Spangler 2017.

14. O'Connor 2011.
15. Kohn 2011.
16. Palmer 2005.

SOURCES

Anderson, Peter. 2017. "To Change Everything While Changing Nothing: Going Gradeless." Teachers Going Gradeless. May 31. https://mrandersonwrites .wordpress.com/2017/05/31/to-change-everything-while-changing-nothing/.

Bradford, John A. 1976. "Policing the Movement of Modern Education." Paper presented at the annual meeting of the Midwest Sociological Society, April 21–44, St. Louis, MO. https://files.eric.ed.gov/fulltext/ED206040.pdf.

Brookhart, Susan M., Thomas R. Guskey, Alex J. Bowers, et al. 2016. "A Century of Grading Research: Meaning and Value in the Most Common Educational Measure." *Review of Educational Research* 86(4): 803–48. https://doi .org/10.3102/0034654316672069.

Donovan, Sarah J. 2017. "Beyond Mandates and Measurement: Lessons from Genocidal Education." Teachers Going Gradeless. June 9. https://teachersgoing gradeless.com/2017/06/09/genocidal-education/.

Geni, Larry, ed. 2018. *Agency: A Teacher's Guide to Self-Directed Learning*. Geni Consulting. http://www.geniconsulting.org/a-teachers-handbook.

Grasgreen, Allie. 2013. "Gender, Jobs and G.P.A." *Inside Higher Ed*. August 20. https:// www.insidehighered.com/news/2013/08/20/study-links-high-school-gpa-gender -gap-collegiate-aspirations.

Hanover Research. 2016. *Best Practices for Equity in Grading*. April. http://www .gssaweb.org/wp-content/uploads/2016/05/Best-Practices-for-Equity-in-Grading .pdf.

Hemphill, F. C., A. Vanneman, and T. Rahman. 2011. *Achievement Gaps: How Hispanic and White Students in Public Schools Perform in Mathematics and Reading on the National Assessment of Educational Progress*. June. Washington, DC: National Center for Education Statistics, Institute of Education Sciences. https://nces .ed.gov/nationsreportcard/pdf/studies/2011459.pdf.

Herron, M. C., and Z. D. Markovich. 2016. *Student Sorting and Implications for Grade Inflation*. September 27. http://www.dartmouth.edu/~herron/sorting.pdf.

Johnson, W., M. McGue, and W. G. Iacono. 2007. "Socioeconomic Status and School Grades: Placing Their Association in Broader Context in a Sample of Biological and Adoptive Families." *Intelligence* 35(6): 526–41.

Katz, Judith H. 1990. *Some Aspects and Assumptions of White Culture in the United States*. The Kaleel Jamison Consulting Group.

Kohn, Alfie. 2011. "The Case against Grades." *Educational Leadership* 69(3): 28–33.

Munk, Dennis D., and William D. Bursuck. 1997–1998. "Can Grades Be Helpful and Fair?" *Educational Leadership* 55(4): 44–47.

National Center for Education Statistics. 2015. *School Composition and the Black-White Achievement Gap*. September 24. Washington, DC: National Center for Education Statistics, Institute of Education Sciences. https://nces.ed.gov /nationsreportcard/subject/studies/pdf/school_composition_and_the_bw _achievement_gap_2015.pdf.

O'Connor, Ken. 2011. *A Repair Kit for Grading: 15 Fixes for Broken Grades*. 2nd ed. New York: Pearson.

Palmer, Barbara. 2005. "Pressure for Good Grades often Leads to High Stress, Cheating, Professors Say." *Stanford News*. September 23. https://news.stanford.edu/news/2005/february23/cheat-022305.html.

Poon, OiYan, Diane Squire, Corinne Kodama, et al. 2016. "A Critical Review of the Model Minority Myth in Selected Literature on Asian Americans and Pacific Islanders in Higher Education." *Review of Educational Research* 86(2): 469–502. https://doi.org/10.3102/0034654315612205.

Spangler, Lisa. 2017. "5 Ways to Increase Student Ownership in Your Classroom." We Are Teachers. January 16. https://www.weareteachers.com/increase-student-ownership/.

Part III

———

REFLECTIONS

Chapter 11

GRADE ANARCHY IN THE PHILOSOPHY CLASSROOM

Marcus Schultz-Bergin

In renovating my 300-level Philosophy of Law course for a new fifteen-student audience, I decided to take a page from the anarchists—those who argue we do not need law or centralized authority—and remove myself as the classroom authoritarian.[1] I would no longer be the sovereign arbiter of grades using threat of an F to motivate my student-subjects to comply. Instead I sought to establish an anarchist classroom where the rules are generated by the community and members of that community feel generally obligated to themselves and to one another. My hypothesis was that this grade-anarchy approach would improve student learning.

My course involved three major changes from a standard course:

1. Students would be provided with a buffet of learning opportunities they could complete at their discretion.
2. The only required assignments would be three reflection essays: an early semester *achievement essay*, a *midterm learning reflection*, and a *final learning reflection*. The aim of these essays was to have students identify what they wanted to achieve and then discuss how they achieved their goals and where they still needed to work.

3. Students would meet with me for two *learning conferences*—one at the midterm and the other at the end of the semester. In each of these, we would discuss the learning reflections and the student's portfolio of work, and end with the student telling me their grade for the course.

In what follows I detail my experiences with grade anarchy as well as my reflections on the successes and failures of the approach. On the whole I will say that while my approach accomplished some of what I hoped for, there are some important changes that would have improved the overall experience. So I encourage everyone to learn from my failures and ideas of how I would improve the structure in the future.

PITCHING GRADE ANARCHY TO STUDENTS

A vital component of a successful classroom experiment is student buy-in. Anytime I introduce an unusual assignment or technique in the classroom, I endeavor to make clear to the students why I am doing it and why I think it will be beneficial to them. The importance of discussing your techniques with students is heightened, I think, when it comes to ungrading. Without such discussions, a potential, understandable reaction from students may be that the professor is simply being lazy or "not doing their job." And so at the start of the semester, I took two interrelated approaches to pitching grade anarchy to my students.

First, we spent part of the first day of class reflecting—individually and collectively—on what we wanted to get out of the course. I had students write about why they were taking the course and what they hoped to learn, and then we discussed these thoughts as a class in order to collaboratively develop course learning outcomes. Common themes arose among the students—a desire to improve their ability to read complex argumentative texts, to improve their ability to communicate arguments and engage in debates, and to gain a deeper understanding of the law and its role in their own lives. Interestingly these sorts of outcomes are by and large the same ones I had written for the course before I decided to have us collaboratively create the outcomes. But now the students exercised their own agency to determine the aims of the class and, as a result, indicated greater interest in what we were doing. Without grades to (externally) motivate students, this activity started the ball rolling on generating internal motivation.

As a result of our collaborative outcome design, I crafted a syllabus for the second class meeting where I also pitched, in more detail, my grade-anarchy approach. Given the nature of philosophy, it made sense to me to present my students with an argument for why we were going to forgo grades in the course and to encourage them to critically evaluate my argument. My hypothesis was that student learning would be improved by eliminating instructor grading, and I presented my students with the following argument to justify that hypothesis:[2]

1. **Grades do not track learning (or anything else of importance).** Grades—whether in the form of letters or numbers or percentages, etc.—do not satisfactorily correlate with student learning or really any other thing we would care about.

2. **Grading reduces student learning.** Grades do at least three terrible things to student psychology: they increase anxiety, place the focus on extrinsic rather than intrinsic motivation, and encourage strategic performance ("How little can I do to still get the grade I want?"). Each of these takes away from learning by discouraging a focus on what you are doing and discouraging taking risks that may lead to failure. But we learn most from our failures, and so you should be encouraged to fail.

3. **Only receiving feedback increases student learning.** The same study has been repeated over and over again: students who only receive feedback on an assignment (rather than only a grade or both a grade and feedback) make the greatest improvement in their learning. Grades end learning opportunities by essentially saying, "This is done." Feedback continues the conversation.

4. **Self-evaluation and self-reflection improve student learning.** Self-evaluation and reflection promote ownership of one's own learning and therefore assist in an individual's development into a self-regulated learner who will be capable of learning and honestly evaluating themselves for their entire life.

Reflection also encourages recognizing how the educational experience is changing you as a person. Self-evaluation and reflection can be done in a graded classroom but are more significant in a gradeless classroom.

As a result of these two interventions, I found most students quite excited by the prospects of a gradeless classroom. This was, though, not unanimous. However, the lack of unanimity largely related to *how* I constructed the gradeless classroom and not *that* it was a gradeless classroom. As the semester went on, I saw how specific decisions I made about course structure positively and negatively influenced student learning. My hope is that the observations I detail below provide some insight into how (not) to create a gradeless classroom.

EFFECT ON ATTENDANCE AND PARTICIPATION

Active engagement is essential to student learning. And in a small discussion course like Philosophy of Law, it is even more important. In similar classes, many professors may make attendance and participation mandatory, enforcing such things through the grading system. I, of course, did not do that, and so one concern is that attendance could be quite poor or there may be a lack of participation (perhaps due to a lack of preparation since there was no grade penalty for not being prepared).

While I do not have direct comparative data with regard to attendance, overall, I would suggest there has been little to no impact—positive or negative. Comparing my course to another 300-level philosophy course taught in the same semester and including some of the same students, I have weeks where attendance is significantly better and other weeks where attendance is poorer. The week after spring break was particularly bad, as was the last week or so of the semester. This, however, appears to be a norm at my university, rather than a reflection of the course structure.

Students have indicated that without the grade pressure to attend, they are a little more likely to miss a class if other things come up. I don't necessarily see this as a problem—it is not the case that students are skipping because they do not feel like showing up. Instead they are making a judgment about other commitments or deciding to take care of their health rather than risk infecting others.

As for participation, things are quite good. Although students are not punished if they are not prepared, most students come having read the material (and often preparing a summary or questions, as I mention below) and attempt to engage in the discussion. Certainly there have been cases where students showed up unprepared, but the benefit here is that the students still felt comfortable showing up since there was no penalty for being ill prepared.

Finally it is worth noting a particular experience we had in the class. We read a classic court case—*Riggs v. Palmer*—and the plan for the day was simply to debate the case. We wanted to understand the arguments the judges presented for their rulings, discuss other possible arguments, and then identify what the case could teach us about the nature of law (the case is referenced by Ronald Dworkin in his criticisms of H. L. A. Hart's legal positivism).[3] On this day I had students who had prepared pages of notes—working to consider possible objections to their position and how to respond—and the debate was vociferous but civil and incredibly detailed. All of this without any grade attached to any part of the day.

EFFECT ON ASSIGNMENTS

Attendance is easy, some may say; the real test is whether the students would complete any assignments for the course, and if so, whether those assignments would indicate any real degree of learning. If students could get away with not completing a single assignment, would they? Similarly if students knew whatever they turned in would not be graded, would they turn in junk work, figuring they could just get by with saying, "Well, I turned stuff in!"?

I will admit that, here, there were both great victories and some significant defeats. Importantly, just as I encourage my students to dig into their failures and learn from them, I believe I learned a lot from these defeats. The lessons learned are ones I was able to consider in making changes midsemester and in thinking about how I would carry out a gradeless classroom in the future. For those considering adopting a gradeless classroom, my hope is this section will give you some indication of what not to do as well as some advice on what will likely work better.

How I Did It

My approach to assignments was one of maximal agency for the students. By providing them a buffet of learning opportunities they could complete as they saw fit, I really put the onus on them to establish an assignment schedule and determine what they needed to do to achieve what they wanted to achieve. This particular approach was great for some, but problematic for others.

As we came around to the midterm, I did have some students who had not submitted any substantial work beyond the required reflection essays. Importantly, they had largely attended class and participated in discussions, so I do not think the lack of work was an indication of them totally blowing off the course. I also had other students who submitted some work leading up to the midterm, but the work did not suggest a significant amount of effort. I think the main aim was just to submit *something* because they knew they should. Of note, and as I will detail below, the students were honest with themselves about the amount of effort they put in, and so even those who submitted little (effortful) work were at least learning something about themselves.

At the other end of the spectrum, I had students who submitted a significant number of assignments—more than I probably would have assigned in a standard course. These students used the freedom of the grading scheme to hone particular skills. For instance, since many students suggested they wanted to improve their ability to extract arguments from complex philosophical texts and I informed them that to do so would require regular practice, I had students submit argumentative summaries for nearly every reading. And these assignments were effortful—while early on I was able to provide a good amount of corrective feedback, the students' abilities clearly improved as we moved on. One particular observation here was that students tended to spend too much time on largely irrelevant information and would end up forgetting about the bigger picture or the more important details. Once I pointed this out to students, they were able to correct the problem, and later summaries showed a much better grasp of distinguishing the important from the unimportant.

Moreover I encouraged (but did not require) students to sign up to be discussion leaders for most class periods. As a discussion leader, the student would be responsible for constructing a one-page handout summarizing the key arguments of the reading and placing it in the broader context of the class, and then facilitating discussion on key issues. This, of course, required a significant amount of work on their part, but I had nearly every available day filled up. Not all students took the opportunity, but some signed up more than once. Some of the students who signed up were largely quiet in most classes or had expressed early on that they knew they were weak public speakers or discussion participants and wanted to get better. And so they signed up to put themselves in an uncomfortable position even though they did not have to, and by and large, they flourished under the pressure. As we instructors (should) know, the best way to learn something is to have to teach it to others, and that is precisely what these students learned as well.

Finally, I had some students who chose to engage in interesting final paper projects, projects it would have been hard for me to make into required assignments in a standard course. In particular, two students decided to engage in a written debate on a topic from the course. One student presented the initial case for a position, the other read that paper and wrote a response, and the process continued a bit so that each student wrote two papers. This is the sort of in-depth and valuable learning I have always wanted to see in a philosophy classroom, but is not something I think can be forced on students. On this front, setting up the class with a make-your-own-assignment approach was quite beneficial.

Some Midsemester Changes

Given the above observations, I will admit that while I was encouraged by the positives I saw, I was worried about those students who had done little or no work. And so after the midterm learning conferences (discussed below), I instituted a few tweaks to the course in the hopes of getting everyone to do more work. Since I had already set things up to promote agency, I did not feel comfortable making significant shifts, so I did not start requiring specific assignments. Instead I simply provided more guidance to the students in order to lower the cognitive cost of completing an assignment.

The first intervention was to provide a suggested schedule of assignments to students. This indicated to them the sorts of assignments they should complete and in roughly what time frame to complete them. My hope, here, was both to eliminate the need for the student to think about *what* type of assignment to do—something that could be a cognitive barrier to doing any assignment—and to provide the students with a rough schedule, so they could perhaps log assignment "due dates" into a planner if that is something they were used to doing.

This change was helpful for some, but not as widely helpful as I had hoped. A few students picked things up a bit after the midterm, but those in the most need (who, interestingly, were precisely the students who asked if I would do something like this) only minimally responded (but, to be clear, they *did* respond).

The second intervention was to provide students with a set of midterm exam questions. These were basically short answer and essay questions that covered all the major ideas we had explored in the first half of the course and easily could have been the basis for an actual midterm exam. But rather than requiring completion of the exam, I made it available to students to complete any or all of it. This intervention was a bit more beneficial, because a few of the students who admitted to not doing enough in the first half of the course had a way, nonetheless, of producing some work that indicated learning throughout that part of the course. And so I did receive a couple of submissions.

The final intervention involved me being explicit and proactive in my recommendations for final paper topics. All of my students agreed on the first day that writing an original argumentative paper was both something they wanted to improve on and something that would indicate achievement of many of the learning outcomes. However, my desire to promote agency led to some being a bit lost about how to engage. And so I went back to the material in the first half of the course and indicated some particular places worth exploring for a final paper, and as we worked through new material, I regularly indicated issues worth further exploration. This has been particularly nice with discussion comments from students, since they get a bit of feedback on how to develop the idea in class, but I make sure to make explicit where they have a possible paper idea.

How I'd Do It in the Future

In a future gradeless classroom, I think I would eliminate the assignment buffet and stick with a precise assignment schedule. It seems to me this is more common among gradeless classrooms (which are often done in K–12, where it seems more obvious too much agency would be problematic), and I think, given my student population, it would be helpful. So how exactly would I maintain a required assignment schedule without the threat of grades?

Technically speaking there would not be any necessary negative result for a student who failed to complete an assignment. However, by getting more precise about what students need to do in their reflection essays and the learning conferences (discussed below), there would effectively be potential negative results for missing (too many) assignments. I still like the idea that a student could miss an assignment without any real repercussions, since these students have a lot going on and I think there can be totally acceptable reasons they couldn't get a particular assignment done on time. This is especially true of students at my university, who are often juggling a full class schedule and a job (at least).

So I would further emphasize the need to create a *portfolio* of work that indicates achievement of the learning outcomes. If a student misses just one assignment—since I prefer to assign many smaller assignments rather than just a few large ones—it may not make any real difference, but if they miss quite a few (or miss just a few of the same type), then it will be difficult to have a complete portfolio.

Now, importantly, I do not want to lose the potential creativity that comes from permitting student agency. I want those students who wanted to complete a written debate to still be able to do that, and so I would have to permit something like the petitioning of alternative assignments. The other benefit to this approach would be that students who came in with a greater skill level or who more quickly achieved certain outcomes could find other ways to challenge themselves. The learning would be more personalized and individualized overall, which was one aim I had in using the assignment buffet.

LEARNING CONFERENCES AND STUDENT GRADES

My university still requires me to assign grades, and so although I am not personally assigning grades on any particular assignment, there still has to be a fair method of assigning course grades. It seems reasonably common among gradeless classrooms for this to be done through some combination of student reflection and conferencing.[4] So I adopted a similar strategy. One particular worry here is that since students are self-assigning their grades, they will just give themselves As regardless of merit. My experience indicated that this may be true of some students, but certainly not all. In particular I found myself bumping some student grades up, because they were (in my view) excessively harsh on themselves. I did not lower anyone's grade from what they assigned themselves, but in one case, I requested a student do additional work given the grade he assigned himself (although I did not *require* he do so).

But, before discussing my observations, it is also worth noting here that if the claim I made in my argument for going gradeless—that grades do not actually track learning—is correct, then the worry that a student will receive an A even though they don't "deserve" it is misplaced. We may mean they don't deserve it because they didn't submit enough work or work of the sort we would assign an A to. If that is what we mean, then fine, it is possible they could receive an A without deserving it. But the skepticism about what grades actually indicate suggests that we *think* grades are an indication of learning, and so our claim of deservingness has to do with whether and how much the student learned. But the evidence shows grades don't actually track that. And so there is no clear connection between what a student deserves (in terms of learning) and what grade they receive anyway. Thus, even if the same is true of a gradeless classroom, that is not really an argument against the gradeless classroom.

How I Did It

Nevertheless, I do think there is a greater possibility that student-assigned grades, as a result of a reflection and learning conference, are more likely to reflect student learning than instructor-assigned grades. This is, in part, because students have a better idea of their starting skill level and so—with the right guidance—can be a better judge of their overall growth. And that guidance is provided by the reflection essays and conferences. My experience indicated that the reflection and conferencing experience was extremely valuable for many of the students.

My setup for the essays and conferences included students submitting a total of three reflective essays: an early semester achievement essay outlining what they hoped to achieve in the course, a midsemester learning reflection, and a final learning reflection. I provided written feedback on the achievement essays, often indicating particular types of assignments students should look to complete in order to achieve what they indicated they wanted to achieve, but I did not conference with them for that essay. The two learning reflections, however, were submitted prior to a short learning conference with me where we discussed their learning in the class, and where, eventually, they would assign themselves a grade.

In writing their achievement essays, my students really considered their intellectual strengths and weaknesses and identified where they wanted to improve. This was especially nice to see, given that I see many of the learning outcomes of a philosophy course to be general philosophical skills, like critically reading complex texts, analyzing and evaluating arguments, constructing arguments, and so on. These are often the sorts of learning outcomes that it is difficult for students to identify with since they are not as concrete as "could state a definition" and the like. Although I regularly include these sorts of outcomes in my syllabus, and craft opportunities to develop and display those skills, some students come away feeling like the activities and assignments are worthless. But in writing these essays, these students really identified with those sorts of skills and considered how they would work on them and display them.

Moreover, some of the students took my advice to *challenge themselves* in these achievement essays. I told them I wanted them to shoot for the moon—they should walk out of the course feeling like they achieved a lot, but not necessarily everything they set out for themselves. That was one of the major benefits of not grading the assignments—they could push themselves and not get anxious about failing or otherwise performing poorly.

For the midterm reflection essays, students discussed those goals they set for themselves, as well as the course learning outcomes, and reflected on their growth up to that point. Those who completed multiple iterations of the same type of assignment—say, an assignment extracting the central argument from a text—would point to how they put into action the feedback I provided early on and how that led to them getting better. Others, particularly those who did not submit much, admitted their failures and set out a plan for themselves for the second half of the course. Either way students were quite honest with themselves and treated their successes and their failures as *on them* in a way I don't always see in a standard class.

Finally what did the grades look like? Well, most students suggested they had thus far earned a C+/B−, with some even suggesting a D and only one claiming to have earned an A. And, by and large, the grades they assigned themselves were about where I would have put them as well. In a few cases, grades were lower than I believed they should be. Midterm grades, of course, don't matter, and so that may have allowed them to be more honest without consequence.

Some Midsemester Changes

Because the reflection and conference setup was mostly successful, I did not make substantial midsemester changes. But I did clarify how I wanted them to construct their learning reflections and regard the conferences going into the final reflection and conference. In particular I made clearer that in writing their reflections, students should explicitly speak to their achievement of the course learning outcomes (which they helped to write) as well as any additional outcomes they had assigned for themselves in their achievement essays. Some students already did this in the midterm reflection, but others neglected to look at the course learning outcomes and mostly focused on their personal outcomes or simply focused on their failures!

By clarifying that students should focus on discussing how they achieved the outcomes, I put greater emphasis on compiling a *portfolio* of their work. For each outcome they needed to indicate either an assignment (or assignments) that spoke to it or note particular experiences in class or while reading that indicated achievement. This would ensure they had clearer evidence for their claims about their own learning and, hopefully, limit the opportunity to inappropriately inflate their own grades. Moreover, as I will explain in more detail below, the process of compiling and reflecting on their portfolios helped them consider what they had achieved in the course and (assuming they did achieve something!) helped them appreciate the work they put into the course.

There was some arguable inflation in final grades, probably reflecting the fact that those grades matter on a transcript. Every student indicated they earned a grade somewhere in the A–B range, with most falling in the A range. While this was a reasonable reflection of performance for many students, a few certainly put in less work than I would have liked. I also believe this was largely a result of my lack of assignment structure and guidance, issues I would fix going forward.

How I'd Do It in the Future

In future courses I would further emphasize the course learning outcomes in the construction of a portfolio and reflection on one's learning. If the class had an assignment schedule, then this would be easier, since I could make sure the assignments would speak to all the learning outcomes (this includes participation-based outcomes, which could involve microassignments that prepare the student for participation or are the result of that participation). Students would then be asked to keep all their assignments—with my feedback—and compile the portfolio in a more formal way. Again I think constructing this compendium of work is not only good practice for what many people have to do in various careers but also a nice way to see one's own growth.

I may also provide additional support for students in assessing their achievement of outcomes. It seems that some gradeless classrooms provide students with rubrics for evaluating their own achievement. The student's job is then to identify how well they achieved each outcome, given the general information provided about what various levels of achievement would look like. This would be helpful for those students who are less skilled at self-assessment, and it could also be helpful in dealing with a student who does not take the reflection process seriously.

A final change, recommended to me by one of the students, is to have some sort of regular check-in, rather than waiting until the midterm or final period to discuss performance. For some students the radical agency an ungraded classroom provides is anxiety producing, rather than reducing. They need more regular input not just on how they are doing on an assignment but also on how they are doing in terms of the number of assignments and overall contributions. Thus, my student offered two possible approaches: (a) a weekly, or biweekly, email check-in, where I give my thoughts on what a student has done since the last check-in and advice on whether I think they should be doing more, and (b) some sort of tracking sheet, where students would regularly indicate what they plan to do for the course each week (or every other week) and share that with me simply to promote accountability. Either of these approaches could be used with or without a set assignment schedule.

CONCLUSION: MUST THE CLASSROOM HAVE A CENTRALIZED AUTHORITY?

My gradeless experiment was carried out in a Philosophy of Law course where one major question we explore is whether human societies *need* a centralized authority, and if so, *what justifies* that authority exercising power over others. Anarchists have argued that human societies can and should function without such centralized authority—any centralized authority is illegitimate anyway, and we can do better if authority is diffused among the members of the community. It was for this reason I titled my experiment Grade Anarchy. It was an experiment into whether a classroom needed a centralized authority in the form of an instructor who authoritatively distributed grades.

And I believe the experiment shows that anarchists are right—at least in regard to a learning community of sixteen people (which, therefore, says very little about any larger implications). By asking the students to be active participants in the creation of the community—we formed the rules through a direct and pure democracy, rather than through the strong-arm of the professor—the students found themselves bound to each other, rather than simply doing what they were told because of the threat of a poor grade. Sure, there are some students who probably would have done more work (understood simply as completing more assignments) in a graded classroom. But it is not obvious to me that they would have learned more. The standard grading system *obliges* students to perform certain tasks out of threat, but I sought for students to genuinely feel obligated—to themselves and to their peers—to perform those tasks that made for an effective learning community. And through reflection on their own actions and work, these students learned quite a bit, even if some of that learning consisted of realizing they did not do as much as they should.

NOTES

1. Recent defenses of philosophical anarchism have come from Robert Paul Wolff (1970) and Michael Huemer (2013).
2. In my syllabus I cited many of the sources discussed in the introduction to this book to support my claims and encouraged my students to take a look at those original sources as well.
3. For Dworkin the case indicates that the law consists of both rules (which Hart recognizes) and principles (which Hart does not), thus showing the inadequacy of Hart's view. This argument is found in Dworkin (1967).
4. Burnett 2018.

SOURCES

Burnett, Andrew. 2018. "Creating a Gradeless Classroom in a School That Requires Grades." Teachers Going Gradeless. https://teachersgoinggradeless.com/2018/08/18/burnett-how/.

Dworkin, Ronald. 1967. "The Model of Rules." *University of Chicago Law Review* 35: 14–46.

Huemer, Michael. 2013. *The Problem of Political Authority: An Examination of the Right to Coerce and the Duty to Obey.* New York: Palgrave Macmillan.

Wolff, Robert Paul. 1970. *In Defense of Anarchism.* New York: Harper and Row.

Chapter 12

———

CONFERENCE MUSINGS AND
THE G-WORD

Joy Kirr

————

This chapter is a series of lightly edited blog posts detailing a seventh-grade teacher's real-time experience introducing ungrading into her teaching. It conveys an immediate sense of what the process feels like.

SUNDAY, SEPTEMBER 2, 2018
THE G-WORD: GRADES

For the life of me, I can't remember how I introduced going without grades at the start of last year. I guess I skipped writing about it, but two years ago I wrote about the day I introduced this idea to my seventh graders.[1] This year, the "discussion" (really just me going on and on and on about how passionate I am about this subject) lasted fifteen to twenty minutes at the end of each period Friday.

First, when students walked in, the question of the day was regarding grades. "Who cares more about your grades?" Answers were "my parents," "both/equally," or "me" (fig. 12.1).

Next, they answered how they were feeling (based on "energy" and "pleasantness") on our mock mood meter, and then we read independently.[2] After, we read, wrote about our books with a prompt, and

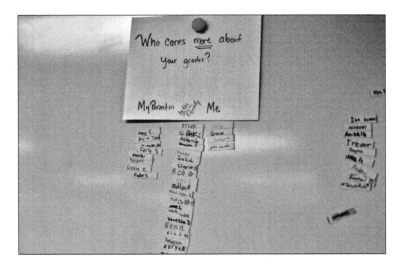

Figure 12.1. Categorizing grades. Courtesy of @MrsSalsinger.

quickly reviewed genres. It was then time to talk about the G-word . . . Grades.

I began this discussion this year by asking students to not say a word . . . I was going to give them *one* word, and I wanted them to write the thoughts that came to mind on a sticky note. I asked them for silence because I wanted twenty-five different ideas, not all one idea just because someone said something aloud. They were fabulous, waiting for the word. I said, "grades," and they all got to work. Some wrote just one word, some wrote phrases, and some wrote sentences. When pencils were down, I asked students to come to the board and categorize their sticky note as "positive," "negative," or "both/neutral."

I then asked if they would've written different things on their sticky, thus moving them, if I added other words to the one word . . . such as "Grades—in ELA [English Language Arts]," or "Grades—in P.E. [Physical Education]," etc. Many hands went up each time I said something different. In one class, almost all hands went up when I said, "Report card grades." I continued the discussion by explaining how grades are very complex, and can be very personal. We all have stories about a grade or points, or a particular teacher. Our parents and their parents all have stories they remember—some still bring up angst, and some are positive. Either way, grading can feel very personal, and I don't want it to be. I want grades to reflect *learning*. I want grades to reflect *achievement*. Not behavior. And not an average.

We went on to talk about averages. How, when one week you may receive 0/5 on your article of the week, but you learn from our reflection of it, the next week you may receive 2/5. That's a 40 percent increase, and yet the grade is averaged out to be 20 percent overall. I had many different numbers on the board, and students saw how, if they were averaged, they wouldn't be able to overcome their first attempt quickly. However, if we did not average them, and instead just worked off feedback and next steps, they could show me how they'd learned. What if their last four assessments showed 5/5? What does that mean?

Then came the explanation of our one-on-one conferences at the end of each term. We'll be looking at all the evidence, and talking about what it means. We'll be looking at growth, revisions, and how students took feedback and did something with it—in order to learn, not for a better grade.

During these fifteen to twenty minutes in each class, I did most of the talking, that's for sure. I had eye contact with all students, however; most seemed to be paying attention, and trying to soak it in. I asked for questions, and they were few, at best. I asked for thumbs up, middle, or down, and got quizzical faces and unsure thumbs. So . . . I passed out the newest parent explanation (appendix 12.1) and asked them to look through it and share their thoughts or findings. One observation was, "This side (the back page right side) has more words on it than the other side." Yes! That led me to explain that our way of grading this year is more work—on me, on them, and on their parents.

This was the time to ask them to talk with their parents about the grading procedure, as they are able to opt out if they'd like. I may have said, at the end, that, "After talking with your parents, if you or they decide you want to opt out, that's fine. You can go back to having the computer average your grades, just like it has for years." It sounded a bit snarky, and I could feel it in my bones as well. I don't drink coffee, and yet I was *buzzing* with passion about how I felt we need to do this in order to portray a more accurate grade to reflect their learning. Phew! This was a *lot*. I still need to refine how I present this to students—this may have been overload for many of them. Should I spread it out over a few days?

I had one more thing to try (new to me, but I'll be doing it again) . . . On the door, I quickly put up a green, yellow, and pink sticky note. (I've seen this same idea with green, yellow, and red hands on the door, but I didn't think of it ahead of time, and stickies work just as well!) On their way out the door, I asked them to high-five the one that best fits how they're feeling about the idea . . .

- Green = Good for now. I may have some questions later.
- Yellow = Okay—I have a question or concern.
- Pink = What are you doing to me, Mrs. Kirr??!!

Students either high-fived the green or the yellow hands. I did not see any using the pink hand. And how am I feeling after this fabulous Friday with this new group of seventh graders? Ahhhh . . . I am pumped up once again believing that I'm doing the right thing for me and my students. I am still worried about parent night (this Wednesday), but having this current discussion fresh in my mind, I can let parents know that I understand grading can feel very personal—to all of us. My principal said he'd stay late during parent night so I could tell parents I will stay late to answer their questions and concerns in person. My hope is that they feel comfortable enough to ask me any and all questions now and throughout the quarter, so they come closer to understanding the reasons *why*.

Want to know what those sticky notes said? See the entry for October 7.

SUNDAY, SEPTEMBER 23, 2018
A TIDBIT OF SUCCESS

In the first quarter of the school year, many teachers don't have a lot of grades. When you're going gradeless, or not putting points or marks to be averaged in the gradebook as I am, it's even fewer. Going into our sixth week, we currently have six assignments that have narrative feedback attached.

The "Article of the Week" actually already has three pieces of feedback embedded in the one assignment. I change the date on that one and move it up to the top when we have a new one to add.

I've got seventh graders, and first quarter for them is all rainbows and unicorns when they're not getting points or marks averaged. In fact, I saw a birthday photo of a tough man as a unicorn on a student's locker the other day and thought, "Yup. That's where we are right now."

Time will come soon enough when I sit one-on-one with each student to look at their evidence and put it all into one little letter. So far, however, there has been no mention of grades. No extra credit, no late penalties . . . we've just been working at learning how to be better readers, writers, and grammarians.

Here's the tidbit I need to share that I heard from a student when they went into the feedback they had for their article of the week . . .

"It worked! The feedback you gave worked, and I did better this time!"

This is why I put myself through the extra work of adding next steps to each student's personalized feedback.

SUNDAY, OCTOBER 7, 2018
SBG COMMITTEE MEETS!

This week, before I headed out to our district office to be in the Middle School Standards-Based Grading Steering Committee, I found Post-its on my desk at home. Post-its from our class discussion noted at the beginning of the chapter. I hadn't taken the time to read them, so I'm going to post them here to see if there's something new I can discover.[3]

In the positive column . . .

- *hardwork, persistavitivity*
- *I try my hardest to keep them all A's!*
- *A+, school, doing my best, working hard*
- *A+ the best grade, 100%, 10/10*
- *A's and B's, 4.0, GPA*
- *Getting As and 4.0 GPA*
- *I like to get grades can se it shows your progress*
- *Are very important*

- *letters / numbers*
- *They may be important.*
- *important*
- *letters, important*
- *more import things*

In the neutral column . . .

- *homework*
- *important, work hard, do good, meaningful, try your best*
- *A+, subjects, stressful, prepared, honor students, quiz, worried, tests, study*
- *low? high? good? bad?*
- *school, classes, teachers, parents*
- *parents, school, A*
- *A, B, C, D, E, F, Ma, Pr, De, Be, Work*
- *Grading policy, As, Bs, Cs, Ds, Fs, parents, school*
- *GPA, school, homework, stress, tests*
- *hard to get*
- *school, academics, my classes, my teachers*
- *How your doing in school*
- *importun and useful, can help U*
- *important, harsh, good, GPA, Pennstate*
- *good, four point o*
- *They make you anscious, some people care and people don't care about them.*
- *Important, Good grades, you have to work hard*
- *try to keep them high I think trying is more important*
- *Grades are what you get in school, they can be bad or good, A, B, C, D, F*
- *I care about my grades, but I also believe you are not a letter or #. You do not define what your grade is.*
- *Powerschool, A, B, C, D, F [The F is circled, with a check mark and smiley face by it]*
- *Good and badd*
- *grades are something that are different.*
- *important, something you work for, assignments/tests*

- *A, B (good), C, +, – (average) F, D (Bad)*
- *Something that measures your academic ability, but it also defines you with a letter.*
- *classes*
- *A+, B, C, D, F*
- *hard work, should be good*

In the negative column . . .

- *Worrying about grades*
- *There ok I don't stress about them too much but when I do its not good*
- *As Bs Cs Ds, I hope I don't get any bad grades*
- *Intence, scary, change*
- *I think they're kinda stupid. I'm getting graded on stuff I don't really like and people kinda treat them like they're this super important thing.*
- *Burn it!!*
- *stressful [on two students' Post-its]*
- *F*
- *G3 = Get Good Grades*
- *A–F, A=good, F=you're a failure*
- *Stress, anxiety*
- *Wait, what are my grades like? When will this grade come in? Do these people all have better grades than me?*
- *Pressure, stress, homework*
- *Something that shows you what understanding your in like a scale. But also can make you feel very sad & happy.*
- *I don't like them when they are lower than an A–. They are good when you work hard.*
- *6th grade report card / PowerSchool. Meh.*

I love this.

I remember these feelings. The successes and the fears.

Their quick thoughts/writing bring me back to when grades mattered to me, personally.

And this is the reason I wanted to be on the standards-based grading committee for our district. The elementary one is finished, and they'll have their first standards-based reports coming out this fall.

We had our first half-day meeting this week, and I had a difficult time not throwing in my two cents after every person spoke. We chatted about how we felt about it, what it was, read some research (how reliable was it?), and came away with the book we'll be studying: *Developing Standards-Based Report Cards* by Thomas R. Guskey and Jane M. Bailey.[4] I'm excited for this next part of my journey in this profession!

WEDNESDAY, OCTOBER 17, 2018
CONFERENCE MUSINGS

Seventh graders—what a mix of minds!

I've conducted thirteen one-on-one "grade" conferences with students this week. I need to meet because even though I've gone all quarter without points or scores averaged together, I still need to put a final letter grade in the online gradebook. The end of the term is next week Friday, so I've reserved five days to have five-minute conferences with students. Some go faster, and some go slower, and they leave a paper trail for students to take home and explain to parents. The first conferences about grades are always tougher than the rest of the year. Students have never done this before, and it's quite the learning curve for some! We use a document (appendix 12.2) to discuss evidence so far.

Here are some snippets from these conferences (all names have been changed) . . .

I see, on our documenting sheet, that Evelyn has earned an A. It's solid. She's gotten proficient or mastery on her writing skills, and she's gotten 90 percent or higher on her reading comprehension checks. I ask, "What do you think your grade should be?"

Her response—again and again—"I don't know."

Cassie knows she should get an A. I ask, "What is your evidence?" She can't find it. We need to look through everything and write it off to the side, so she can see what I see. We end up deciding a B– is more representative of her learning right now. I look at last year's grades when I have time. Uh oh. I might be hearing from parents. She had all As last year . . .

Jimmy starts by saying, "I've never done this before, so I'm going to do my best, but I might make mistakes. So . . . ," and he goes on and on about his skills, how he's doing, where he could improve . . . He's got three goals for next quarter and wants to narrow it down to one that will have the most impact . . . I don't have to say a *thing*.

Norman has been in trouble this year. Only once from me. I "let him get away" with things that do not impede other students' learning. I pick my battles, and I think we have an okay relationship. He seemed scared, yet put on his tough face. He seemed surprised to know I agreed with his assessment of himself and did not bring behavior into the mix. Behavior doesn't belong in a grade, yet he looked me in the eyes the entire time we talked. I can't measure that, but I can recognize how important it is.

We have different seating options in our room. I make sure to sit on a chair that is the same height as the student's chair. I want them to know this should not be scary. It's just a conversation about how they're doing right now, and where they can improve. I *love* these conversations. Some are tougher than others, but I feel like I learn so much about the students, and I feel that we build more of a bond of trust with each other. If (when?) we do go to standards-based grading, I'd love to keep these conversations going at the end of each term.

NOTES

1. Kirr 2016.
2. The Mood Meter was developed by Marc Brackett and Robin Stern of the Yale Center for Emotional Intelligence (http://ei.yale.edu/ruler).
3. My students' comments are presented here unedited.
4. Guskey and Bailey 2010.

SOURCES

Guskey, Thomas R., and Jane M. Bailey. 2010. *Developing Standards-Based Report Cards*. Thousand Oaks, CA: Corbin (SAGE).

Kirr, Joy. 2016. "Introducing Feedback in Lieu of Grading to 7th Graders." *My Own Genius Hour*. September 8. https://geniushour.blogspot.com/2016/09/introducing-feedback-in-lieu-of-grading.html.

APPENDIX 12.1: GRADING INFORMATION FOR ELA CLASS

Dear parents,

I have the pleasure of teaching your child in English Language Arts (ELA) this year. I'm writing to briefly introduce myself, and to introduce a change I have made to our ELA classes the past few years. Please read through this lengthy explanation. When you finish, if you'd like to meet one-on-one to discuss it further, let's set a date and time.

This is my twenty-fourth year of teaching—my seventeenth year teaching in District 25, and my tenth teaching ELA. In addition to my years at TMS, I taught for seven years as a teacher for the deaf and hard-of-hearing. I have tried on many hats at TMS, including yearbook editor, reading specialist, and department head. I am also National Board Certified (renewed in 2016). More information about me and our ELA class can be found at www.scholarsrm239.weebly.com.

In an effort to encourage a more student-centric learning environment and to better replicate an independent learning style encouraging *lifelong* learning, I have implemented a different grading system in your child's ELA class. This will be the third complete year of implementation.

There will be no points assigned to tasks, there will not be individual grades in the online gradebook, and final grades will not be determined by a computer. I will provide ample feedback (much more than typical classes) on coursework, writing prompts, and classroom participation; objective assignments (i.e., multiple-choice reading checks) may include a numeric score, but will not be entered in the gradebook in a way that averages these scores. We will only use the most current evidence of student achievement.

At the end of each quarter, students and I will meet individually and look through their evidence of learning. We will assign a final grade together, and write goals for the next quarter. This process will include considerable reflection, and will help us to focus on achievement. The following categories will be taken into account:

- quality of writing (including grammar),
- performance on reading comprehension checks,
- independent reading at home,
- class participation and preparedness,
- daily engagement in content, and
- the use of feedback to improve performance.

This change was inspired by a number of researchers, who are/were teachers first. I encourage you to watch my video explaining the research and changes to grading in my classroom here: tinyurl.com/Kirr Grading. Consider reading more at tinyurl.com/FeedbackBinder to get a better understanding of why I have made these changes. This system has yielded more authentic, intrinsically motivated learning. One student last year told her mom, "I might not get an A in ELA this year." When asked why, she responded, "Because I'm going to have to actually *learn* something." Using feedback alone deters students from "playing the grading game" at school, helps to take the focus off of a grade that can be very arbitrary and actually *misrepresentative* of what has been learned throughout the year, and helps students focus on *improvement*.

I am thankful for support from our administration and previous parents, and am happy to discuss with you your student's progress or anything happening in our classroom at *any* point during the year. After you've looked through the resources, please contact me via email or phone with *any* questions or concerns. This is a big change for parents and students, and I'd love to continue this conversation, as I'm very passionate about it.

Respectfully,

Mrs. Joy Kirr

"Typical" ELA Grading vs. Feedback System

Similarities

Same assignments as the other ELA class on the team.

All assignments will be in the gradebook.

One to two polished writing pieces will be formally assessed each quarter.

Revisions on writing assignments are encouraged.

Reading comprehension checks may not be redone, as we review them as a class.

Habit/behavior feedback (w/o a grade attached) will be in the comments section of the gradebook.

Differences

Typical	Feedback
Less time-consuming for the teacher.	More time-consuming for the teacher. (Mrs. Kirr believes it's worth it, or she wouldn't try it.)
Less time-consuming for students.	More time-consuming for students, as they look at the feedback comments under each assignment (and many use it to improve).
Grades updated with each assignment—may fluctuate from day to day, depending upon activities included.	Grades not updated—students and parents will need to go a step further into comments section for each assignment and update.
Assignments will have points/grades without feedback in the comments section.	Assignments will not have points/grades—narrative feedback will be in the comments section of each assignment.
Reading: Points on comprehension checks will be averaged. No feedback will be included in the comments section of the gradebook.	Reading: Points on comprehension checks and feedback for improvement will be in the comments section of each assignment and not averaged.

Differences	
Typical	**Feedback**
Writing: Students will receive a grade based on the rubrics we use, and two pieces of feedback will be included in the document itself. Mastery = 100% Proficient = 90% Developing = 75% Needs Improvement = 50%	Writing: Students will receive a link to video feedback of their writing (in the comments section of each assignment and in the document itself).
Grammar in Writing: Students will receive a grade based on the rubrics we use. Mastery = 100% Proficient = 90% Developing = 75% Needs Improvement = 50%	Grammar in Writing: Students will receive grammar feedback in the same fashion as writing feedback (see above).
Grammar: Grades for sporadic grammar checks will be included and averaged. No feedback will be included in the comments section of each assignment.	Grammar: Narrative feedback for sporadic grammar checks will be in the comments section of each assignment.
Final Grade: Will be averaged by a computer.	Final Grade: Will be determined by the student and teacher in 1:1 conference the last week of each term.

Thank you so much for reading this far! If, after watching the video suggested on the first page and discussing it with your child, you and your child do *not* want to be involved in the feedback system, you may, of course, opt out. Please send me an email at jkirr@sd25.org explaining that you would like for me to use "typical" grading with your child, and it will be implemented.

APPENDIX 12.2: END-OF-TERM CONFERENCE

Name: .... Quarter: 1

Evidence of my current **reading** habits and comprehension skills:

I read .... min. on average each night.

I bring my book with me to class . . .

  a. every single day.
  b. most days.
  c. infrequently. (I need to get my book at least two days a week.)
  d. almost never. (I need to go back to my locker often.)

During independent reading time . . .

  a. I never have to be reminded to read. I begin reading right away and read the entire time.
  b. Either I've talked w/ a peer or something else has distracted me once or twice.
  c. I've been asked to read, be quiet, or move away from distractions a few times.

I've completed .... books during the past seven weeks.

When asked to write in response to my reading, here's my current effort:

Needs Improvement: You barely write in your notebook / off-topic.	**Developing:** You write in your notebook infrequently. You write one sentence most days. You are off-topic some days.	**Proficient:** You write in your notebook regularly and on topic. You write two or more sentences every day. Ideas are developing.	**Mastery:** You write in your notebook consistently and on topic. You write at least one developed paragraph every day.

My comprehension checks average to .... % literal and
.... % inferential.

Notes about comprehension checks: ....

Evidence of my current **writing** habits:

Focus

Needs Improvement:	**Developing:**	**Proficient:**	**Mastery:**
Almost every sentence raises a new topic or describes a different moment. There is no underlying emotion or idea to connect the moments.	Some sentences refer to the same moment, or are smoothly connected because they all focus on the same underlying idea or emotion.	Most sentences refer to the same moment, or are smoothly connected because they all focus on the same underlying idea or emotion.	Almost all sentences refer to the same moment, or are smoothly connected because they all focus on the same underlying idea or emotion.

Showing

Needs Improvement:	**Developing:**	**Proficient:**	**Mastery:**
No use of strong verbs, sensory details, or unique observations to create a vivid picture in the reader's mind. Slow-Mo and/or dialogue is missing.	Very little use of strong verbs, sensory details, and unique observations to create a vivid picture in the reader's mind. Slow-Mo and/or dialogue is attempted.	Some use of strong verbs, sensory details, and unique observations to create a vivid picture in the reader's mind. Slow-Mo and/or dialogue effectively develops the plot and/or character.	Effective use of strong verbs, sensory details, and unique observations to create a vivid picture in the reader's mind. Slow-Mo and/or dialogue effectively develops the plot and character.

Grammar and Conventions

Needs Improvement:	**Developing:**	**Proficient:**	**Mastery:**
There are multiple distracting errors in grammar and usage that often impede understanding.	There are multiple distracting errors in grammar and usage that occasionally impede understanding.	There are a couple of distracting errors in grammar and usage, but meaning is clear.	Meaning is clear throughout the piece. This is ready to publish!

I currently practice these habits in ELA (circle any that apply):

perseverance	**optimism**	**self-control**	**courage**	**curiosity**
I stick with things, even if they're difficult.	I have a positive attitude.	I can control my silliness or blurting out.	I participate and/or share my ideas.	I ask questions.

The saying goes that goals not written down are just wishes—and are likely to stay that way. Recent studies have backed up this theory when they showed students who wrote down their goals were more likely to achieve success.

My grade: .... This grade is based on the evidence provided, and was decided after having a discussion about the evidence with my ELA teacher on ....

Goals for Next Quarter
Goals can be based on the evidence provided on the other side of this report, or on comments chosen from the comment list on the next page.

My plan to improve my skills further:

....

....

....

....

.... I should be able to reach these goals by the end of next quarter.

....

Signature   Date

Teacher Notes:

....

....

....

....

Chapter 13

———

WILE E. COYOTE, THE HERO OF UNGRADING

John Warner

———

I would think of them as the "lost" weekends, the six or seven spots during the semester when I would take in an assignment on a Thursday and need to have them graded by the next Tuesday. Depending on the semester and the stop along the road in my career, this meant between a low of 60 and a high of 120 pieces of student writing to read, provide marginal comments on, write a concluding summary for, and issue a numerical grade.

There is a lot of advice in this book about how to ungrade your classes, as well as arguments for how and why ungrading will benefit your students, but I want to write about how and why ungrading will benefit the instructor, particularly the overburdened instructor, the never-enough-time instructor.

The instructor I spent my entire time being as contingent faculty at four different institutions over the course of seventeen years.

At the start of the lost weekend, I would try to set a quota—eighty essays over Friday, Saturday, Sunday, Monday meant *only* twenty per day—totally doable. Of course because contingent faculty positions often pay less than a necessary wage, I filled my time with nonteaching work writing and editing to bolster my income. Having time to respond to twenty essays on a Friday when other work called for my attention that day was a pipe dream.

I'd be lucky to do ten.

This is when I'd start to do the more detailed math: seventy essays over three days at fifteen minutes per essay (a pretty good clip) adds up to seventeen-and-a-half hours of grading, which is a lot, but okay. Six hours or so per day. Sure, that's a huge chunk of my Saturday and Sunday, but it's not the *whole* day.

Right?

Except keeping up the four essays per hour pace isn't sustainable for hours at a time. Sometimes a particular essay requires extra attention. Sometimes you just need a break. Sometimes the word-processing program you use to make digital marginal comments will crash midway, requiring a restart and a ninety-second period where you pray that AutoSave captured your work.

It didn't. Do you pound the desk in frustration, startling the dogs? Does your family know when it's a grading weekend because you're a misery to be around? Does knowing you have a pile of work to grade affect what you choose to say yes to? When you say yes to something that sounded fun, is it significantly less fun as you contemplate the grading you've left undone?

Does even 80 essays seem like not so many because sometimes it's 100 or 120 or 140?

Grading becomes something one simply tries to get through. I decreased the burden in literature classes by assigning four essays a semester, but dropping the lowest grade, in the hope students would take advantage of not having to turn in a paper at all.

This felt crappy, but I knew students wouldn't complain about such a policy in a gabillion years provided I gave out a generous share of B+'s, the mark that says, "If you don't bother me, kid, I won't bother you."

I would craft template responses and assign them macros in Microsoft Word, pulling them off the digital shelf and inserting them into student work. If an essay was seriously off the rails, I would stop reading it at some point, assign the letter, summarize what I saw in the wreckage following the derailment, and move on, relieved of the burden of response but simultaneously aware I was denying a student something they could reflect on and then build upon. I no longer teach full time, and yet I can conjure the angst I experienced in having to employ these strategies by merely typing these sentences.

Grading was something to be managed, something to be survived. It was the worst part of the job, often the only truly bad part of the job, but it was just one of those things you had to do, right?

But why was I doing it? Years earlier, after reading Ken Bain's *What the Best College Teachers Do*, I asked the same question of my attendance policies. Every absence over four class periods (on a Tuesday/Thursday schedule) during the semester would result in a one-third-of-a-letter-grade deduction on the final mark, no exceptions, I mean it now, don't you test me.

I meant it, I suppose, but I never really *believed* it. I'd been a serial class skipper as an undergraduate myself, and managed to do just fine with deciding when a class was or was not useful to achieving my educational goals. I especially didn't believe in my own policy when, halfway through the semester, I'd look up and see an empty seat and see that a student was flirting with the limit, and didn't they realize they were going to make me dock their grade, that I didn't want to do it, but for the sake of fairness and in their own best interests I'd have to?

Don't you test me.

Why did I have a knot in my stomach over enforcing my own attendance policy? Why would I then spend ten minutes preaching to the choir of students present in class about the necessity of attendance?

Late in the semester, I would see not empty seats necessarily, but absent minds, students present in body and little else. Often these students were visibly ill, red-eyed and snuffling, sometimes even sleeping through class not out of lassitude but virus-induced exhaustion, and I would try to convince myself that at least they were there, as though that mattered.

As I snuffled myself through one of my lost weekends of grading, Kleenex shoved up my nose to stop the dripping, I would curse them and their germs.

Why was I doing it? My attendance policy was part of what I call teaching "folklore," the practices handed down instructor to instructor. I was doing what had been done unto me, no matter whether I thought it was effective. Class was important; students won't come to class if you don't punish excessive absence; therefore, absence must be punished.

Except, reading *What the Best Teachers Do* not long after it was published, I found that these best teachers do not have mandatory attendance policies. They concentrate much more on making sure class is not only worth attending but also vital to the learning process. Students both *want* and *need* to come to class. Attendance takes care of itself.

I already strived to meet the want-and-need bar with my class periods, so what was stopping me from committing to my values, other than some folklore I'd never been too sure about to begin with anyway?

I dropped my attendance policy the next semester and never looked back, except that I did keep track to see how it affected attendance.

It went up slightly. It went up for a couple reasons, I believe. It went up because saying you can miss four classes without penalty essentially signals to students that it's okay to miss class, as long as you don't miss more than four. My instructor authority was used against me. "Prof says we can miss four classes, so I'm going to miss four classes."

When absences were not explicitly punished, I was signaling that, indeed, every class mattered and students needed to make a choice consistent with *their* goals and desires, not mine. Dropping attendance increased the rigor of the course by forcing students to make affirmative decisions, rather than outsourcing them to me and my perceived authority.

Best of all, I had no more anxiety about enforcing a system, which I never believed in, on students I thought should instead be treated like the autonomous adults they are. Win-win.

I wish I can say I jumped into alternative grading with the same confidence and gusto, that having been bolstered by my experience with dropping my attendance requirement, I instantly ditched the folklore attached to grading and bounded into the verdant fields of this brave new world.

I did not.

WILE E. COYOTE: HERO

Ungrading is a leap of faith, and there is no guarantee that after the leap, you won't go splat, no matter the amount of preparation, enthusiasm, and confidence you bring to the task. Here I am thinking of Wile E. Coyote chasing the Road Runner off a cliff, successfully running twelve feet from the edge before realizing he is actually bound by the laws of gravity.

Splat!

Even as a child, I had great sympathy for Wile E. Coyote. He is a creature merely pursuing his biological imperative of catching his prey. Wile E. Coyote is a source of additional pathos in that he has been consigned to a landscape in which his prey is the fastest, cleverest roadrunner in history. Surely he could catch even an average roadrunner, but this is not Wile E. Coyote's lot in life.

Even worse, his prey is an asshole who seems to take active pleasure in whatever misfortunes befall Mr. Coyote, his *beep-beep* a taunt, ringing across the desert landscape.

Despite his eternal haplessness, Wile E. Coyote is not a terrible model for thinking about how we should approach any pedagogical experiment, including ungrading or alternative grading.

The most notable aspect of Mr. Coyote is undoubtedly his resilience. Even when he straps his Acme roller skates to his feet, and the Acme rocket powering his pursuit of the Road Runner to his back, only to have the rocket explode upon lighting it, singeing all the fur from his body, his ears dissolving entirely into dust, we see him in the next scene, unbowed in pursuit of his goal of at last catching that stupid bird.

Wile E. Coyote is a planner, an iterator, each failed initiative giving rise to the next. His plans are often quite sound in concept. Why shouldn't painting a black arch on the side of a cliff, simulating a tunnel, cause the Road Runner to smack into the rock face, stunning him sufficiently for Wile E. Coyote to seize his prey?

How could Wile E. Coyote possibly have known that through some kind of necromancy, the Road Runner is capable of making the fake tunnel opening real (for himself), only to have the rock face return to stone while Wile E. Coyote continues his pursuit?

This is quite literally unforeseeable, a defying of all that was previously known about the rules of the physical world, and yet it is Wile E. Coyote who must pay the full brunt of the price.

Lastly, Wile E. Coyote commits fully to his plan. There are no half measures for Mr. Coyote, no dipping his toe in the water and seeing how it goes. Wile E. Coyote sees that if we want to achieve the ultimate prize, we must commit fully, even as history indicates this may not be sufficient.

As much fun as I'm having with my analogy, I will now make the message clear. Perfection in teaching is the Road Runner. We are never going to catch it. We need not be as pathetic as Wile E. Coyote in his failures, but we must vow to be as dogged in pursuit of our mission. Embracing this reality is not only a key to having success in making such a radical shift but also the key to not losing control of your emotional experience of the world as you make that shift.

There may be many forces stacked against maintaining the spirit of Wile E. Coyote as you ungrade. The Road Runner cartoons lose their comic potency when or if we sympathize with Mr. Coyote. We are meant to know he is a fool, his errand impossible, and the fool deserves to be scorned. Depending on where you teach, the culture in which you work, it is possible you will be looked on as a fool. One of the advantages of being a lifetime contingent instructor was my ability to go largely unnoticed in my work. I often did things that, in hindsight, might have caused turbulence if they had needed explanation and justification in a tenure dossier.

(Let us pause for a moment to note the irony that as a contingent/adjunct instructor I had far more freedom to experiment in my pedagogical practices than the average assistant professor.)

Even with my relative freedom, it took connecting via social media with many of the folks you're reading in this book to muster the courage to make my initial attempts at ungrading. I had to know I wasn't entirely alone, at least spiritually.

If one is being evaluated for tenure, the incentive to go along to get along is strong, and to appear to be a fool of the Wile E. Coyote variety could be fatal to one's career. Even if there is some support among some of your colleagues, it may take only a small handful to cast doubt. No one is ever punished for sticking with the default.

Students may also think you're being foolish. In some cases they are cynics (for good reason), believing that anyone who tries to mess with the game of school is a dreamer with stars in their eyes. More often, in my experience, they are merely comfortable with the systems to which they have become accustomed. They do not necessarily care for these systems, and can articulate many ways in which grading is unfair or confusing and definitely not linked to learning, but what kind of fool thinks school has anything to do with learning?

Others have simply figured out how to play in the system they're used to, and any upset to that system is unwelcome.

We're here to perform man, not learn!

I wish I could report that I tackled changing my grading policies with the commitment of Wile E. Coyote, but I did not.

I was timid, cowed in the face of the teaching folklore around grades, worried about deviating from the default. Even though I was 100 percent convinced the grading folklore was 100 percent BS, I could not commit to the idea that someone like me—a contingent instructor without a credential in teaching writing, armed only with my experiences, my wits, and a bunch of reading—could possibly undo generations of practices.

I talked myself out of success even before I started.

In hindsight my approach embodied some of the worst of Wile E. Coyote's plans, overelaborate schemes with too many moving parts and a variety of components.

Following in the wake of Asao Inoue's "labor-based" grading contracts, I adopted a grading contract that attempted to value *how much* students did during the semester.[1] The more writing, more class-related work, more revision and reflection, the better the grade. It used an elaborate point system where everyone started with a B and could then rise or fall on the grading ladder depending on how much they were completing.

It took half a class period to introduce the system, and numerous reminders of how it worked every step of the way for the rest of the semester. Students never fully grokked it. I'm not sure I did either.

Worse, while I eliminated letter grades, I instituted a proficiency scale where "proficient" was neutral in terms of points, "above proficient" advanced students up the grade ladder, and "below proficient" sent them down a rung or two.

In my head it made sense. I was introducing something new while giving students the comfort of the old. Without going into too much unnecessary (and frankly humiliating) detail, I'd worked out the system so a student could earn an A either (a) by doing all of the "extra" writing assignments, demonstrating their commitment to doing more, or (b) by scoring above proficient on all of the major assignments, demonstrating their competence.

In practice it did not go as badly as I am making it sound, but I spent the bulk of the semester disappointed in my failure of nerve, and students were the first to identify the mismatch between what I claimed to value and my stupid proficiency scale. I was trying to foster a culture of intrinsic motivation around writing while using a metaphor of a grade ladder one had to climb.

WTF? As the kids used to say (maybe they still do).

That proficiency scale; what was I thinking? I am no fan of proficiency or competency as animating values in the classroom, never have been. Proficiency is too low a bar, and an uninspiring one to attempt to jump over to boot. Proficiency is a lousy way to help people learn in ways that resonate beyond the immediate assessment.

"But," people ask me, "don't you want to make sure your doctor is proficient?"

"Heck no!" I reply. I want my doctor so far beyond proficient that proficiency can't even be seen in the rearview mirror. I don't want my doctor even flirting with proficiency, let alone settling down with it for the duration of their career. I want my doctor obsessed with being the best doctor possible on a day-to-day, moment-to-moment basis. I want my doctor inhabiting their "practice"—the skills, attitudes, knowledge, and habits of mind of doctors—as though it is a second skin.

I want students seeking this same state as writers, which is why I frame learning to write around developing "the writer's practice": the skills, attitudes, knowledge, and habits of mind of writers. To settle for proficiency is to focus only on one aspect of one's practice, the skills. Often, in classrooms subject to top-down administrative diktats, the pursuit of proving proficiency in those skills actively stamps out any attention to other aspects of the practice. Even worse, students are often incentivized to produce what I call writing-related simulations, highly prescriptive exercises that allow us to pretend students are learning something, but once the students are asked to work without the prescriptions, everything seems to fall apart.

Doctors are significantly motivated by attitudes that invoke values like caring for others, a sentiment embodied in their professional oath. In writing I value attitudes like curiosity, thoroughness, and fairness, none of which directly deal with skills associated with proficiency. Yet if those values are attended to while practicing one's writing practice, my belief is those skills will develop far beyond what is possible when aiming for mere proficiency, or its close cousin, competency.

If there is no terminal proficiency in writing—and I know this to be true from my own experience—why would I pretend such a thing is true for students? I want my class to be a launchpad for the writing challenges students will face in school and beyond, not a terminal where they are stamped "proficient" and I pretend as though that's a worthy goal.

I have spent the intervening years trying to fully understand the roots of my mistake, and I have come to the following conclusion: I am human.

I am human, students are human, and no matter how noble our intentions, no matter how thorough our preparations, we cannot guard against our own humanity and its penchant to cause us to do the wrong thing. My desire to give students something familiar while introducing them to something new and strange was well intentioned. It was also a mistake.

NO, REALLY, IT GETS BETTER

I realize that at the outset I promised to tell you how ungrading your class will benefit you as an instructor, but I have spent the bulk of this essay describing how you are likely to be burnt, blown up, flattened, or possibly even compressed into an accordion-like shape, causing you to make a faintly musical wheezing sound as you walk.[2]

Still, some other things we must cover before we get to the good part.

I cannot promise that ungrading will lead to less work. It did not in my experience.

I cannot promise that students will greet your ungrading as though they have been liberated from tyranny, throwing ropes around the statuary of traditional grading, pulling them off their pedestals, and dragging them through the square as they shout your name in hosannas. While some students do respond this way, others may be resistant throughout, and this resistance may even show up in your teaching evaluations.[3]

Depending on your teaching load, you still may have those weekends where you spend a huge chunk of your time responding to student writing.

But here is the difference: no longer will those weekends feel lost. They will instead feel like a vital part of your pedagogy, not the bitter pill you must swallow, over and over, in order to get to the good stuff.

Several things changed for me once I fully embraced ungrading.

For one, while I was still reading everything students completed, I was not necessarily scoring it against a grading scale, which allowed me to better appreciate what students had accomplished in their writing, rather than feeling honor bound to pick out and remedy their defects. This is simply a more pleasurable reading experience.

Two, the ratio of my summative to formative feedback changed almost instantly from 50/50 to 2/98. I'd always been a big believer in formative feedback, believing the highest purpose for my comments was to help students diagnose what may have gone awry in order to remedy the issue in future writing, but when giving grades, I felt it necessary to justify the letter or number. And let's be honest, if you are giving out letters and numbers and not telling students how you arrived at this judgment, a ball is being dropped.

Three, while the total time I spent reading student writing didn't drop appreciably, I found that I approached the pile of student writing not with dread but with curiosity. Rather than asking, "What have they done?" I was focused on "What are they doing?"

I believe this distinction is important. The first question is retrospective, suggesting that whatever has happened is fixed in place and, let's face it, is likely to be a disappointment. The latter question is forward looking, an eye toward what's coming next. Quite simply the reading and responding to student writing felt less like a distasteful chore to get through in order to enjoy the good parts of teaching. Instead I experienced my responding to student writing as one of the high callings of my personal pedagogy.

Here is where I could do the kind of work I'm uniquely positioned to do—read and respond to student writing while helping them realize their potential as writers. This is an expertise that cannot be done by just anyone or anything, like a computer algorithm. Grading became no different from how I would treat the professional writers I worked with in editing McSweeney's Internet Tendency for many years, where my goal was to help them maximize the effectiveness of their piece, in that case, to make the writing as funny as possible.

Rather than having an attitude oriented around statements like "Look what you've done," I was focused on "What is it you're trying to do?" Agency transferred from me as the instructor back to the students, who would have to clarify—to themselves above all—why they'd made a specific writing choice in the context of what they were trying to achieve.

It was a great weight lifted. I don't know what to say other than my mood improved because I was doing the work not of a writing evaluator but of a writing teacher. The quality of my assignments improved as I strived to give students experiences worthy of their time and effort, challenging tasks written for authentic audiences.

Please don't read this as a suggestion that I finally caught the Road Runner and was enjoying a nice meal of a drumstick roasted over a slow fire. Some students will continue to resist this shift, quite possibly for the entire duration of the class. Student writing doesn't instantly turn into something other than what it is, the work of apprentices often in the early stages of their journey. In fact a less prescriptive process sometimes resulted in some very confusing and confounding work indeed. Every semester revealed some aspect of my approach to course and assignment structure and feedback that could be improved.

There will always be frustrations because teaching and learning is a human endeavor, and as stipulated previously, I am human.

In the end the benefits of the change were not so much practical—though they were very real—but spiritual. Similar to changing my attendance policy, ungrading became a truer expression of my pedagogical and life values. I was at last walking my walk, and before the change I did not fully appreciate the emotional toll of adhering to a set of practices that were not reflective of what I believed to be true or important.

I also noticed that having taken on the teaching folklore regarding attendance and grading, I felt empowered to question all aspects of the folklore. Why am I assigning a research paper even though it's always a disappointment? Why do I care whether students use MLA formatting correctly down to the last parenthesis and comma? (I don't.)

Why should I worry about first-year writing as a course meant to prepare students for the rest of college? Why can't I have autonomy over what *I* think students should experience?

Having felled a couple of sacred cows, I soon found myself knee-deep in entrails as I also took on how the five-paragraph essay hinders student progress, how I believe the fundamental unit of writing is not the sentence but the idea, how the labor structures of academia are likely the biggest barrier when it comes to improving writing instruction, and all kinds of other things that had always bothered me but I didn't realize I had the standing to take on.[4]

Fully drunk on my new knowledge, feeling as though I was just approaching the height of my teaching powers, I made one final discovery: I could no longer teach full time as a contingent instructor.[5] In fact I might've been done teaching in a higher education context altogether.[6]

It was a terrible paradox to recognize that I could not reconcile the conditions under which I was working with the work I believed to be so important, but having opened the floodgates of questioning the folklore, having felt as though I'd made myself into a highly effective instructor working in ways consistent with my values, I couldn't manage to reconcile my second-class status with those values.

For sure, external events played a role in this as well. I had applied for a tenure-track position as an internal candidate at College of Charleston and not gotten the job. The visiting position I thought I'd held contentedly for four years suddenly seemed not so satisfactory. The writing that had resulted from taking on the teaching folklore seemed to hold potential for changing my professional trajectory as a public voice on issues of writing pedagogy. Perhaps it was time for a change.

Mostly, though, I recognized how the work of teaching as contingent faculty was inconsistent with my values, and that disconnect was going to result in me resenting the work I felt was more important than anything else I had done or will do. Does this mean I held teaching sacred in a way that goes beyond good sense? Quite possibly, but the feelings were sincerely held, and I was no longer in a position to deny them.

I do not mean to suggest that others who work under the circumstances I once labored under should be required to make the same choice, and here I must acknowledge how fortunate I was to be able to make that choice. My extracurricular writing and editing (and my wife's career) had already been financially subsidizing my teaching "habit" for years. I had the freedom and slack to make a choice that was consistent with my values. Far too many of those laboring inside our educational institutions do not have this same freedom.

If anything, my experience had only further radicalized me on this front, but this is a topic for a different essay, a different book.

Ungrading my courses was one of the most important steps I've ever taken. It was liberating in all senses of the word. It fulfilled a previously obscured lifelong goal of teaching in a way that was consistent with my values. It also revealed the ways the status I'd been afforded by the higher education institutions in which I worked could not be reconciled with my values.

The whole process was difficult, emotionally fraught, and often frustrating. I went *splat* many times. I'm pretty sure a rocket exploded in my face at least once, and the wheels flew off my roller skates sending my legs in opposite directions in a manner defying physical anatomy. And even though I have come out the other side looking objectively successful, with two books and a lucrative career outside of academia underway, I am often plagued with doubt that leaving full-time teaching was the right thing.[7]

But I wouldn't, and couldn't, change a thing.

NOTES

1. Inoue 2019.
2. That reference belongs to Ian Frazier's masterful "Coyote v. Acme" which is truly LOL funny.

3. "Warner thinks his grading stuff is cool, but it's just confusing."
4. All apologies for the extended metaphor, but I'm frankly committed at this point.
5. I am surprised this essay went here. It was not my intention, but one of the things I preach to students is that writing involves the process of discovery, and I think being asked to write about my experiences with ungrading for this volume has unearthed some connections I was not ready to grapple with at that time.
6. This turns out not to have been true. In fall 2019 I taught a first-year experience course focused on humorous writing. I was overjoyed to be back in the classroom, and hope to make teaching the first-year experience a regular staple of my life.
7. I am a senior analyst and communication strategist for Willow Research of Chicago, Illinois.

SOURCES

Bain, Ken. 2004. *What the Best College Teachers Do.* Cambridge, MA: Harvard University Press.

Frazier, Ian. 1990. "Coyote v. Acme." *The New Yorker.* February 26. https://www.newyorker.com/magazine/1990/02/26/coyote-v-acme.

Inoue, Asao B. 2019. *Labor-Based Grading Contracts: Building Equity and Inclusion in the Compassionate Writing Classroom.* Fort Collins, CO: WAC Clearinghouse and University Press of Colorado. https://wac.colostate.edu/books/perspectives/labor/.

Conclusion

———

NOT SIMPLE BUT ESSENTIAL

Susan D. Blum

———

You have read the baker's dozen of approaches to ungrading, with very honest and sometimes emotional accounts of each educator's own experience and the reasoning that led them to embark on the ungrading journey. You've read about our failures too. (We believe that failures contribute to learning—ours and our students'.) We do not have all the answers; any approach to something as complex as human learning—emphasis on *human*—must accept that unlike factory products, humans bring multiple and often unpredictable dimensions to the adventure of learning in institutions of secondary and higher education. Any classroom—face-to-face or virtual—has both foreseeable aspects and completely magical alchemy, that mysterious mix of the students, teachers, classroom, time of day, subject matter, season, and more that makes each course its own unreplicable experience. We've tried to be clear about what has been consistently successful and what still requires tweaking.

Though ungrading isn't necessarily a time-saving approach, nor does it emphasize efficiency, it does tend to lead to both greater learning and more positive relationships. Nobody pretends it's simple, especially at first. But all agree it is worth it. As bell hooks put it so forcefully in her essential book *Teaching to Transgress: Education as the Practice of Freedom*, "The classroom remains the most radical space of possibility in the academy." She urges us to "think and rethink, so that we can create new visions," and in so doing, make "education the practice of freedom."[1]

RISKS

Educational experimentation has been generated from both elite or advantaged positions—think of the Chicago Lab School begun by Dewey or Brown University—and from people working among groups in poverty: from Maria Montessori to Paulo Freire, generator of liberatory pedagogy (*Pedagogy of the Oppressed*) who worked among nonliterate Brazilian laborers, and from Herbert Kohl to Christopher Emdin.[2] But only certain teachers feel themselves secure enough professionally to take these risks. Secondary school teachers may have an administrator urging them to adopt new practices or one who is skeptical of them. In higher ed, it is usually individual faculty who embark on these changes, sometimes supported and sometimes resisted by administrators.

The advantage of tenure—which some of the authors enjoy—is that we lucky (and diminishing) few have some protection against unpopular speech.[3] I have nonetheless been nervous. The first semester I went full-out ungrading, I essentially held my breath for four months, worried that something terrible might happen. And I'm a full professor, white, neurotypical, cisgender, straight, a native speaker of English, and citizen, at a private university with every possible advantage. I had research to back up my methods. And I had Starr Sacktein's book *Hacking Assessment: 10 Ways to Go Gradeless in a Traditional Grades School* to wave in the air, like Mao's *Little Red Book*, at the enforcers coming to arrest me for violating expectations. Still I was worried, deeply worried.

But it was worth it, and transformed my teaching fundamentally. In fact this is the experience of every person writing in this book.

OBSTACLES, OBJECTIONS, AND CHALLENGES

It is not all sweetness and light when we attempt to change something as apparently timeless as the assessments in our classrooms. Obstacles and objections—many of them discussed in the book's chapters—are numerous.

One objection to the decrease of a focus on grades, or to total elimination of them, stems from the utility of grades to sort and rank students, for the convenience of employers and admissions committees, and sometimes for practices such as selecting valedictorians or awarding fellowships. Despite these fears, moving to the next level of employment or schooling has been less of a challenge than expected. At the secondary level, the Mastery Transcript Consortium is attempting to create a legible set of nongraded rubrics that will facilitate college admission.[4] Colleges like Hampshire and Evergreen State have been quite successful in placing their graduates in graduate and professional programs.

Some argue—and here I am sympathetic—that grading diminishes the potential for bias. Sometimes, the argument goes, a less advantaged student will stand out because of high grades just as much as already advantaged students, who tend to have higher scores and more polished self-presentation simply because they can avail themselves of tutors and other forms of cultural capital. (That presumes, though, that grades are meaningful and consistent—something the research shows is not the case.)[5] The possibility that grades provide greater justice is one I take very seriously, that grades provide a way to communicate students' accomplishments, especially if they lack the cultural and social capital that allows them to promote their own achievement. However, given what we know about the inconsistency of grades, perhaps faith in this approach is unwarranted.

Beginning to ungrade is not an easy undertaking; challenges are many. One significant challenge is the time required to communicate richly to every student. But if we cannot, because of overwork, engage with students to communicate their strengths and challenges, then what is the point of the entire system? Surely meaningful educational experiences are the true goal?

FUTURE RESEARCH

This book does not exhaust all possible considerations and questions. (Since I issued the first invitations to contributors, I've learned of many more educators at all levels of schooling who engage in ungrading and are entirely gradeless. I wish I could have included them all—and had a thousand-page tome with true physical heft.)

There are several topics that deserve additional research. Preliminary comments follow each.

Scale

Riesbeck reports that he has nearly always taught classes with fifty to one hundred students, with no teaching assistant, but given his technological systems, he is able to give feedback at scale. Some advocates of ungrading, such as Stommel, suggest having some assignments that aren't graded at all. Why must everything be graded? Students may be responsible to peers rather than to a teacher. But the scale of higher education is a genuine consideration. If there are suboptimal class sizes, those charged with creating successful learning conditions—administrators, trustees—must take this into account.

Subject: STEM versus Non-STEM

It is no accident that many advocates of ungrading work in fields such as writing or humanities, where there tends to be more flexibility. But as the chapters by Riesbeck, Chu, and Sorensen-Unruh demonstrate, there are possible methods for either complete or partial ungrading that people teaching STEM subjects can employ. In "real-world" practices outside school, such as engineering, singular right answers are few. Preparing students to face the nuances of ambiguity is not irresponsible; it may, in fact, be exactly what students need if one of the goals of schooling is work preparation. Experiments with clickers, think-pair-share, and many innovations in math, chemistry, physics, and other subjects are abundant and deemphasize grading.

Sequences or Group Curricula, or Required Courses

This is a larger subject, but how "gen eds" or sequential courses play out in students' education intersects with methods of assessing and with motivation. Some initial findings point to improved learning, as the chapters have shown, but how do these findings vary when ungrading in electives is compared with ungrading in required courses? How does motivation change if students are not interested at all? Could this be positive? Some comparison between the same course taught graded and ungraded would be helpful—but faculty who have embraced ungrading would be loath to teach with conventional grading, and different instructors aren't exactly comparable.

Student Reactions

Given students' backgrounds, some—often the highest achieving—may respond with dismay when their familiar benchmarks are removed. Others will be relieved. Some find lack of numbers the opposite of transparent. "How am I doing?" may be legible only through familiar metrics.

Diverse Academic and Social Backgrounds

One of the greatest challenges in contemporary education is how to foster equity—not necessarily equality or uniformity—among ever more diverse student populations. Given different backgrounds, they may require different kinds of feedback—adding to the mandate that educators' educational practices occur in conversation with participating students. This mandate makes generic practices untenable. To the extent that learning in schools involves relationships, they must be remade with each new cohort.

Time to Revamp One's Teaching

If new pedagogical practices are found to improve student learning, how are overburdened faculty to find the time and support to rethink their own teaching? Sabbaticals for research are relatively familiar, if precious and diminishing; sabbaticals for teaching are rare. But it may take months, years, of careful planning and experimentation to eliminate old practices and incorporate new ones, with guidance from mentors and the scholarship of teaching and learning. But with increasingly casualized employment for faculty, the burden falls entirely to motivated individual faculty to undertake this transformation. However, it may be that new faculty are much more drawn to ungrading and may have less unlearning to do. (In my own department, several recently finished doctoral students have come to ungrading on their own, often discouraged by senior faculty.)

Student-Faculty Relationships

We often speak as if there is a single relationship between faculty and students, but there are many models. One shorthand has "sage on the stage" versus "guide on the side," but there are many others: mentor, coach, expert. How much of an authority should the instructor be? How much of knowledge is fixed, known once and for all? Therese Huston advocates in her book *Teaching What You Don't Know* against faculty always taking an expert position—an appeal for modeling *learning*, rather than modeling *already-knowing*.[6] Students may desire to be told whether something is good enough, but there is also an argument for students figuring out what standards apply, and understanding why, rather than simply reacting passively to a preset list of requirements that appear arbitrary.

The Connection between Assessment and Learning

One of the possible subtitles I thought might work for this book is "assessment for learning." What are the relationships between assessment and learning, and what measures aside from testing and giving grades are there? Feedback is a form of conveying assessment, which is more informative than a simple score. Must all assessment be formal?

ISOLATED NO MORE: COOPERATION AMONG TEACHERS

I had not necessarily realized how difficult it was—mostly in terms of morale—to be the only person I knew in higher ed undertaking this fundamental change in pedagogy until I had company. This is not my challenge alone. An article about critical pedagogy puts it clearly: "There are several challenges to maintaining a dedication to critical pedagogy, whether one teaches in K–12 or postsecondary educational settings. A major challenge is isolation. Even if one is able to work within a program that shares one's values, that program is often philosophically and sometimes physically separated from the rest of the school or university."[7]

But the risks are not uniform: "Having full time faculty take the lead [in a certain project] was strategic because they were the least vulnerable among the group members and instrumental for advancing the vision of the new curricular and pedagogical approaches."[8]

It is not merely that full-time, tenured faculty are more able to take risks. It is also that college faculty generally have more time available for research and writing than K–12 faculty.

Yet K–12 and higher education educators rarely speak to each other.

The line between K–12 and higher education was created in the early twentieth century when colleges and high schools competed for the same students; age was not the determining factor.[9] The Carnegie Foundation aimed to create a "standardized, vertically integrated, and rationally planned" system without the chaotic, decentralized, unsystematic realities where there was no clear differentiation between different levels of schools—something that has been so thoroughly transformed in a mere century that we cannot imagine that high schools and colleges were essentially two different ways of preparing young people for life in trades or professions, or for class reproduction. The Carnegie Foundation, the National Education Association, and the College Entrance Examination Board together then created something called the "Carnegie unit"—a quarter of instructional time during an academic year. In order for a college to qualify for a very desirable Carnegie pension, it had to require fourteen Carnegie units of secondary school for admission. Thus the Carnegie Foundation—a private foundation that helped shape national public schooling—"established for the first time a clear and hierarchical relation between secondary and higher education and at the same time established a unit of educational progress defined by student seat time rather than a demonstration of content mastery."[10] Interestingly the line between secondary and higher education is blurring slightly in the twenty-first century, reverting to the predifferentiated era with increased calls for "early college" and simultaneous college and high school credit ("dual enrollment") for highly ambitious students—or those wishing to save money on required classes in college.

Yet whatever the historical contingencies that have brought us our relatively recent educational system, all formal education shares the basic question of how to create optimal conditions for learning. If we are concerned about how people learn—see Eyler's *How Humans Learn* and the National Academies' *How People Learn II: Learners, Contexts, and Cultures*—then insights from one setting might have relevance for another setting.[11]

Further, most of the pioneering work on ungrading has been done by teachers in and researchers of K–12 classrooms. Also K–12 teachers are trained in pedagogy (which is often disparaged as unintellectual [hah!]).

Their thinking is informed not only by their own experience but also through engagement with principles of educational psychology. Faculty in higher ed usually make it up as we go, possibly reading a little about pedagogy and sometimes forced to attend, or sometimes voluntarily attending, workshops on teaching and learning (such as those taught by Joshua Eyler, James Lang, Jesse Stommel, Cathy Davidson, Sarah Rose Cavanagh, Jessamyn Neuhaus, and Laura Gibbs).[12] David Gooblar calls pedagogy training "the missing course" in doctoral programs.[13]

Still there are notable differences. Secondary school teachers have parents as constituents, and earlier levels of schooling have even more parental or familial involvement. In some ways their work is more intimate and holistic than that of university and college faculty, where we generally teach a single course. Despite the helicopter or snowplow parent trope of overinvolved parents, because of FERPA (Family Educational Rights and Privacy Act), student information is protected and adult students' information is generally not discussed even with parents—with some exceptions made for medical or safety emergencies, or for violations of under-twenty-one drinking laws. (For the most part, college students are adults—emerging adults, or sure-enough adults, or what my students call "a grown woman/man."[14] It's important to recall that only about a quarter of college students are "traditional" now: attending straight from high school and aged approximately eighteen to twenty-two. They may or may not live on campus, and may or may not be supported by their families.) Many lower levels of school are accountable to state standards—essentially, statewide learning outcomes. Individual teachers often have little control over their textbooks, assignments, and more. (This is true for higher ed faculty in many contexts as well.) Some classes are part of professionally mandated curricula, and the content is outside the control of the instructor.

But we share the conviction that within the realm of our responsibility, we have an obligation and an opportunity to improve our facilitation of student learning. We hope that by reporting on our separate experiences, our suggestions will be understood not as *the one way* that works for everyone but as a multitude of possible approaches. We recognize the challenges that accompany moving through schooling while keeping our eyes on the prize, the true bottom line: student learning.

There is a growing recognition (a movement, almost, maybe?) that the current models of teaching and assessment often fail. They fail to promote learning. They fail to provide useful feedback. They fail to produce joyous cooperative learning. They fail to produce positive relationships among students, or between students and teachers. They fail to meet the needs of diverse students, and they fail to promote equity.

Alfie Kohn states that when we work in an unjust system, we have to proceed at two levels at once: "You do what you can within the confines of the current structure, trying to minimize its harm. You also work with others to try to change that structure, conscious that nothing dramatic may happen for a very long time."[15] The essence in the meantime, waiting for grades to disappear, is that *"teachers and parents who care about learning need to do everything in their power to help students forget that grades exist."*[16] This does require a revolution, but it also requires daily action.

We offer this book as evidence of several committed teachers who have attempted to work within the current structure, and as a contribution toward the structural change that will make schools about rewarding students with learning.

What did *you* learn today?

NOTES

1. hooks 1994: 12.
2. Emdin 2016; Freire 2005; Kohl 1994.
3. Childress 2019.
4. See the consortium's website: https://mastery.org/.
5. Brookhart, Guskey, Bowers, et al. 2016.
6. Huston 2012.
7. Foley et al. 2015: 124.
8. Foley et al. 2015: 126.
9. Labaree 1997: 114.
10. Labaree 1997: 114.
11. Blum 2019. See Eyler 2018; National Academies of Sciences, Engineering, and Medicine 2018.
12. I'm grateful to an anonymous reviewer for some of these names.
13. Gooblar 2019.
14. See Arnett 2000; Lythcott-Haims 2015.
15. Kohn [1993] 2018: 206.
16. Kohn [1993] 2018: 206. Italics in original.

CITED SOURCES AND FURTHER READING

Arnett, Jeffrey Jensen. 2000. "Emerging Adulthood: A Theory of Development from the Late Teens through the Twenties." *American Psychologist* 55(5): 469–80.

Blum, Susan D. 2019. "Why Don't Anthropologists Care about Learning (or Education or School)? An Immodest Proposal for an Integrative Anthropology of Learning Whose Time Has Finally Come." *American Anthropologist* 121(3): 641–54.

Brookhart, Susan M., Thomas R. Guskey, Alex J. Bowers, et al. 2016. "A Century of Grading Research: Meaning and Value in the Most Common Educational Measure." *Review of Educational Research* 86(4): 803–48. https://doi.org /10.7916/D8NV9JQ0.

Childress, Herb. 2019. *The Adjunct Underclass: How America's Colleges Betrayed Their Faculty, Their Students, and Their Mission*. Chicago: University of Chicago Press.

Emdin, Christopher. 2016. *For White Folks Who Teach in the Hood . . . and the Rest of Y'all Too: Reality Pedagogy and Urban Education*. Boston: Beacon Press.

Eyler, Joshua R. 2018. *How Humans Learn: The Science and Stories behind Effective College Teaching*. Morgantown: West Virginia University Press.

Foley, Jean Ann, Doug Morris, Panayota Gounari, and Faith Agostinone-Wilson. 2015. "Critical Education, Critical Pedagogies, Marxist Education in the United States." *Journal for Critical Education Policy Studies* 13(3): 110–44.

Freire, Paulo. 2005. *Pedagogy of the Oppressed*. Translated by Myra Bergman Ramos. New York: Continuum.

Gooblar, David. 2019. *The Missing Course: Everything They Never Taught You about College Teaching*. Cambridge, MA: Harvard University Press.

hooks, bell. 1994. *Teaching to Transgress: Education as the Practice of Freedom*. New York: Routledge.

Huston, Therese. 2012. *Teaching What You Don't Know*. Cambridge, MA: Harvard University Press.

Kohl, Herbert R. 1994. *I Won't Learn from You: And Other Thoughts on Creative Maladjustment*. New York: New Press.

Kohn, Alfie. [1993] 2018. *Punished by Rewards: The Trouble with Gold Stars, Incentive Plans, A's, Praise, and Other Bribes*. 25th anniversary ed. Boston: Houghton Mifflin.

Labaree, David F. 1997. *How to Succeed in School without Really Learning: The Credentials Race in American Education*. New Haven, CT: Yale University Press.

Lythcott-Haims, Julie. 2015. *How to Raise an Adult: Break Free of the Overparenting Trap and Prepare Your Kid for Success*. New York: St. Martin's Press.

National Academies of Sciences, Engineering, and Medicine. 2018. *How People Learn II: Learners, Contexts, and Cultures*. Washington, DC: The National Academies Press. https://doi.org/10.17226/24783.

ACKNOWLEDGMENTS

This book exists as the result of many people's work, some direct and some indirect. The most obvious gratitude is due to the contributors, all of whom are deeply committed educators who bring scholarship and reflection to their interactions with their students. It has been a delight to work with all of you. Thank you for your initial enthusiastic reactions, your ongoing encouragement, your prompt responses to many rounds of revision, your feedback, and just your general ways of being in the world of schooling with conviction, passion, and compassion. Your support has made a difference both in the production of this book and also in my ongoing efforts to improve my own classroom activities.

My journey into ungrading has several origin stories, but one of them involves my first reading of *Punished by Rewards: The Trouble with Gold Stars, Incentive Plans, A's, Praise, and Other Bribes*, which literally changed my life. The fact that its author, Alfie Kohn, responded immediately to the request to write the foreword and produced his usual dazzling and thought-provoking work feels like I've been the recipient of a bit of magic. Thank you for your words here, your editorial suggestions, and mostly for all that you have done and continue to do to change education on behalf of its actual beneficiaries, in a humane way. I am honored by your serious engagement with the book and am sure that your foreword will itself have a life far into the future.

Other steps on the way to this particular project include my children's experiences in many institutions of education, from the Jewish Community Center preschool and John J. Cory Elementary School in Denver to John Marshall Elementary School and John Adams High School in South Bend, Indiana, and from the Montessori Academy at

Edison Lakes in Mishawaka, Indiana, to Hampshire College, which continues to inspire fresh and deep thinking about education. I am grateful to the educators and administrators who continue to show alternatives to business as usual.

For several years, since the publication of my book *I Love Learning*, I have given talks about pedagogy and learning. Each time I introduced the topic of ungrading, that's all anyone paid attention to or wanted to discuss. I am grateful to the audiences at the Society for Values in Higher Education; the department of anthropology at the University of Notre Dame; Cornell University; the College of the Holy Cross in Worcester, Massachusetts; and Carthage College for pushing the discussion about ungrading. I am grateful to the University of Notre Dame, which has provided a stable and supportive environment for my research and teaching. The indexing for this book is made possible in part by support from the Institute for Scholarship in the Liberal Arts, College of Arts and Letters, University of Notre Dame. Agustín Fuentes did not balk when I waved Starr Sackstein's *Hacking Assessment* in his office, and I thank you for your willingness to tolerate this dangerous experimentation.

I want to thank my colleagues, near and far, and especially my Twitter and Facebook communities, which have demonstrated the positive side of social media connections. Because of the robust, generous spirit of sharing, I was introduced to journalists Colleen Flaherty at *Inside Higher Ed* and especially Beckie Supiano at the *Chronicle of Higher Education*, who wrote a fabulous story about our efforts to produce a more humane form of education, including assessment. Thank you, Beckie, for visiting and thinking through this whole conundrum with your experienced journalist's mind. The Human Restoration Project, led by Chris McNutt and Nick Covington, also showed interest in this, as have Cara Ocobock and Chris Lynn in their podcast, *The Sausage of Science*. The whole WVU Press Teaching and Learning in Higher Education community has been a new family of learners and mentors and partners, and I can't wait to meet you all in person someday. My new "learning team," the group thinking up a Theory of Public Higher Education, has been a group of interlocutors straight out of my dreams. Oscar Fernandez, Mays Imad, Ryan Korstange, Tom Nelson Laird, and Kate Pantelides, plus Eric

Bain-Selbo, you have been the most extraordinary companions on this ongoing journey of ours!

The WVU Press staff have been an absolute and consistent pleasure to work with. From the first contact, when I suggested this book to Derek Krissoff and James Lang, to the appearance of the book you are holding in your hand, I have been treated with nothing but enthusiasm—even though the groundbreaking series on Teaching and Learning in Higher Education that Jim edits had committed from the beginning to avoid publishing edited volumes. Thank you for your willingness to be flexible in the face of an apparent need in the world of education. Charlotte Vester took on the responsibility of masterfully tackling the formatting details for these sixteen items, which was a great relief to me. Sara Georgi copyedited these disparate fragments brilliantly! Thank you, all.

This book is written for the colleagues who suspect there's something wrong with business as usual but aren't quite sure what to do, whether it will work, whether it will be acceptable. I've spoken with some who are intrigued by the prospect of an alternative approach to assessment, including Cara Ocobock, Amanda Cortez, Rieti Gengo, Julia Kowalski, and Marc Kissel. I hope we continue to talk about this in the coming years as well. I invite others to think with us too.

My family, especially Lionel Jensen, Hannah Jensen, Elena and Gerson Coronado-Jensen, listened to me talk about this topic endlessly, and never told me to stop! Baby Estrella so far can only listen, and inspire, but her vulnerability is a reminder that this matters. Thank you for this, and for everything. My extended Blum family and the local Sinai family have also been essential in making me feel connected and rooted.

I especially want to thank my students. You have been subjected to my experiments for the past decade, leading up to my current versions of ungrading. You have been sometimes patient and enthusiastic, on the one hand, and sometimes suspicious and wary, on the other. This has encouraged me and also forced me to improve my methods and to refine my explanations. I hope you find this longer explanation, finally, satisfying. And most of all, I hope future students, in all our classes, will be rewarded by deep and humane experiences of learning. What else are we here for after all?

CONTRIBUTORS

Aaron Blackwelder is a high school English teacher, a Washington State English Teachers Fellow, a Washington State Teacher of the Year nominee, and founder of Teachers Going Gradeless.

Susan D. Blum is a professor of anthropology at the University of Notre Dame. She has been writing books critical of higher education since 2009 (*My Word! Plagiarism and College Culture* and *"I Love Learning; I Hate School": An Anthropology of College*). She's been ungrading since 2016.

Arthur Chiaravalli has taught high school language arts, mathematics, technology, and media arts. He is the cofounder of Teachers Going Gradeless, an international group of educators convinced that teaching and learning is better when we grade less. Arthur serves as house director at Champlain Valley Union High School in Hinesburg, Vermont.

Gary Chu is a high school mathematics teacher in a racially and culturally diverse suburb just outside of Chicago. He is passionate about disrupting the inequities in schools. He's on Twitter at @mrgarychu.

Cathy N. Davidson founded the Futures Initiative at the City University of New York in 2014 and is a distinguished professor at the Graduate Center (CUNY) in the PhD program in English, the MA program in digital humanities, and the MS program in data analysis and visualization. Previously she taught courses in American studies, technology, neuroscience, and the history and future of higher education at Duke University.

Laura Gibbs is an online instructor at the University of Oklahoma, teaching courses for the general education humanities program. She has been ungrading (and teaching online) since 2002.

Christina Katopodis is a Futures Initiative Fellow and PhD candidate in English at the CUNY Graduate Center and a prizewinning adjunct at Hunter College. Her dissertation is titled "Sound Ecologies: Music and Vibration in 19th-Century American Literature." She was awarded the Graduate Center English program's 2019 Diana Colbert Innovative Teaching Prize and the New Media Lab's 2018 Dewey Digital Teaching Award.

Joy Kirr is a teacher of middle schoolers in the northwestern suburbs of Chicago and the author of *Shift This: How to Implement Gradual Changes for Massive Impact in Your Classroom*. She has been shifting teaching since 1995.

Alfie Kohn is the author of fourteen books, including *The Schools Our Children Deserve* and *Punished by Rewards*, as well as hundreds of articles about education and human behavior. He lives (actually) in the Boston area and (virtually) at www.alfiekohn.org.

Christopher Riesbeck is an associate professor of computer science at Northwestern University and codirector of the Center for Computer Science and Learning Sciences. He has been doing critique-driven learning since 1997. He is now working on computer-assisted coaching to help struggling students create artifacts worth critiquing.

Starr Sackstein was a high school English and journalism teacher in New York City public schools for sixteen years and then the director of humanities in West Hempstead schools for two years. She is currently an educational consultant and speaker helping schools build capacity around assessment reform. She has been throwing out grades since 2013.

Marcus Schultz-Bergin is an assistant college lecturer in philosophy at Cleveland State University. As a philosopher and teacher, he regularly questions the dominant assumptions of our education system and seeks innovative ways to enhance student learning. This has included experiments with a variety of grading systems or no grading system at all, as well as experiments with a variety of instructional techniques.

Clarissa Sorensen-Unruh has been full-time chemistry faculty at Central New Mexico Community College since 2002. She is also a PhD student in learning sciences and recently began teaching statistics in addition to chemistry.

Jesse Stommel is cofounder of *Hybrid Pedagogy* and the Digital Pedagogy Lab. He's been teaching in higher education and ungrading since 2001. He has a husband; a rascal pup, Emily; two clever cats, Loki and Odin; and a badass daughter, Hazel. He's on Twitter at @Jessifer.

John Warner started the process of ungrading in 2011 when he began to question the folklore surrounding the teaching of writing. That questioning led to two recent books—*Why They Can't Write: Killing the Five-Paragraph Essay and Other Necessities* and *The Writer's Practice: Building Confidence in Your Nonfiction Writing*—and continues to this day at the College of Charleston where he is an affiliate professor.

INDEX

The letter *t* following a page number denotes a table; the letter *f* following a page number denotes a figure.

accuracy-based grading, 140
advanced placement courses, 12,
    164
advantaged students, 34, 221
agency, 174, 178, 180, 181, 214
    ungrading and, 27, 141, 159, 186
alienation, 57, 107
anarchy, 173–74, 186
    See also grade-anarchy experiment
Anderson, Peter, 164, 165
anxiety, 4, 186
    about grades, 29–30, 33, 34, 94,
        98, 175
assessment
    alternative approaches to, 27–29,
        36–40, 167
    formative and summative, 13, 40,
        76, 156, 165, 166, 213
    grading *vs.*, 36, 76–77
    grappling with, xviii
    and learning connection, 13,
        74–75, 224
    neutral vocabulary of, 75t
    performative and quantitative, 34
    See also critique-driven learning
        and assessment; self-
        assessment or self-evaluation
assimilation, 162
assumptions, 34, 36, 95, 140, 162
attendance
    college, 226

norms of a gradeless classroom,
    176–77
penalties, 112
points for, 10–11, 142
policies, 63n26, 116, 206–7, 214
attitude, 59, 211–12, 214
authority, 136, 163, 167, 207, 224
    centralized, 173, 186
autonomy, 10, 48, 105–6, 108, 215
averages, 74, 190
    See also grade point average (GPA)

badge system, 109–10
behavior, 9, 56, 190, 196
bell curve, 7, 9, 163
    See also grading on a curve
Berthoff, Ann, 36
biases, 34, 221
Bickman, Martin, 27
binary grading, 85, 142
Blackboard, 26, 93
Blackwelder, Aaron, xvii, 15–16, 96
blogs, 112–14, 142
    on ungrading, 140, 157–58
Blum, Susan D., 16
Bock, Laszlo, 83
Breakfast Club, The (1985), 43, 44f
building relationships, 42, 46, 49–51,
    123, 223
    See also student-faculty relationships
Butler, Ruth, 3, 13, 46–47, 82–83

Cambridge University, 6
Camus, Albert, 83
Canvas, 26, 93
Carnegie Foundation, 225
Cavanagh, Sarah Rose, 8, 226
challenges
  of conventional grading, 10–14
  of critical pedagogy, 224
  of critique-driven learning, 134–35
  educational, 3, 226
  in teacher-student relationship,
    49–51, 107
  of ungrading, 61–62, 220–21
change
  gradual *vs.* rapid, xiii
  revelation of, 42–45
  structural, 164, 165, 227
  in student practice, 135–38
cheating, 12, 46, 56, 99, 103, 168
Chemaly, Soraya, 34
Chiaravalli, Arthur, 16
China, 6
choice in coursework, 163–64
Chu, Gary, 16, 222
classroom equality, 106, 108
Clifford, John, 9
coercion, 95–96
collaboration, 28, 32, 45, 109, 114,
  148
college admission, 83, 221, 225
color categorization, 191
community, 38, 106, 118, 119, 173,
  186–87
competition, xiv, 4, 8, 28, 45
compliance, 78, 164, 165
computer-graded assessments, 10,
  190, 197, 200
computer programming, 123, 124–25
  agile retrospective practices, 135–37
  analytic rubrics, 131–32, 132t
  plagiarism, 134–35
conferences
  learning, 174, 182–83, 184
  one-on-one "grade," 167, 190,
    195–96, 201–3
  portfolio, 59–60
  student-led, 78, 165

confidence levels, 149f, 149–51, 150f,
  157
contract grading, 38, 60, 210
  badge system for, 109–10
  Collaborative Peer Evaluation model,
    108, 116–20
  community aspect of, 106
  institutional implementation, 106–7
  Twenty-First-Century Literacies
    model, 108, 110–16
control
  grades as a form of, 31, 95
  institutional, 30
  students', 48, 60, 108
  teachers', xviii, 13, 61, 77, 226
course evaluations, 93–95, 120, 213,
  217n3
Covid-19 pandemic, xxi
creativity, 51, 78, 83, 99, 106, 181
critical thinking, 10, 32, 35, 116, 146,
  147
critique-driven learning and assessment
  applications and data analysis,
    128–30
  categorization and tallying, 130–31
  challenges and solutions, 134–38
  course work and expectations, 124–25
  overview of, 123–24
  portfolio-based assessments *vs.*, 123,
    130
  students and instructor reactions to,
    126–28
  submissions and feedback, 125f, 127f,
    129f
cultural capital, 221
curiosity, 3, 56, 212, 213
curriculum/curricula, 107, 164, 224,
  226
  grappling with, xvii–xix
  sequences or group, 222
  student-developed, 49
  value of, 47

Dartmouth University, 5
Davidson, Cathy N., 15–16, 26, 32, 226
  contract grading, 38, 60, 107,
    108, 110

Deci, Edward L., 1, 10
default systems, 209–10
Dewey, John, 8, 101, 220
dialogue, engaging in, 15, 31, 35, 37, 40
  colleagues and administrators, 80
  on grading and ungrading, 157–58, 188–91
  on learning outcomes, 145, 174–75
  parents and teachers, 77–78, 162, 190, 191, 197–98, 226
  See also conferences
divergent-thinking tasks, 13
diversity, 223, 227
Donovan, Sarah, 165
do-review-redo submission process, 123, 124–28
  categorization and tallying, 130–31
  challenges of, 134
  example with feedback, 125f
  student/teacher summary views of, 127f, 129f
Dweck, Carol, 83
Dworkin, Ronald, 177, 187n3

Elbow, Peter, 11, 25, 34, 37, 39, 120
emergent outcomes, 30
emojis, 149f, 149–50, 150f
employers
  performance reviews, 148
  preferred competencies, 146t, 146–47
  ratings of recent college graduates, 147t, 147–48
English Language Arts (ELA), 189, 197–98
  grade conferences, 195–96, 201–3
  "typical" grading *vs.* feedback system, 199–200
equity/inequity, xxi–xxii, 8, 12, 164, 223, 227
essays
  achievement, 173, 183–84, 185–86

feedback on, 79–80, 180–81
  grading strategies, 45–46, 54, 204–6
  paragraph structure, 215
ethnicity, 162, 163–64
Evergreen State College, 4, 221
examinations
  in China's history, 6
  feedback approach to, 142, 143–44, 151, 153–55, 158
  grading by confidence level, 149f, 149–51, 150f
  grading by points, 7, 152t, 152–53, 158
  as optional, 180
  at Oxford and Cambridge, 6
exhaustion, student, 206
expectations, 29, 38, 47, 80, 105, 164
  reframing of, 155
  tacit, 34
Eyler, Joshua, 8, 225–26

failing grades, 44–45, 115
failure, 14, 108, 134, 135, 154, 209, 211
  of current teaching models, 227
  learning from, 174, 175, 177, 219
  success and, 46–47, 184
Farish, William, 6
Fast, Amy, 29
Fast Times at Ridgemont High (1982), 49–50, 50f
feedback
  efficacy of comments, 3, 13, 46, 82
  in exam ungrading process, 143–44, 151, 153–56
  as judgment, xiv, 74
  learning assessments and, 166–67, 224
  in lieu of grades, 78–80, 83, 92–93, 116, 175
  logs, 79
  for making improvements, 57, 78, 84–87, 97–98, 104, 198
  narrative, 76, 191–92, 199–200
  objectivity/subjectivity and, 31, 35

feedback (*continued*)
  peer, 110, 111–12, 117–20
  scale and, 222
  social backgrounds and, 223
  student reactions to, 93–95, 120,
    157–58, 192
  supportive, 95–96
  systems, 25
  types of, 82
  "typical" grading *vs.*, 199–200
FERPA (Family Educational Rights and
    Privacy Act), 226
film courses, 37–38
freedom, 60, 94, 101, 209
  academic, 36
  bell hooks on, 107, 219
  for learners, 95–97
  to make choices, 216
Freire, Paulo, 101, 106, 220

"game of school," 53, 78, 162, 198, 210
games, 56
general intelligence, notion of, 7
Geni, Larry, 163, 164, 165
Gibbs, Laura, xxiin1, 15–16, 31, 226
GitHub, 116, 135
goals, 12, 55, 212, 221, 222
  achieving, 112, 118, 145, 173, 206
  learning, 13, 15, 80, 96, 106, 116
  pedagogical, 214, 216
  setting, 58, 72, 184, 203
Gooblar, David, 226
Google applications
  Docs, 72, 79, 86, 118
  Forms, 85, 86f
  Keep, 128
  Trends, 29, 30f
grade-anarchy experiment
  approach to assignments, 177–82
  arguments for, 175–76
  attendance and participation, 176–77
  authority and community, 173,
    186–87
  collaborative outcome design, 174–75
  course requirements, 173–74
  future recommendations,
    185–86

  student grades and learning
    outcomes, 182–85
gradebooks, 45, 85, 195, 197, 199
  LMS, 26, 92–93
grade compression, 5
grade-free institutions, 3–5, 54, 221
grade-free zones, 36
grade inflation, xiii, 83, 144, 164, 185
  criticism and combating, 5
  institutional control of, 30
  teaching evaluations and, 13
grade ladder, 210–11
grade point average (GPA), xix, 4, 28,
    83, 104, 163
  booster courses, 13–14
  contract grading and, 108
  meaning of, 12, 55, 100
grades (general discussion)
  as arbitrary and inconsistent,
    10–12, 56–57, 76, 104, 198,
    221
  categorizing, 188, 189f
  deemphasizing or minimizing,
    164–65, 220, 222
  exchange value of, 83–84
  as a form of coercion, 95–96
  Google Trends search for, 29,
    30f
  meaning of, xxi–xxii, 40, 83,
    163
  as motivators, 31–32, 55–56,
    163, 173
  negative effects of, xiii–xvi,
    12–14, 27–28, 45–47, 97,
    163–64, 168
  origin of, 6–7, 25, 162
  reasons for eliminating, xvii–
    xix, 53–55, 84, 91, 140, 168,
    175–76
  students' feelings about,
    189–90, 192–94
  vocabulary, 75t
grading on a curve, xiii, 7, 9, 11, 28,
    32, 163
grading systems
  automated, 26
  challenges of, 10–12

efficiency of, 32–33
objective approach to, 25–26
obligations and, 187
punitive, 97
scales, 37, 143, 210, 213
See also letter grades; points
    system; rubrics
group work, 109, 117–20
in computer programming,
    137–38
growth mindset, xv, 81, 83, 84, 92
grubbing, grade, 31, 120

Hacking Assessment (Sackstein),
    54, 75, 220, 230
Hampshire College, 4, 221
Hart, H. L. A., 177, 187n3
Harvard University, xxi, 4, 7
HASTAC.org, 113–14, 116
hierarchies, 26, 28, 40, 106, 225
higher education faculty, 16,
    224–26
hiring companies, 146t
    See also employers
Hochschild, Arlie, 59
Holt, John, 27
hooks, bell, 36, 107, 219
Hughes, John, 43
Hurst, John, 101–2
Huston, Therese, 224

individual development plan, 58
Inoue, Asao B., 38, 120, 210
institutional requirements, xv–
    xvi, 33–34, 106–7
intelligence quotient (IQ), 7
intrinsic/extrinsic motivation, 3,
    10, 60, 198, 211
    grades and, 55–56, 163, 175
    growth mindset and, 83, 84
    praise and, 13
isolation, 62, 224

judgment, xiv, xvii, 11, 38, 39,
    177
    grades as, 78, 96, 213
    language and, 74–75

peer evaluations and, 109–10,
    116–17, 118–19
in teacher-student relationship,
    45, 47, 54

K–12 educators, xix, 16, 220, 224–26
Katopodis, Christina, 15, 16, 38, 60,
    107, 116–17, 119
Kirr, Joy, 16, 197–98
knowledge, tacit *vs.* explicit, 141,
    149
Kohn, Alfie, 3, 36, 45, 120, 141, 168,
    227
    on the ideal characteristics of
        classrooms, 10
    on the negative effects of grades,
        46
    "The Trouble with Rubrics," 31, 39
    on the value of the curriculum, 47
Kruglanski, Arie, 56
Kvale, Steinar, 13

labels/labeling, xiv, 4, 74, 78, 84, 132
Lang, James, 8, 226
language
    of grading, 32–33, 75
    judgment and, 74–75
    programming, 124, 136
language courses, 14, 66–73
    See also English Language Arts
        (ELA)
law schools, 4–5
leadership, 114, 117, 118, 147, 179
learning
    and assessment connection, 13,
        74–75, 224
    communicating, 75, 77, 81
    compliance and, 78, 165
    cooperative, 226–27
    different ways of, 53, 56, 81, 173,
        197
    feedback approach to, 78–80,
        92–93, 166–67, 175
    feminist views of, 9
    grades correlation, 25, 28, 140,
        175, 182, 190, 210
    habits, 99

learning (*continued*)
    human aspect of, 219
    impediments, 140, 163, 175
    optimal conditions for, 225
    ownership of, 87, 145, 175
    performance and, xvi–xvii, 1,
        75, 107, 141, 210
    positive reactions to, 93–95
    research and scholarship, 8–9
    and teaching divide, 123
    See also critique-driven learning
        and assessment; learning
        outcomes
learning management systems
    (LMSs), 26, 92–93
learning outcomes, 12, 30, 53, 116,
    183
    achievement of, 181–82, 184–85
    collaborative creation of, 174–75
    solutions and approaches, 14–16,
        59–60
    statewide, 226
    uniformity of, 55
    See also reflections
Leonard, George, xviii
letter grades, xxi, 47, 84, 93,
    167–68
    in contract grading, 108, 111,
        112–15
    descriptive criteria for, 85–86,
        86f, 87f
    elimination of, 100, 102, 140, 210
    meaning of, 4, 5, 40, 74, 83, 99
    negative effects of, 97
    origin of, 6–7, 25
    student fixation on, 104, 105
levels of school, 4, 6, 225–26
life skills, 110, 111

make-your-own-assignment
    approach, 179
marking, term usage, 1–2
Marzano, Robert, 83
mastery, 10, 11, 32, 48, 79, 83, 200
    demonstrated, 85–86, 201
    emphasis on, 4, 133, 136
    of learning, 81, 138, 157

Mastery Transcript Consortium, 221
medical schools, xxi, 4
memories, grading, 91, 103–4
metacognition, 29, 36, 145, 152–53,
    166, 167
    meaning, 59, 108
minimal grading, 37, 165, 222
mistakes, making
    educators', 80, 212
    freedom of, 95, 97
    learning from, 57, 92, 97
motivators, grades as, 31–32, 55–56,
    163, 173
    See also intrinsic/extrinsic motivation
Mount Holyoke College, 7
Muller, Jerry Z., 3
MythFolklore.net, 92, 93

narrative evaluations, xiv, 4, 12, 13
    feedback on assignments, 76,
        191–92, 199–200
    in lieu of report cards, 168
neoliberalism, 16n2
Neuhaus, Jessamyn, 8, 226
Newton, Jen, xxii
Northwestern University, 123, 124,
    125, 126
numerical grades, 4, 7, 28, 132, 175,
    213, 223
    See also grade point average
        (GPA)

objectivity and subjectivity, 14, 31, 35,
    57, 167
occupational performance, xxn4
O'Connor, Ken, 165
Odyssey, The (Homer), 48
online course instruction, xxi, 16, 26,
    84, 92, 125
oral examinations, 6
Oxford University, 6

parent-teacher night, 77–78, 191
participation
    importance of quality and, 143
    norms of a gradeless classroom,
        176–77

outcomes, 185
points, 10–11, 31, 94
policy, 112, 116
reflections on, 70, 73, 118, 119
pass-fail (not pass) system, xvi, xxi,
    6–7, 93, 100
    at Democratic Education at Cal
        (DECal), 101–2
    in medical and law schools, xxi,
        4–5
pedagogy, xviii–xix, 33–34
    critical, 27, 39, 224
    of equality, 106
    ideas of freedom and, 95–97
    innovative, 8–9, 220
    liberatory, 61, 220
    personal goals and values, 214–16
    revamping practices, 223
    training, 225–26
    Wile E. Coyote approach to,
        208–10
peer evaluation, xvii, 39, 84–85
    badge system for, 109–10
    contract grading and, 106, 107,
        110–12, 116–19
    sharing, 120
    use of rubrics, 132
perfectionism, 77, 97, 98, 209
performance *vs.* learning, xvi–xvii,
    1, 75, 107, 141, 210
Pink, Daniel, 10, 48, 83
plagiarism, 56, 134–35
points system, xvii, 7, 25, 44, 56
    for assignments, 92–93, 126,
        199–200
    based on proficiency, 210–11
    for exams, 144, 151–53, 152t,
        158
    See also grade point average
        (GPA)
portfolios, 58, 63n19
    conferences, 59, 76, 174
    contents of, 67
    critique-driven learning approach
        vs., 123, 130–31
    learning outcomes and, 181, 185
    online platforms, 38, 84

power dynamics, xv, xvii, 31, 40
praise, 13
Princeton University, 5
privilege, 32, 34
problem-based learning, 15, 48–49
process letters, 35, 37, 39
proficiency scale, 210–11
programming. *See* computer
    programming
progressive education, 3, 8
punishment, 57, 83, 97, 98, 207
purpose, sense of, 10, 48, 83, 108

race, 162, 163–64
ranking, 27, 33, 34, 163, 220
    on a curve, xiii–xiv
    at Oxford and Cambridge, 6
    practices in China, 6
    students against one another, 28, 32
recent college graduates, 146–47,
    147t
reflections
    in blog format, 142
    educational value of, 175–76
    end-of-semester, 58, 65–71, 173,
        183–84
    feedback on, 79, 83, 116
    on learning outcomes, 184–85, 187
    metacognitive, 107–8
    mid-semester, 58, 72–73, 173,
        183–84
    on ungrading, 60, 161
relationships. *See* building
    relationships; student-faculty
    relationships
report cards, 76, 77, 97, 103, 162,
    168, 189
required courses, 222
revision work, 97–98, 104
Riesbeck, Christopher, 15–16, 222
risk-taking, 13, 57, 60, 175, 220, 224
Riter, Aviah, 56
rubrics, xvii, 15, 31, 38, 200, 221
    analytic and single-point, 131–33,
        132t, 133t
    student-made, 39
Ryan, Richard M., 1, 10

sabbaticals, 223
Sackstein, Starr, 2, 15–16, 54, 230
Satisfactory/Unsatisfactory grades,
  103, 132
  badging method for judging,
    109–10
  peers determining, 110, 111–12
scale, 7, 26, 222
  grading, 31, 37, 143, 210, 213
  percentage, 25
  proficiency, 210–11
  ternary, 143
Scantrons, 103
Schank, Roger, 135
Schinske, Jeffrey, 25, 120, 140
scholarship of teaching and
  learning (SoTL), 8–9
schooling *vs.* learning, 57
Schultz-Bergin, Marcus, xix, 16
scientific management approach,
  7–8
scoring, term usage, 76
secondary and higher education,
  line between, 225
secondary school teachers, 16, 220,
  224–26
Seesaw, 84
self-assessment or self-evaluation,
  xvii, 39, 54, 72, 175
  as a continual process, 36–37
  feedback cycle and, 84–85
  individual development plan,
    58–59
  peer evaluation and, 116, 117–19
  on reading and writing
    comprehension, 201–2
  as a space of dialogue, 35
  syllabus statement on, 29
  See also reflections; self-grading
self-grading, xv–xvi, 59, 71, 73
  contracts, 108, 111, 112–15, 117
  descriptive criteria for, 85–86,
    86f, 87f
  exams, 151–53
  reflections and conferences,
    182–85, 195–96, 201–3
  student feedback on, 94–95

student-teacher dynamics of, 167
  underestimating, 35–36, 153,
    182, 184
sequential courses, 222
Shor, Ira, 107
Singham, Mano, xxn3
skill development, 135–36, 138,
  145–48, 178, 183
  writing practice, 211–12
Slack, 67, 70–71, 72
software developers, 136–37
Sorensen-Unruh, Clarissa, 16, 222
special education, 163–64
standardized tests, 7
standards, 106, 134, 226
  developing, 58
  for evaluation, 7, 39
  learning, 76, 77
standards-based grading (SBG), xiv,
  165–66, 192, 195, 196
Stanford University, 4–5
static groups, 117
Stein, Chana, 56
STEM (science, technology,
  engineering, and
  mathematics) subjects, 16,
  222
STEM ungrading case study
  employer *vs.* student
    competency ratings, 145–48,
    146t, 147t
  exams, 149f, 149–53, 150f, 152t
  implementation of ungrading,
    141–45, 149
  instructional design model, 156f,
    156–57
  reframing of expectations,
    153–55
  student feedback, 157–58
  summary, 158–59
Stevenson, Dean, 11
Stommel, Jesse, 15, 16, 120, 140,
  222, 226
stress. *See* anxiety
student-faculty relationships,
  42–45, 123, 223–24, 227
student information, 226

success, 47, 105–6, 184, 210
Successive Approximation Model
    (SAM), 156
suicide rates, 4
syllabi
    description of contract grading, 15,
        110–15
    statement on self-assessment, 29
    student cocreated, 116
    ungrading scheme, 142–44
systemic oppression, 34

Tanner, Kimberley, 25, 120, 140
Teachers Going Gradeless (TG2), 2
Teachers Throwing Out Grades, 2
teaching evaluations. *See* course
    evaluations
tenure, 101, 209, 215, 220, 224
Thoreau, Henry David, 27
Thorndike, Edward Lee, 7
time-consuming, grading and
    ungrading as, 33, 158–59, 199,
    204–5
true-false questions, 92
trust, 15, 28, 61, 145, 196

ungrading (general discussion)
    additional research topics, 221–24
    administrative support for, 101, 220
    and assessment distinction, 36
    benefits, 98–100, 204, 212–16, 219
    cooperation among educators, 224–26
    meaning and principles, xv–xvi, 140
    movement, 2–3
    objections and challenges, 61–62,
        220–21
    reasons for, 27–28, 40, 53–54,
        175–76

skepticism of, 60–61
student reactions to, 1, 157–59,
    223
Wile E. Coyote model for, 208–10
See also contract grading; grade-
    anarchy experiment; STEM
    ungrading case study
Universal Design for Learning
    (UDL), 15, 58
University of California
    Berkeley, 5, 33, 101–2
    Santa Cruz, 4
University of Michigan, xxi, 7

values, personal, 207, 214–16
verbal reports, 162

Warner, John, 16, 60, 98, 217n3
weighted grades, 12
What the Best College Teachers Do
    (Bain), 206, 207
wiki, use of, 113–14
Wile E. Coyote analogy, 208–10,
    214
Wiliam, Dylan, 82–83
workshops, 8, 226
writing courses, 42–43, 48, 92, 99,
    107
    habits, 202
    pedagogical values and, 214–16
    process of discovery and, 217n5
    proficiency in, 211–12
    reflections, 72

Yale University, 4–5, 7
YouTube, 77–78, 114

Zhao, Yong, 12